M000232930

How to
Leave Your
Psychopath

For my Mum and Dad, Catherine and Laurence,
who gifted me protection, education, and unconditional love.

My twin, Tom, who has saved my ass
since we were wombmates.

My sister, Claire, your strength
and wisdom inspire me daily.

My love for you all lasts a million lifetimes.

How to Leave Your Psychopath

The essential handbook for escaping toxic relationships

Maddy Anholt

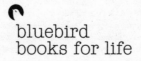

bluebird
books for life

First published 2022 by Bluebird
an imprint of Pan Macmillan
The Smithson, 6 Briset Street, London EC1M 5NR
EU representative: Macmillan Publishers Ireland Ltd, 1st Floor,
The Liffey Trust Centre, 117–126 Sheriff Street Upper,
Dublin 1, D01 YC43
Associated companies throughout the world
www.panmacmillan.com

ISBN HB 978-1-5290-7593-9
ISBN TPB 978-1-5290-7594-6

Names and identifying details of all individuals have been changed in
all circumstances to protect confidentiality.
Situations and descriptions of events in the author's past have
also been changed in some instances for privacy reasons.
This book contains potentially triggering themes of graphic domestic abuse,
sexual, physical and emotional violence and suicide.

Typeset in Minion Pro by Palimpsest Book Production Ltd, Falkirk, Stirlingshire
Printed and bound by CPI Group (UK) Ltd, Croydon, CR0 4YY

Visit **www.panmacmillan.com** to read more about all our books
and to buy them. You will also find features, author interviews and
news of any author events, and you can sign up for e-newsletters
so that you're always first to hear about our new releases.

CONTENTS

INTRODUCTION

Are you forever finding yourself in the stranglehold of shitty spouses, controlling companions, and dominating dickheads? Well, fear not, because once you've finished reading this book, you'll be able to wave ta-ta to unhappy and unhealthy relationships for good. Consider me the Psycho Sprucer, Bad Boy Buster, the Hot Mess Assessor – ready to leave your love life sparkling.

You see, this is a book about controlling relationships. It's about everyday Narcissists and Psychopaths who hide in plain sight. It's about the men, and sometimes the women, who contribute to everything from low self-esteem to suicide.

I'm not a psychologist or a doctor – sure, I once examined someone's perineum with latex gloves but, as they told me in court, that doesn't mean I'm medically trained. I spent ten years tumbling in and out of controlling relationships; each time I vowed it would be my last. When I finally hit the depths of despair, I decided enough was enough. I worked with a host of superb psychologists, experts and counsellors to learn why I was a magnet for these toxic twerps. The culmination of that knowledge is this book. This is my lived experience, here is my truth – advice from the field if you will. I have written what I wish had fallen into my lap a decade ago.

I hope this book will educate as many people as possible about these dangerous personality types before they eat up your life. There's nothing to be afraid of: with knowledge comes power, and awareness will be your shield.

You may not have reported the abuse you suffer or suffered. You may never have been hit or physically attacked in any way. Perhaps you're not convinced it's domestic abuse at all. I get you – this is something far subtler. Something that often you're not sure is happening at all. But you're certain of one thing and that's that you can't keep playing with these poisonous pricks. You are weary of getting your life upturned. Perfect. I'm glad to say, you're exactly where you need to be – here, reading this book. Congratulations and welcome along.

I'm going to go out on a limb here and assume one of three things about you, dear reader:

1. You're in a relationship right now that doesn't feel right. You can't quite put your finger on it but it's icky and uncomfortable.

2. You know someone – sister, brother, mother, father, friend – who is trapped in some sort of diabolical partnership and you want to help.

3. You've escaped a toxic relationship – it doesn't matter how long ago – and you're keen not to fall into another cataclysmic coupling.

(Extra category: You've been given this book as a half-joke but, really, you have begun to realize there's some work to be done to perish past patterns.)

Whoever you are, I have done everything in my power to make this book your ticket to healthy love. I want you to know it's possible not only to survive, but to thrive.

Let's do it together, one step at a time.

If you wish to seek help or further advice on the issues covered in this book, you will find a full list of organizations and domestic abuse charities listed at the back.

This book contains potentially triggering themes of graphic domestic abuse, sexual, physical and emotional violence and suicide. All names, locations and dates have been changed to protect the privacy of individuals. Any resemblance to actual persons, living or dead, or to real events is purely coincidental.

CHAPTER ONE

PSYCHOMETER

The Empath–Psychopath Scale

Raise your hand if you've been in a controlling relationship. Raise your hand if you're in a controlling relationship now. Raise your hand if you have to ask the person that you're with if you're in a controlling relationship.

Don't worry, you're in safe hands now. You're in the hands of a Super Empath. A Super Empath is not the next shit Marvel franchise, because that would be a film about a superhero with relentless anxiety, psoriasis flare-ups and occasional insomnia.

Nope. In fact, Empaths are highly sensitive people, often gauging their mood on how others are feeling. We have our spaced-out sci-fi friend, author J. T. McIntosh, to thank for the term – he was first to cite it in his 1956 book *Empath*. *Star Trek* then brought it to an even wider audience. Rather beautifully, both McIntosh and *Star Trek* meant it to convey a person with 'emotional telepathy'. You feel me? Then you're one too.

In the past I had a tendency to get into what you might call 'controlling relationships'. After each one of these romances had ended, I'd be convinced I'd learnt my lesson . . . and then a matter of days later would find myself right back where I'd started.

It'd always be the same: I'd see a broken man and I would want him. 'A new project!' I'd squeal as Lady Gut Instinct shook her head, rolled her eyes and walked in the opposite direction. You know that tingly feeling you get when you see someone across the room you like? Yeah, well for me that was all the common sense leaving my body.

I had a real knack for finding these shattered souls; an inner radar that would alert me to their proximity: beep, beep, beep – incapacity to love, commitment-phobe, once punched a wall in a Wetherspoon's toilet? DING, DING, DING! I should have created a dating app for broken people, I was that good at discovering them. I could have called it Unhinged, Crumble or Grindherdown.

I thought that was my 'thing', you know, like doing a headstand, being able to say the alphabet backwards or eating broken glass. I accepted my role was to fix these lost souls; I was the Mother Teresa of unhealthy relationships. Void of emotion? Come here, my child, let me bless you.

On top of being an Empath, I'm also a perfectionist – the two usually go hand in hand. I really like to be sure I've given a situation everything. I'm stubbornly persistent, to a fault. I once spent a straight two hours learning to fold a fitted sheet. I watched a tutorial and everything. Still can't do it, but then, who can?

Being an Empath and a perfectionist meant I stayed in toxic relationships for far longer than I should have, in the hope that with enough 'hard work' I could achieve some form of stability.

I saw red flags as signs of encouragement – be a little more dedicated, you're doing great, keep going, you can fix this! As the glaringly glowing flags whacked me in the face then flew back to wind me.

Chumming up beside my Empath babe is a little friend called 'Codependency'. Codependency in its purest form is a strong desire to fix others – usually at any cost. Codependents require constant validation from anyone and everyone that they are 'doing a great job'. Are your ears burning? Don't worry – we'll tie up these Codependent ends later.

Now the toxic relationships I'm talking about are not just with your standard dickhead. You know the ones. Those that take days to reply, don't hang up the bath mat, and ogle your best mate. These pricks are annoying, upsetting, and general wastes of space, but you get over it, learn from them and chalk it up to an unlucky experience. No, the people I am talking about are far more dangerous than leaving you on read.

THE PSYCHOMETER

The easiest way to discuss these personality types is by simplifying them down through a scale of 1–10. Let's call it our Psychometer. This is a spectrum I have invented which goes from Super Empath at one end, all the way up to Psychopath on the other. It looks like this:

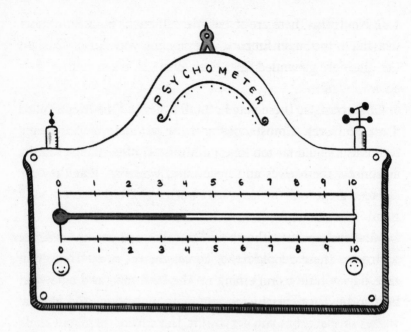

Now of course, there are many strands off this scale, and it certainly isn't as simple as one straight line. There is a variability within the characteristics of Empaths, Psychopaths and everyone else. However, for the purposes of clarity, the Psychometer will be our benchmark.

0–2: Super Empaths. These are the compassionate souls that cannot do enough for others. They feel what others are feeling as if they were experiencing those emotions themselves.

2–4: Empaths. There are varying degrees; not all Empaths would give themselves piles from sitting on a luggage rack for a six-hour train journey so someone else could have a seat.

4–6: Neutrals. There are those that fall in the middle, neither swaying to the Super Empath side, nor the extreme Psychopath side; they are grounded folks who have got it just right.

6–8: Narcissists. These people think the world revolves around them and seek almost constant gratification for their ego. Narcissists spend far too long pointing out other people's faults to console themselves and have an unwavering sense of self-righteousness.

8–10: Psychopaths. The most dangerous of the personality disorders. These people have no conscience, remorse or guilt, and display little to no empathy. The Psychopaths cannot feel fear, and live for ever-increasing, often violent acts, for thrills.

SOCIOPATHS AND PSYCHOPATHS

It's important that we look at the differences between a Psychopath and a Sociopath. The distinction has been heavily debated and many psychologists, criminal lawyers, police officers etc. often use the words interchangeably. It has been argued that Psychopaths are Sociopaths but with more extreme symptoms. The simple fact is – there's a hell of a lot of overlap. I interviewed clinical psychologist Professor Hilton Davis, who said: 'For all practical purposes there is little need to pursue the subtle academic differentiation of these terms. I avoid the disputed theoretical differences by simply using the term "Psychopath".'

German psychiatrist J. L. A. Koch coined the term 'Psychopath' in 1888. In the late 1920s American psychologist George E. Partridge invented an alternative term, 'Sociopath'. He used it to describe someone whose main trait was that they could not conform to societal norms, in such a way that presented a danger to others.

In essence, the two terms share many parallels, so for my purposes in this book, I will be referring to Psychopaths and Sociopaths using the umbrella term 'Psychopaths'.

We'll also be talking about Narcissists in detail later. But the fact is this – I can tell you from first-hand experience that you won't give too much of a shit if the person who is obliterating your life is a Psychopath, a Sociopath, has learned psychopathic behaviour, narcissistic personality disorder, is just plain toxic, or all the above, when you find yourself in a state of total devastation from these tyrannical twat-toasties.

CONTROLLS

What I am discussing in this book are **controlling personality types**. These people – both Narcissists and Psychopaths – employ many of the same campaigns to control, a lot of which I encountered. Their aim is to plunder your power through coercion and manipulation. They pluck you from a calm life, rip you into tiny pieces and chuck you into moving traffic. I needed a name to encapsulate *all* these controlling personality types; a term for the vast and varying range, preferably without offending the psychologists amongst us.

I found that there wasn't one inclusive term. Yes, we talk about these personality types in a strictly psychological and scientific way, but there was no colloquial name for the layperson to describe ALL controlling people. The world of controlling personality types felt clinical and remote, when actually, millions upon millions have their lives upended on a daily basis by these malicious monsters.

I decided I needed to create my own term. I was determined for this new word not to add to their pre-existing dark and devilish mystique. We should not be in awe of these people.

I pondered this for a while. What did these controlling types actually *do*? I recalled experiences I'd had. Times I'd been in arguments, sprung from seemingly nothing, the constant feeling of treading on eggshells, the air heavy with tension. These people have an instinctive ability to consume every inch of you. They coerce, deceive and con. They provoke, prod and push. They troll your life, wreaking havoc on everything you believe about yourself and the world.

They are Controlls.

Definition

Controlls (kɒntrɒls) *Collective Noun* Singular: Controll
The group term used to describe controlling personality types, particularly those who are at the helm of abusive relationships. They could be narcissistic and/or psychopathic, either learned or predisposed to be. NB. These people lack the ability to love, and most are unable to show empathy.

In a sentence: *'My exes are all Controlls; I'm going to stop dating until I work out why.'*

Throughout this book, I will refer to controlling personality types as CONTROLLS.

THE WORLD'S BEST ACTORS

The further up the Psychometer we go, the more treacherous the individual becomes and, if you have dalliances with them, the more liable your life will be to implode. To be clear, no one is beyond their grip. *Everyone* is vulnerable. That includes other Psychopaths too – where they are concerned, like attracts like.

As no two individuals are the same, no two Psychopaths and no two Narcissists are the same. Each one is unique, like fingerprints, the veins of leaves or lies my exes told me – always kept me on my toes.

The closer to 0 we are, the higher the chance we'll fall into the path of a controlling personality type – the partner, the boss, the Controll. If you're on the Empath side you're likely to be a tad too trusting; I don't want to use the word 'naive' but I'm afraid it's somewhere close.

Listen, it's not your fault if you come a cropper with a Controll because they are Oscar-worthy actors, masters of disguise. At the beginning of your relationship, anything you want them to be, they can. Oh, and they don't need to train for it, it's a completely innate set of skills they deliver with impeccable artistry and finesse.

They learn what is attractive to you and mirror it.

Fond of big displays of affection? They can do that. What about if you're desperate for someone to sit and listen to you for once? They're the champ. Have you been endlessly searching for a man that will cook you a biryani, have a laugh with your mum and give you a foot rub whilst gossiping over soap storylines? They'll do it standing on their head, mate. But once they're sure you're invested . . . the act falls fast. This is called love-bombing and it's the very start of one of the worst journeys of your life. Strap yourself in.

Controlls are more charming, more alluring, more self-confident than the average person.

EMPATHS VS CONTROLLS

Let's look at the attraction between Empaths and Controlls. Empaths luuurve to fix broken people. Controlls use mock-vulnerability to make people believe they are not a threat and could do with some help. Ted Bundy famously put his arm in a sling or his leg in a fake cast when approaching women. A good-looking guy with a physical injury? Little darling, Mama's here!

It's very important to know where you are on the Psychometer because if you are an Empath, it is in your very nature to help others, and if a charming, hot man with an injury requires your aid, it's likely you'll be there before the judge has even picked up the gavel.

Ideally, we'd all sit around 4–5 on the Psychometer. I don't want you thinking that 10 = all bad and 0 = all good. It's not that clear cut. A dose of narcissism every now and again is healthy. It's also not so fantastic to be a high and mighty Empath all the time either. More on that later.

If you are still unsure where you live on the Psychometer, I'd like you to read the below anecdote and note your reaction:

It was 8.45 a.m. on a sharp September morning and Amanda was in the car, running extremely late to take her two-year-old daughter, Imani, to nursery. Imani was the sweetest, happiest little toddler – curly hair, round cheeks, always gripping her favourite, chewed bunny toy.

When Amanda pulled up at the nursery gates her boss called. She tucked the phone between her shoulder and ear as she unbuckled her little daughter and popped her safely on the pavement. As Amanda went to grab her bag from the driver's side, tiny Imani realized she'd left her bunny in her car seat. She saw Mummy was busy, so reached up, putting her tiny toddler fingers on the door frame to get it. Amanda, still talking to her boss, hands full, kicked Imani's door shut behind her and Imani's delicate fingers went crunch.

Now if, like me, you have an almost visceral reaction – you squeezed your hands, feeling little Imani's pain, I would suggest you are 0–3 on the Psychometer.

If you had a reaction similar to 'of course that's bad, but it's just a story', that's OK, perhaps you may be higher up the scale, more like 4–5.

If, however, your reaction was, 'yeah, but what car was it?' then we may need to have a little chat . . .

THREE KILLER QUESTIONS

A decade ago, I didn't have a clue about any of this Psychometer business, all I knew was that each destructive relationship I entered intensified in terms of control.

First Ollie, then Shiv, then Damien.

The pattern became boringly obvious: I would find an ostensibly broken man, try to fix him, get mistreated, then we'd eventually break up. The men went away stronger whilst I came out a crushed cabbage.

This cycle persisted from the ages of 18 to 30 (which sounds like the shittest Benidorm package holiday that I definitely didn't buy tickets for). When the pattern peaked, I found myself utterly, wholly and totally exhausted and very nearly annihilated. I was faced with two options – find a way to make the cycle stop or free-fall into the clawing darkness.

I was the one who had become broken and, holy fuck, I was shattered into a million pieces. It took me a long time to get to the bottom of why I was so attracted to these corrosive Controlls.

Fundamentally, I was desperate to have these three questions answered:

1. How did I get into these controlling relationships?

2. Why didn't I leave them earlier?

3. How can I stop the cycle?

I'd lost all hope of ever being able to enter a 'normal' relationship. I couldn't understand where I was going wrong.

- What was it about these men, these personality types, these Controlls, that made me a target?
- Who were these people and why were they every place I looked for a partner?
- How could I love and be loved in a healthy relationship?
- Why was everyone else getting it right except me?
- Was I destined to end up either single and lonely or in a relationship and miserable?

I didn't have the answers then, but I knew I was ready to do everything it took to break the cycle. Over the coming years I worked with some brilliant professionals and slowly, very slowly, I began to educate myself . . .

I learnt why you can *never* have a healthy relationship with a Controll.

I mastered Controlls' trails of destruction and observed how ultimately they could be the end of people like you and me. Yes, it is that deep.

We're going to solve all the questions above and more, but first I need you to come with me. Take my hand. Are you ready? It's time to meet Damien.

CHAPTER TWO

SOMETIMES YOUR WORDS JUST NORMALIZE ME

The Art of Normalizing

The first time I meet Damien is at a networking event in a bougie, obscure bar in East London. In the run-up to the party, I've been working flat out trying to hone a column I'm writing. I'm being paid in 'experience' which, weirdly, my landlord doesn't accept as rent. I'm overtired and generally pissed off with life. But the thought of free alcohol and those bits of salmon on tiny pancakes with chives sprinkled on is enough for me to set out into the blustery night.

After fifteen frustrating minutes of turning in a circle waiting for Google Maps to calibrate and show me which direction to walk, I find the ironically named bar – Happiness Forgets. The Universe clearly tries her best there to lay out a warning sign, but I ignore it and merrily walk down the twisting, wrought-iron staircase, into the darkness below.

When I enter the dingy, uber-hip speakeasy I feel a flutter of

17

anxiety. I pull the green jumper dress away from my stomach. Already self-conscious at my absolutely fine outfit choice.

After a bag check and confusion about the guest list, an unfriendly Czech woman permits me entry. The bar is one of those low-lit places where you get cataracts trying to read the menu and go blind attempting to spot a pal.

It's half full and sounds of the Gotan Project ooze through the space. I walk in and squint, just about making out my friend Clara leaning over the counter and shouting, presumably a drink order, to the man-bunned barman.

I say 'friend'; Clara is a former colleague. A raging alcoholic theatre booker in her seventies who I worked with on a show. During that performance she got blind drunk, plunged the theatre into total blackout and took four minutes to find the lights. To be fair, the audience weren't responsive that night so at least she created some excitement. Clara is my excuse to be here. I'm not particularly fussed to see her but I never seem to be able to quench the thirst of FOMO that haunts me when I turn down an invite. What if I miss out on a job? Or meet my husband-to-be? I could find a tenner on the floor if I'm lucky.

I take off my coat and drape it over my arm, now nervous there's a definite VPL situation happening behind me. Trying to act as unfazed as possible, I walk to Clara and, as I do, I clock a man in his late thirties, white-shirted and navy-blazered, looking at me and grinning. We lock eyes momentarily. A flash of confidence. I smile and look down. I estimate I have less than a minute to quickly speed-plan our life together . . .

How I'll meet him later by the toilets, we'll chat and have everything in common. We'll date for four years then he'll propose, probably on Hampstead Heath with a picnic and a bottle of Dom Perignon he'll have inscribed to me. Our now-mutual friends would've been hiding in the bushes for three hours and they'll jump out and start an acoustic cover of 'You Do Something to Me'. Or something. Whatever, not bothered, haven't thought about it that much.

I've often mused back to that Sliding Doors moment. What would have happened if I'd spoken to Navy Blazer Man that night instead of the man I was about to give four painful years to? Presumably, because I hadn't yet educated myself on the cycle of control, exactly the same set of circumstances that did happen would follow, but with Navy Blazer Man instead.

I reach Clara, now talking to a tall guy with fiery red hair. She turns to me and smiles, then gives me an awkward shoulder pat, like she's trying to put out a tiny, tiny fire on my clavicle. She's got purple red wine stains at the corners of her mouth. I hate red wine. I nod at the man who is unremarkable looking but there is . . . something about him that I can't quite put into words. Believe me, I've tried.

She introduces us: 'Of course you know Damien.'

I haven't a clue. 'Mmm,' I say, extending my hand.

'She doesn't,' he says, then chuckles. I laugh, heat rises to my face.

He's broad and muscular, with an understated dress sense that's not in accordance with what I later learn is his relatively esteemed position at work.

Four hours pass. He's a raconteur and I'm completely and utterly disarmed by his charisma. He tells me about his role in tech marketing and his dreams to start a magazine, all of which he manages to make humorous. I'm impressed by his ambition, the way he side-eyes me to give cheeky grins and how *he takes me firmly by the waist and guides me to the bar when he wants a drink. It's as though I'm in an illustrious members' bar where he and I are the only patrons. I focus on nothing else that night. He's a foreign creature from outer space – there's no one more interesting, electrifying or captivating than him.*

My whole world has turned technicolour.

Everyone knows Damien. But I've always been terrible with names. At the end of the evening, he places his hands on the small of my back, draws me close and tells me he finds my obliviousness endearing.

'Endearing' changes months later to 'obnoxious' as he spits the memory back.

At the outset, he's enamoured. Once the last gaggle of guests depart and we're forced to leave, we walk together to the train station, our fingers sparking like they're being welded together. Then we ride the escalator to the underground. He's a step below and as he turns back and looks up, I see a definite glimmer in his eyes. He tells me about his 'crazy exes' and how nice it is to meet a normal woman. I grip my hands together to stop myself taking his face between my palms and kissing him intensely.

We quickly tumble into a relationship. I barely know a thing about him, but I've never experienced the kind of romantic love he shows in the first few weeks. He bulldozes me off my feet. There's no one like him. I'm so lucky.

'I've been waiting for someone like you. I see our whole future together,' he says, after two weeks of dating. It's magical.

My diary is suddenly full of social events with Damien. He knows everyone, or rather, they know him, and he's always got a witty remark or intelligent observation. Damien walks into the party like he's walking onto a yacht. I am honoured to be with him, a proud addition to his arm. That's early on in our relationship. After only a few months we barely go anywhere together.

'Different social circles,' he says, on his way out. 'You'll only get bored. Have a good night, yeah?' The door closes behind him.

The interest he shows in me dissipates by the day, but I dismiss this as part of the 'settling in' process. Soon other women will no longer be a distraction. Soon he'll stop hiding his phone. Soon it'll go back to how it used to be. Soon he'll remember how much he loved me on that escalator. Soon he'll stop being pissed off all the time, and soon I'll be his whole future again. Soon.

On the odd occasion we do go out together I frantically try to shore up our connection. I make sure I look my best, spending hours doing my hair and make-up, false lashes, new dress, manicure – the full shebang. I ruthlessly criticize my appearance – often things I can't change, like my height. 'Guys like petite women. I wish I was shorter, maybe I'll just crouch a bit.' Still his eyes wander. 'Men are visual creatures,' I reassure Lady Gut Instinct as she eye-rolls and exhales.

Many years later, I laugh as my therapist advises me to 'delete all photos of the two of you together'; she doesn't get the joke. 'Um . . . there, there aren't any,' I say. There were a few treasured photos on my phone that I snapped before he could tell me it wasn't a good time, but that's it. Certainly none on any social media platform. I called him out on this once and his reason was that it saves all the humiliation of the public

break-up that will inevitably happen when shit hits the fan.
That's some cripplingly low relationship confidence. It's like
walking into a gym with your neck in a brace: 'I've put this on
because I'm pretty sure I'm going to fall off the treadmill and
career into the weights section, so I'm making sure I'm covered.'

I only know a handful of his mates – mostly names from
stories. A few I've met and have relentlessly done my best to
make a good impression. I play out in my head them telling
Damien what a catch I am, him finally realizing how good he's
got it.

A year into our relationship Damien presents me with tickets
to a music festival. I'm eating cereal on a high bar stool in my
kitchen and nearly cause myself spinal injury from the jerk. I
try to play it cool:

'Oh, nice one, yeah sounds good; some all-right bands
playing, I think,' I say, choking on a huge mouthful of
Shreddies.

My inner child meanwhile has her head in the dressing-up
box, digging out fairy wings and face glitter, excitedly throwing
outfit choices on her bright blue bubble chair (she's from the
nineties, don't judge).

When Damien and I see the billowing, bright red flags at
the festival gates and hear the distant, pulsating bass, I'm on
top of the world. This is the 'soon' I'd wanted. I knew we'd get
here.

The dusty paths are bustling with nose-ringed, dreadlocked,
tattooed festival-goers, all carrying huge camping backpacks
and the obligatory Red Stripe. A tiny woman in her
mid-twenties walks towards us, carrying a thin mattress on her
head like she's returning to the village to provide bedding for

her sleep-deprived family. I turn to Damien, about to make a witty comment, but his eyes are fixed on her with what I gauge as a longing. He quickens his pace, he's now a few feet in front of me. He's heading directly towards her. What's he doing? My heartbeat mirrors the speed of his walk. When he reaches her, he's out of earshot, but I see him crouch under the mattress and slink an arm around her waist, kissing her dangerously close to the mouth.

I puff my way next to the two of them, feeling that familiar pang of hurt and jealousy.

'Hi,' I say, emphatically. I try to conceal my breathlessness but the 'hi' comes out far deeper and more sixty-a-day-ish than intended. They look at me like I'm deranged.

'Er, hi,' she says, smiling and glancing to Damien. I can see her up close now. She's stunning. Heterochromatic eyes – one brown, one blue – tanned skin with a sprinkle of freckles. Damien once told me how he loved freckles on a woman. I don't have any.

'Right, let's go,' says Damien, the annoyance in his voice unmistakable.

'I'll message you, Eve,' he says in a softer tone to Freckle-Mattress-Head.

As we walk away, I regret my actions immediately. Why did I have to say anything? I should have let it go. Blaming myself is survival instinct. It's easier to self-flagellate, then apologize to him. I know better than to ask who she is. But deep down, Lady Gut Instinct tells me. Months later, when I see her name come up on his phone as he shoots me a 'don't you dare' look and takes the call in another room, I have her identity as 'another woman' confirmed.

HOT COALS

You accept a high degree of powerlessness being in a relationship with a Controll. A lot of keeping quiet in order to cling at calm. Don't say anything, don't do anything, if you have an issue with their behaviour, you're best to bite your tongue rather than call it out. It's not just walking on eggshells; it's walking barefoot on red-hot coals.

I wanted Damien to want me. I wanted him to want me like he wanted me in our first few months together. I wanted him to want me like he wanted Eve and all the other women. I could offer him something they couldn't and that was true, devoted, no-holds-barred love. Little did I know, this wasn't what *he* wanted. He needed a fresh supply of women cascading through his life – not one. He'd soon get bored of one.

Over time, he became more distant and these 'Eves' popped up more frequently. I learnt it was easier to keep my opinions on them to myself, rather than question him. And so it went on. It wasn't until many years later that I realized:

What you put up with at the end of the relationship is not what you would have put up with at the beginning.

Read that again.

What you put up with at the end of the relationship is not what you would have put up with at the beginning.

THE ROAD TO NORMAL

Very quickly into my relationship with Damien I normalized his womanizing behaviour, his sporadic temper which caught me off guard, and his micro (and macro) aggressions.

Normalizing is the act of placating, reducing and returning events, circumstances and ideas back to a label of 'normal'.

**Normalizing is normal . . .
and extremely dangerous.**

It can happen on a global scale: world leaders can have populations normalizing destructive, racist, sexist, fascist behaviours relatively quickly. This is cultural normalization, where nations exposed to, say, radical terrorism or warfare will eventually consider it a 'normal' part of life.

Those in relationships with Controlls swiftly file their partner's abuse as normal. You see, 'normal' is a safe place to be, 'normal' is our comfort zone, we welcome 'normal' into our lives, it's what we're used to, so we know how to cope with it. It's easier for us to normalize abusive, vitriolic behaviour than to confront it.

If you think about cultural normalization, living in a war-torn country, you're already dealing with the day-to-day hell of trying to survive, and over time it becomes extremely unlikely you would spend time thinking 'this doesn't feel right'. You would be exhausted and terrified, your minimal energy spent, consistently readjusting the 'norm' to cope.

Similarly, being in a relationship with a Controll, you are regularly up against some form of terror. After all, emotional abuse from being in a relationship with a Controll is also known as . . . **Intimate Terrorism**.

Those in a relationship with a Controll can be living in a penthouse suite in an upmarket suburb, but still be desperately trying to survive and stay safe whilst confronted by their own terror. To cope, to manage, to survive, we normalize.

DENSENSITIZING AND DOWNPLAY

Alongside normalizing, the Controll will use methods to desensitize us and take the sting out of their bad behaviour with lines like:

'Calm down! I wasn't angry, just upset! What, I'm not allowed to show my emotions?'

'You need to rein in your paranoia about me and other women, it's all in your head.'

'Yes, I shouted and swore, but you drove me to do it. It's only because I care!'

It's all in the downplay. It wasn't that bad, was it? Your standards for what is acceptable diminish and normal boundaries that you have relied on from a young age get stomped down. You learn it is much harder work to assess, question and speak out, than it is to accept the situation and normalize it.

There is no way I would have gulped down some of the abusive behaviour from my Controlls if they had displayed it when we initially met. Can you imagine on a first date, your potential partner sneering at you, telling you you'd look better with no make-up on and giving the waitress a kiss? His bread roll would be wedged up his arse and you'd be in a taxi before the mains arrived.

No, normalizing takes time, it's a methodical process. I'll say it again: what you put up with at the end is not what you would have put up with at the beginning.

Normalizing abusive behaviour at home can bleed into other areas of your life too. If you subconsciously normalize behaviour like being sworn or shouted at and you learn to turn the other cheek to abusive actions and normalize that feeling of walking on hot coals, then what happens when you come up against a dictatorial character in a work environment? You've learnt to swallow it, tolerate it, and not speak up. You've already normalized it. As time goes by, your self-esteem and emotional welfare take a battering not only from the Controll at home, but at work too. There is no respite.

The more terror that comes your way, the better you get at normalizing abusive behaviour and its impact. This is something in life you'll improve at that you don't deserve a gold star for. Because normalizing fear that an explosion may happen at any minute allows it to go on longer and worsen. You can develop what's called **Hypervigilance**.

Hypervigilance is a state of extreme, heightened alertness. Have you ever watched a horror movie then heard a creak in your house and been so on edge you couldn't breathe? This is a small nod towards hypervigilance. Your senses have been pushed to such an elevated place because your fight-or-flight responses have kicked in, thinking you're in danger. You're insanely sensitive to any noise and, no matter what, you can't shake the feeling something terrifying is lurking in the shadows. Now imagine this all, or almost all the time. This can be exactly what it's like living with a Controll. Exhausting, right?

What can you do if you recognize that you have normalized toxic behaviour? Well, the first call of action is to start . . . **Noticing**.

There is power in noticing. Noticing precedes action, which precedes change. Noticing areas of your life where you have normalized abusive behaviours is the key to starting the journey to change.

Depending how far down the Controll course you are, this could be difficult. If you've been with a Controll for a long time, and/or you're an A* Normalizer, then you may have no point of reference to realize their behaviour is damaging. In this case, pay attention to how friends and family react to your Controll's behaviour. Do they raise their eyebrows or seem taken aback when you tell them some of the things they have done? This can be a good place to start the noticing process.

Later we'll discuss dating post-Controll, which is quite the obstacle course to navigate, but possible. One of the things that makes it so tricky is that you could have unknowingly worked hard on rehashing what is 'normal' to you whilst with your Controll. Things like being cheated on, spoken down to and intimidated will be your standards of what is acceptable even after the relationship is over. You need to unpick your 'normal' before you look for another partner.

We've got a way to go yet though, so hold fire on the dating apps.

Seriously, stop swiping.

CHAPTER THREE

SPILL THE GENES

Why are Psychopaths, Psychopaths?

A few months before meeting Damien, at the wet-behind-the-ears age of twenty-four I am momentarily single, having tumbled head first out of another toxic relationship with someone called Shiv. Shiv was, I'm sure still is, a wannabe singer-songwriter. On our first date he played me his album of covers which he recorded in the local leisure centre toilets for reverb. He liked to pretend he was 'from the streets' yet was annoyingly dripping in family money. He was absolutely convinced he was destined for success. Unfortunately, his only true assets were a wardrobe of designer jumpers, a burner phone, and an impressively high sex drive.

I'm happy to be single again. Really, I am. High on a heady mix of a week's worth of insomnia and a share bag of Haribos, all before 9 a.m. I'm walking through a relatively quiet Waterloo station. A few stragglers from last night sit on the chairs blearily staring at the departure boards, carb-cramming overpriced cheese croissants and guzzling coffee.

My platform flashes up and I board a train to visit my parents in the countryside – a welcome escape from city life. It's a sunny Sunday morning and the carriage is nearly empty; I spy a lovely, free double seat. It's far enough away from the toilets and close enough to the door to see when the food trolley comes and to have time to mentally prepare my extra snacks order. This is not my first rodeo.

I plonk my cabin-size suitcase on the racks above, take out my Meal Deal and prepare to do the usual 'eat everything before we reach the next stop' challenge. I don't want to boast, but I always win.

The electric doors from the next carriage slide open with a whoosh and a burly, bald man who looks like Oddjob from Goldfinger *walks through and spots me. I catch his eye, mid-BLT, then look down, pretending to be engrossed in the nutritional information of the Shapers prawn swirls in my hand.*

'Sit here?' he says in a deep, gruff, Cockney accent. He stops directly to the right of me. You've got two choices: deliberately look at the almost entirely empty train carriage, shrug and do a lot of pondering until he gets the message; or, if you're Peak Empath like me, gulp, quickly move all your belongings, knock the bacon out of your sandwich and nod furiously.

Obviously, I do the latter and the man, who I'll learn shortly is called Bill, slumps heavily onto the seat next to me. His gargantuan frame squeezes me closer to the grubby Perspex window. He gets out a copy of the Daily Mail *which he proceeds to manspread over me, so now I have 'EMMA WATSON SHOCKS IN SEE-THROUGH DRESS' on my lap.*

I side-eye Bill and see he's missing half a finger and a thumb.

Something awful has also happened to the tips of his fingers, like he's been in a really terrible accident. This is when I start feeling sorry for him.

He has letters tattooed across his hairy knuckles which read P-A-T-I-E-N-C-E. I reflect later that 'patience' may have been a 'reminder to self'.

Eventually we start chatting because, well, because that always happens to me. I have one of those 'tell me your life story' faces. I'd make a great talk-show host. He tells me he's on his way to get a heart transplant, he even pulls out his ECG scans.

I get the courage to ask what happened to his finger and thumb. Bill stiffly swivels round to me (he has very little neck to turn), and comes out with what I think is one of the most chilling sentences I've ever heard. He holds up his half-finger and thumb and says:

'What vis? Shot me own fingers orf in a bar brawl,' and with a wink adds, 'still managed to get the bouncer, though.' Then does a slow hangman's gesture paired with a gaping smile.

'Oh . . . no,' I say, 'did – did you get in any trouble?'

Bill, who has now turned back to Emma's nipples, shakes his head and waves his remaining fingers, then gives a self-satisfied:

'No fingerprints, no crime. Burnt 'em orf didnih?'

There we go, I am now most definitely sitting next to a homicidal maniac. What do you do? Get out, go to the loo, jump off the moving train, even if you're in Stockport . . . Or, if you're like me, give him your number to make sure his heart transplant goes OK. I must have been struck so many times with red flags from the whole happening that I got concussed and lost the ability to think clearly.

Bill and I sit for a while in silence. I'm playing out in my head what may have happened the night of that bar brawl when he shot and potentially murdered a bouncer. Is it weird he makes me feel kind of . . . safe? I should really address this. Reminder to self.

Whether our friend Bill (he's mine, so now he's yours too) murdered or maimed the nameless bouncer or not, he is obviously still an extremely shady, potentially psychopathic character.

Did he knock the bouncer off to protect himself? Possibly. Wrong place, wrong time? Maybe. Or was he in with a dangerous crowd and absorbed what it took to survive in the hellish criminal underworld? Not sure. Either way, it doesn't serve us to chuck around the term 'Psychopath' willy-nilly just because someone is more two-faced than some carnival mirrors.

NATURE OR NURTURE: PSYCHOPATH EDITION

How does someone become a Psychopath, all the way up there at 10 on the Psychometer? Well, there are a few ways. And there is no one single cause. There are some people who have the genetic predisposition of Psychopaths. These guys have different wiring in their brain to those who are not Psychopaths. This cannot be altered, fixed or healed – it's the way they were born.

Let's talk about brains, baby, let's talk about you and me. There are three key factors that may help you understand the behaviours of someone who has the predisposed genetics of a Psychopath.

Researchers at King's College London Institute of Psychiatry

(IoP) looked at brain scans and were unable to tell the gender, sexuality, geographic origin or race of a patient but realized they could, in fact, easily spot the brains of Psychopaths.

The team found the brains on these MRI scans had:

1. A shrunken Amygdala, which leads to a lack of feeling fear.

2. An enlarged Striatum, which controls reward-seeking – so for those on the far end of the Psychometer, the bigger the risk, the bigger the reward.

3. Reduced activity in the Insula, which is the part of the brain that should activate when seeing someone express emotions – this is a key component of the social brain. Quite literally, Psychopaths cannot read emotions like you or I.

There's another interesting difference between 'typical' brains and Psychopaths and that's a chemical called Oxytocin. This little fella is what regulates our emotional responses like trust, positivity, and the ability to bond with others. **It also contributes to how we experience love.**

Psychopaths do not process Oxytocin in the same way we do. Now don't start feeling sorry for them, but do start understanding why a desperate bid to stick around and change them is pointless.

The fact is: not all Psychopaths are bad people. That's right, you heard me – not every Psychopath is a horrific serial killer. Some have all the neurological characteristics but may simply be quietly living their lives, not out to cause pain and harm to others. They may merely seem detached or present a lack of emotional responses. As we've seen from our Psychometer, it's all scalable.

OUR PLASTIC BRAINS

The brain is a frighteningly malleable organ. This is known as 'synaptic plasticity', which means the synapses in the brain have an ability to strengthen or weaken over time due to increased or decreased activity. There's something else that shapes the brain too – hard blows or injury like those sustained in car accidents, by boxers, or in other contact sports.

If we look at the case of American Footballer Aaron Josef Hernandez, we see a successful, fit, personable guy who had a young daughter and fiancée and was rising to the top of the NFL. But in 2013, at the age of twenty-four he murdered line-backer Odin Lloyd; he was charged and received a life sentence, then he took his own life at twenty-seven.

What went so wrong, so quickly? Post-mortem brain scans of Aaron revealed he had Stage 3 CTE – Chronic Traumatic Encephalopathy, which is a progressive brain condition thought to be caused by repeated blows to the head. Some of the symptoms of CTE are depression, frustration and short-term memory loss. Although, of course, Aaron's actions cannot be excused, his case displays how impacts to the brain can have significant, long-term and sometimes devastating consequences to the recipient's behaviour.

Scientists have found that psychopathic behaviour can be caused by traumatic blows to the head, and damage to a specific part of the forebrain can result in inability to feel fear and lack of emotional responses . . . i.e., the creation of a psychopathic brain.

A study by Dr Simone Shamay-Tsoory[1] found that: 'people diagnosed as Psychopathic have difficulty showing empathy, just like patients who have suffered frontal head injury.' And vice versa, 'people who have Psychopathic symptoms behave as though they are suffering frontal brain damage.'

So, anyone can become a Psychopath. I don't mean any of us could wake up one day and decide to murder Karen in the office for making fish in the microwave for the fourth lunchtime in a row (though we've felt inclinations), but you can see how in one fell swoop, personalities are darkly transmuted due to brain injury.

PSYCHO SCHOOL –
LEARNING TO BE A PSYCHOPATH

What about the ones who don't have the genetic disposition for Psychopathy? Is there some kind of Controll Training Camp, a Psycho School run by a dictatorial figure with flashy PowerPoints and end of term exams? Angry face stickers for the ones who pass? Not as far as I know (not unless you count some private schools), but there's research that shows a person's environment can have a huge impact on whether that person develops and executes psychopathic behaviours.

Let's talk about those displaying psychopathic behaviour – that's those who don't necessarily have that different wiring in the brain. It's all about conditioning. Psychopathic traits can be

learnt from peers, media, family, environments, pretty much anywhere you can think of. What that means is, it's also possible to unlearn them. Learning is about altering neurological pathways, and though unlearning is not necessarily a quick and easy process, it's conceivable. If someone is a womanizer, you can't just ask them to keep it in their pants and show some respect; it may take a lifetime of psychotherapy to change their behaviours. Often, it's not so much the unlearning that's the problem but the desire to do so in the first place.

But let's be clear . . .

If someone is displaying psychopathic behaviour, then no one can make them change.

ARE YOU A PSYCHO?

We have all at one stage in our lives displayed psychopathic traits. If you're shaking your head, well then, you're lying, and that in itself is a bit psychopathic, mate. Perhaps there have been times you've surprised yourself with a lack of emotion when dealing with an intense situation. You may have acted without thinking and convinced yourself that it was acceptable to cheat, lie or steal. Have you sought some form of revenge or felt utterly remorseless in a situation that should have warranted it? These are all up there as behaviours on the latter end of the Psychometer.

Men that constantly beg for nudes, who cheat, never live up to their promises, and don't introduce you to their friends or family, also known as fuckboys, could well have learnt that behaviour. It may have been from observing their father not being faithful when they were growing up. Perhaps they formed a clique of equally gormless mates who lauded their actions, or maybe they were just gifted with the emotional intelligence of a damp flannel.

Where else can learned psychopathic behaviour come from? Well, aside from shifting the blame onto bad role models, shit parenting and a bad environment, you could argue that our friend Capitalism has quite the hand to play.

SHOW ME THE MONEY!

You see, Capitalism, by its very design, demands us to acquire more, show more, be more. It's dog eat dog. The very ecosystem rests on the questionable morals and ethics of a handful of individuals who, more than likely, fall at the latter end of the Psychometer themselves.

Ingrained within Capitalism is the notion that if you are not one of the hyper-elite puppeteers pulling the strings on the world economy, you're the puppet, exhaustedly trying to keep up with demands. You can see then that it would be relatively easy to fall prey to some learned psychopathic behaviour: undercutting people, lying, cheating, feeling a secret glee when your colleague gets fired because it may mean you get a promotion and, hence, move closer to being a puppet master yourself.

The idea of success, financial abundance and wealth beyond our wildest dreams is touted to us in all manner of ways through the Capitalist system. Is it our fault then if we surprise ourselves with a lack of remorse for pocketing that tenner we found on the street corner instead of handing it to the homeless guy who was too exhausted by the system to see it?

DR ROBERT HARE'S PSYCHOPATHY CHECKLIST

Look, here's the thing – if you're getting your self-esteem sucked on the daily then it's unlikely you'll be umming and erring over the perp being diagnosed as a Psycho or how they came to be that way. But to show us the definitive traits of a true Psychopath, so we can get clearer on who we're looking out for, allow me to bring you the Hare Psychopathy Checklist.

In the 1970s, criminal psychologist Dr Robert Hare devised the Hare Psychopathy Checklist-Revised (PCL-R) – a diagnostic tool used to assess the severity of a person's psychopathic tendencies.

This is considered the gold standard for assessing psychopathy. Although I must say that this checklist should only be used by qualified practitioners to assess a person's propensity for psychopathy. It's very helpful for us – the victims of Controlls – to understand the list, but I'm not going to suggest writing the traits on your hand and diagnosing, say, the bus driver for not letting you on because you forgot your fare. So here goes, the twenty traits assessed in the Hare Psychopathy Checklist-Revised:

1. **Glib and superficial charm**
    The smooth schmoozers, they talk the talk.

2. **Grandiose (exaggeratedly high) estimation of self**
    Think God Complex. I'm all for self-love, but we're talking sky-stretching egotism. An unshakeable belief they are the greatest thing that walks the planet.

3. **Need for stimulation**
    They are bored, bored, bored. Often taking part in illegal activities, chasing potential sexual partners, or indulging in substance abuse.

4. **Pathological lying**
    So good they're fooling everyone. If you catch them, they'll gaslight their way out of it.

5. **Cunning and manipulative**
    Crafty and divisive, they are smarter, savvier, and far more deceptive than you can dare to imagine.

6. **Lack of remorse or guilt**

   The word 'sorry' is not in their vocabulary. They will cheat, lie, steal, abuse and worse, with no attachment to morality.

7. **Shallow or flat affect (superficial emotional responsiveness)**

   That lifeless look. Watching notorious Psychopaths, their faces will seem totally expressionless. They are blank.

8. **Callousness and lack of empathy**

   Don't expect them to change their ways because they're hurting you. They care for no one but themselves. They are not capable of compassion; they will never see things through your eyes.

9. **Parasitic lifestyle**

   They feed off others, taking whatever they can get: sex, money, drugs, the list is infinite. They believe they are owed everything they desire.

10. **Poor behavioural controls**

    There's no off switch. Their moods swing violently, they fire up faster than a Porsche 911 and you do not want to be in their way when they shift gear.

11. **Sexual promiscuity**

    Sex addicts. They'll cheat and chase their sexual partners indiscriminately and certainly will not be satisfied being monogamous.

12. **Early behaviour problems**

    They were trouble growing up; they could have been

diagnosed with ADHD. They may have been overly aggressive, defiant, or emotionally maladjusted.

13. **Lack of realistic long-term goals**
They have no aspirations, or if they do, they are completely overblown and unachievable, such as: 'I'm going to be the next President of the United States.' Oh no, wait . . .

14. **Impulsivity**
They act without thinking; their behaviour is 'spur of the moment' and they make rash decisions without caring how it affects others.

15. **Irresponsibility**
Nothing is ever their fault; they will shame others into submission. They act recklessly and are negligent of any responsibilities.

16. **Failure to accept responsibility for own actions**
It's always everyone else's fault. They will never accept the consequences of their behaviour on themselves or others.

17. **Many short-term marital relationships**
They can't hold down a partner. I would argue this is not only marital. The thrill of the chase is just too great.

18. **Juvenile delinquency**
They will have participated in criminal activity as a young person; this doesn't necessarily mean they were caught.

19. **Revocation of conditional release**
A probation or freeing from prison has been cancelled due to their inability to stay within the laws and rules of their probation.

20. **Criminal versatility**
They will commit a variety of offences, thieving, raping, murdering, or more. Whatever floats their boat and they'll take great pride in getting away with it.

For each of these traits, the subject is assessed on a 3-point scale. 0 = doesn't apply, 1 = applies somewhat and 2 = definitely applies. The scoring measures a maximum of 40 points. A person in the US that measures 30 and above, or 25 and above in the UK, is likely to be a clinical Psychopath.

An important point to stress here . . .

Just because your Controll doesn't tick every single one of those traits, it doesn't mean they are not abusive.

I see you: don't be looking for the ones they don't line up with, wiping your brow and cheerily marching into oblivion. We have to be far more astute than that. There are many tones and hues to Controlls, one is not a carbon copy of another. Awareness will be our shield.

As I said, it won't make any difference if you hear that person is 'officially' a Psychopath or not. Similarly, unless you're able to take along an MRI scanner to a first date (I've tried, and they ask you to leave it in the cloakroom), then you only have one detecting power to sniff out the psychos . . . your gut instinct. If it doesn't feel right, if you're intimidated, suspecting that you're losing yourself, step back, assess and prepare to get out. Don't worry – we're going to be working on our gut instinct later.

It's not fair for us to let Psychopaths take all the shade. No, it's time to move on, because these next folk we're even more likely to come into contact with. In fact, we're more likely to become them ourselves . . .

CHAPTER FOUR

DON'T BE AFRAID OF THE NARC

Narcissistic Personality Disorder

After my train journey with Bill and a few weeks in the countryside, I am rejuvenated. As I step back onto the bustling city streets, I'm pretty certain this is what it feels like to have your shit together. Little do I know that only a few nights later I will plummet into four painful years with the most callous and cruel Controll yet: Damien. But at this moment, I have my shit together.

I blink into the morning sun and allow myself a browse around a pound shop to buy stuff like a hot pink salt shaker, some highlighters and a toothbrush holder shaped as a giraffe. You know, the crap you really need – the mark of a twenty-four-year-old who, as I say, really has her shit together.

I've shied away from performing any comedy over the last few years. Being in a relationship with a Controll takes a steaming turd on your self-esteem, so I haven't felt I have it in

44

me to bravely face the public and attempt to make them laugh. There hasn't been much to laugh about. But tonight I've been booked for my first gig in a long time and I'm nervous, but ready.

It's a venue I've performed in a few times before – an old man's pub that thwacks you with a sweet, yeasty smell when you step in. The kind of place you definitely squat and hover whilst using the loo. I go to the back room to check the running order. I already know it, but I triple-quadruple-check facts when I'm anxious. As I go into the green room, which is actually the backroom store cupboard with some sticky spirit dispensers stacked against odd, third-hand chairs, I swallow hard and re-remember that familiar feeling of being the only female on the line-up and walking into a roomful of blokes. I must give off 'please don't interact with me' vibes because no one does.

I start gliding my hands along my chin with nervousness and feel the bristle of one of those tough hairs that you won't be able to get off your mind until it's out.

There's a surprise headliner; I don't know who it is, and I don't really care – I am planning to leave straight after my set. I head to find the bathroom to do some breathing and deal with what I'm sure is a Miss Trunchbull hair on my chin but is most likely unnoticeable.

As I head along the musty, narrow corridor a large man in his early fifties approaches from the other end of the walkway. He's wearing a faded brown leather jacket, a slogan T-shirt saying 'POLICE THE POLICE', which barely holds his beer belly, and too-tight dark jeans. There isn't enough room for us both to pass and he doesn't look like he's going to make space

*for me, so I stop and press my back to the wall. As he comes
closer, I know what's about to happen. Call it second sight.
Unfortunately, through years of similar experiences, females
have intuition for this kind of thing. As he presses his body up
against mine, I feel the ridge of his belt on my crotch and smell
his acrid aftershave.*

*'Nice and tight,' he breathes into my face, with a laugh. I
smell the lager I'm sure came straight off the tap downstairs.
His legs are wide and encasing mine. So close he could poke
out his tongue and lick me. And then he does. His sandpaper
slug tongue draws a trail across my cheek, touching the
corner of my mouth. It happens slowly. At first, I don't react.
Then I shove him back and say, 'Hey!' With a laugh,
immediately trying to make light of the situation. My face
turns crimson. He grins. Ace, set and match for this
autocratic arsehole.*

*Ideally, I should knee him in his tiny dick, wrap his arm
around his back, tell him he's pathetically clawing at youth with
his age-inappropriate clothes, and call the police. But I don't. I
minimize. I play along like I'm in on the joke, most likely to
grapple for some kind of control in the hope it won't escalate.
Fighting back is not part of the 'smile sweetly' rhetoric that's
been ingrained in us since desperately working towards the title
of 'good girl' at six years old. Now I would argue a 'good girl' is
a woman that finds a way to safely react and speak out. That's
what I'm doing right here.*

*Later I learn he's the headliner. I had no idea who he was
until then. This won't be the last time I come across him. Even
though his story is out there on the lips of many other
unfortunate women, he's still working. Still getting booked by*

the higher-ups. Fondles don't count. That's just his way. He's being friendly.

He has another gig afterwards, so his headline spot has been moved right after mine. I see it ruffles the booker but what is he going to do?

My set is dry. A few laughs here and there but nothing spectacular. The words of my recent ex, Shiv, echo in my head as I wait for my pay envelope: 'Maybe you're not cut out for comedy.'

As I stand side of stage I watch the headliner at work. I have to admit – it's quite the sight. Although his material is dated and there's no particular craft to his jokes, he has the audience in the palm of his hand. He works them like putty. Obnoxiously flirting with wives as their husbands feign smiles and cross arms. Locating, then ripping the piss out of the 'weaker' members of the crowd. They love him. He goes way over his allotted time slot, so much so that another act is axed.

'He always does this,' the booker whispers with a shake of his head as he hands me my thin envelope.

On the bus home I can smell him on me. I feel sick. I rummage in my bag and pull out a cheap roll-on deodorant which I use around my neck like an expensive eau de toilette. I sit wondering how he did it. How did he have so much confidence, so few fucks to give? He used the audience like pawns, the venue his chess board, he was not the king or the knight, no, he was the player – totally in charge.

That night I took two showers before I could get to sleep.

*

The headline act was winning in that world because, undoubtedly, he was a Narcissist, with a capital 'N'. He was definitely between 6 and 8 on the Psychometer, I would hazard an 8.

Narcissism is not a new concept, and it certainly doesn't only thrive in the airless corridors of crumbling comedy clubs.

THE NARC ORIGIN STORY

The term evolved over 2,000 years ago when this dude called Ovid wrote the legend of Narcissus. Basically, it goes like this:

Narcissus was the warrior son of a god. He became besotted with his own reflection in a lake. Echo, a nymph, fell in love with him but he was too absorbed in his reflection to notice. Echo was having a 'mare talking – she'd had a spell cast on her, but Narcissus paid no attention. He died, she died. The End.

A few years ago, I realized I had the propensity to fall in love with Narcissists, but on reflection, it wasn't the best idea. See what I did there? 'Reflection' because he fell in love with his . . . Forget it. Narcissism ain't pretty, even if Narcissus was.

There's a scale to narcissism, as with psychopathy – it comes in different shapes and sizes. Unfortunately, Narcissists are a little harder to spot because we've all become a tad narcissistic, and it's turned into an epidemic.

THE SCOURGE OF SOCIAL MEDIA

You could argue one of the main reasons for the rise in narcissism is social media. In the wrong hands, social media is a precarious creation. Everyone can say and do things and be the people they would never have the confidence for IRL.

We use the barrier of a screen to showcase the best versions of ourselves, reeling in netfuls of validation. The screen is a barrier between self and conscious thought, and social media facilitates exhibitionism and the thirst for superiority. Narcissists love to exert their power, and what faster and more detached way is there than online from the comfort of their mum's basement?

Being 'narcissistic' is a throwaway insult; but when narcissistic traits become so apparent that they lead to uneasiness, anxiety, and worse, for the Narc's partner, this can indicate narcissistic personality disorder (NPD).

HOW TO SPOT A NARCISSIST

Narcissists are in awe of themselves. They cannot tell enough people how brilliant they are and how many admirers lust after them. But Narcs are crippled by their own fragile self-confidence. There is mixed research to suggest that, ironically, Narcissists could suffer from alarmingly low self-esteem, desperately needing others to prop them up. It's perhaps more apt to say Narcs have:

Fragile high self-esteem.

This means their beliefs about themselves are dependent on external validation, praise, and their own self-deception. Their demand for attention and grandiose sense of self-importance make them exhausting to be around.

You can't spot a Narc by noting their phone gallery is all shirtless selfies, there's more to it. There are subcategories within narcissistic personality disorder. The main two being Grandiose and Vulnerable. Many psychologists and health professionals would argue there are up to eight other subcategories, but as of yet there is no clinical diagnosis for these, so let's look at the two main types.

Overt Narcissists, also known as Grandiose Narcissists, are exactly what we would imagine the typical Narcissist to be. The loud, brash types that demand attention and compliments. They have fantastical ideas about who they are, what they represent in society and what their future holds. Often Overt Narcissists are obsessed with the idea of fame and recognition and are 'slighted' when they're not where they think they deserve to be.

These people tend to be, but are not always, in public-facing roles, preferably in the limelight where they can harness as much appreciation as possible. They become frustrated if they do not receive the acknowledgement they require. The Overt Narcissist will use tactics like love-bombing, gaslighting and baiting (where they wind you up and prime you for an argument) to insert excitement into their days.

Covert Narcissists, also known as Vulnerable Narcissists, are extremely difficult to recognize because they are the lesser-spotted variety. They appear extremely vulnerable; they are experts at appealing to your compassionate side and masters at playing the victim. They behave very differently to an Overt Narcissist, and could even seem meek, mild-mannered and humble but, and this is important . . .

Their end goal is exactly the same.
They are Controlls – controlling personality
types who seek to dominate your life.

Do you see how they would be harder to spot? You wouldn't imagine that self-effacing, quiet soul to be a Covert Narcissist, but they very much could be.

The Covert Narcissist could use their seemingly self-critical, low self-esteem chat to make you pity them, perhaps ensuring you empathize with their bad financial situation to the point where you offer them money. In order to exist, they need your backing.

A Narcissist can only function with other people
around them – as their mirror or their echo.

All Narcissists relish mind games, including gaslighting and other abusive behaviours. We're going to cover gaslighting in more detail later.

Although difficult to ascertain, because it's a hard case to prove, there is an unquestionably significant correlation between suicide and the partners of Narcissists. Victims are left in emotional tatters when or if the relationship ends.

There is something else – a key trait that will help us spot them if we look very carefully and that is flat affect, or lack of emotion. Underneath their bravado or self-effacement, they are hollow.

FLAT-PACKED

Flat affect is where someone has a severely reduced aptitude for expressing emotions. They may speak in a monotonous voice, have diminished expressions, or appear 'flat' when conveying themselves. When Narcissists – particularly Overt Narcissists – are not performing their loud, bombast, in-your-face routines, their act drops, and they can present flat affect.

It's like they don't see you, they look through you, they're blank. Their 'emotions' muted, they don't really laugh or smile and if they do it seems fake. Their face is almost motionless, even when expressing anger, there's something very still, yet chilling about it. Imagine it like a person with low energy. They stare through you, not at you.

It's worth noting that if someone presents flat affect it doesn't necessarily mean they are a Psychopath. It can be a feature of those with autism spectrum disorder, for example – those with ASD can interact or communicate differently. They may appear uncaring or unresponsive but they are not.

But – and it's a big but – not everybody who has narcissistic personality disorder also has flat affect; however, it was an indicator for me with some of my Controlls. In essence, it felt like they weren't present.

The lights are on, but nobody's home.

Controlls can't register emotions: the higher up the Psychometer they are, the less they sense, or rather, truly understand emotions. There was even a case where a Psychopath was taught to read emotions using emojis.

Then there are those who struggle to communicate at all. I once dated a guy who texted me using nothing but 'lol' and that goddamn cry laughing emoji. I can tell you that he was definitely a gym-grunter, he had a cheeky Nandos, and his Instagram handle was @[hisname]official – official what? Official bellend.

CRY, BABY

You'll often feel confused when dating a Controll, wondering if they do truly love you and if they enjoy your company at all. Controlls see other people as extensions of themselves, so any

love they show is misdirected to where they need it most –
themselves. They're using you as a prop for their ego.

Controlls are often perplexed by emotions because they do
not sense them in the same way that you or I do. I had an ex
that would tell me I put on 'crocodile tears' when he upset me.
I later concluded that he couldn't connect high emotional states
with the physical emotions they induced. He figured I was acting;
he just didn't get it.

Although I have been using the umbrella term 'Controlls' for
all controlling personality types, it's important you can tell your
Psycho from your Narc.

THE DIFFERENCES BETWEEN
A PSYCHOPATH AND A NARCISSIST

There is a great dichotomy between those with antisocial person-
ality disorder (Psychopaths) and narcissistic personality disorder.
The main aspects that differentiate a Narcissist and a
Psychopath are:

1. **Empathy**. A Psychopath has minimal to no empathy.
   Narcissists, however, do understand what empathy is and
   can sometimes display it, but it is usually aligned with
   themselves. For example, a Narcissist may cry when
   their pet dies but only because that animal was an
   extension of them. Narcissism has been described as
   'empathy's evil twin'.

2. **Regret**. A recent study suggests that Psychopaths can feel regret but what they cannot do is use it to guide their future decision-making, like you or I would.[1] Essentially, they don't tend to look back and learn from their mistakes. A Narcissist experiences guilt in the guise of shame. They feel shame for their behaviour, but only because they know it will mar their self-image.

3. **Fear**. Psychopaths cannot feel fear. For them, the bigger the risk, the bigger the reward. Narcissists can feel fear, but their anxieties are different to normal worries (loss, illness, suffering, death). Narcissists have an intense fear of humiliation, failure and loss of admiration from others.

4. **Emotions**. Psychopaths cannot read emotions like you or I.[2] They can pick up on social cues but only if it benefits them. For example, if they want to score a promotion or climb the social ladder, Psychopaths can attune themselves with how others are feeling, but only to manipulate them. Narcissists can read emotions but are confused by them. Both will use people's emotional responses as tools for control.

5. **Social standing**. You will most likely find those with NPD in public-facing roles, as they like to be seen, heard and appreciated; whereas a Psychopath may choose a more covert lifestyle, often watching from the shadows, not to be seen nor heard.

LET'S GET MYTHICAL

There's another element of Controlls that we haven't put a name to yet. You see, there's actually something else happening on the Psychometer. Up there between the Narcs and the Psychos lives a lying leech called . . . Machiavelli. Machiavellianism is the third side of the Dark Triad. OK, I understand you may be wondering if you've accidentally picked up some dusty ass mythical book that's about to begin detailing a princess boning a dragon . . . you haven't, stick with me.

The Dark Triad looks like this:

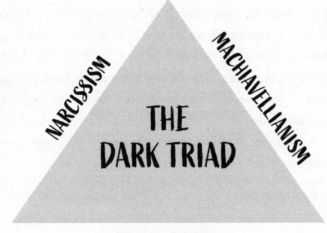

The Dark Triad comprises three closely related but independent personality traits: narcissism, Machiavellianism and psychopathy.

- **Narcissism:** tends to be an egocentric obsession with oneself, lack of empathy.
- **Machiavellianism:** those who lie and manipulate, they are unemotional and self-obsessed.
- **Psychopathy:** those who display continuous antisocial behaviour with little to no remorse.

THE DIRTY DOZEN

Two psychologists at the University of Western Florida concocted 'The Dirty Dozen' scale, which is a look at how to measure the Dark Triad traits.[3]

Here are the twelve criteria they used to assess participants:

Narcissism
- I tend to want others to admire me.
- I tend to want others to pay attention to me.
- I tend to expect special favours from others.
- I tend to seek prestige or status.

Machiavellianism
- I have used deceit or lies to get my way.
- I tend to manipulate others to get my way.
- I have used flattery to get my way.
- I tend to exploit others towards my own end.

Psychopathy
- I tend to lack remorse.
- I tend to be callous or insensitive.
- I tend to not be too concerned with morality or the morality of my actions.
- I tend to be cynical.

Essentially, the higher the person scored across each test, the greater the propensity for Dark Triad tendencies. There are shared aspects to these three types, such as lack of empathy, hostility, and general dog-eat-dogness (probs not the technical term). So here we are again – it's great for us to be aware of the differences, but I care about the victim, not the perp, so our focus is on arming ourselves with the knowledge in order to live a free, healthy and boundary-filled life.

NO RESET FOR THE WICKED

It is difficult to put a figure on the number of Narcs there are in society. Often, if someone suspects that another could be diagnosed with NPD, then the person with potential NPD will dispute it, heaping blame on others. If they do go to therapy, it is nigh-on impossible for them to have the capability to analyse themselves and address their flaws.

Many years ago, I once suggested one of my exes, Shiv, went to see a therapist, even though ironically it was me who needed one. I didn't think I deserved one back then, which, of course, is bullshit. At that point I didn't fully understand the subtleties and complexities of the Controlls I dated. But I sure as hell knew that when they wanted to turn on the charm they could, and you didn't want to be around when it was off.

Shiv returned from that session and proudly told me there was nothing wrong with him and it was all in my head – another dose of gaslighting – and I didn't mention it again. In reality he had probably stopped off at KFC for chicken thighs and then got between another female's thighs whilst I sat at home patting myself on the back for 'solving the problem'. Sigh.

All righty. I reckon we're pretty damn sussed on the higher end of the Psychometer now. We can spot Controlls, and we've learnt the plethora of differences between them. Next up, in order to further protect ourselves we need to go deeper and get inside their heads.

It's time to learn how *they* find *us*.

CHAPTER FIVE

PREY FOR ME

How Controlls Find Their Prey

I love love. It's less Disney, more Destiny. I estimate that before the age of twenty-five I am absolutely guaranteed to find my Mr Darcy-Cum-Elba (that's the lovechild of Fitzwilliam Darcy, Benedict Cumberbatch and Idris Elba, obviously).

I'm fifteen and plans for my destiny are on track as I find myself with my first serious boyfriend, which makes it sound like I got a rash. I suppose in some ways, I did. Chris is a guy in the sixth form, a few years above me at school. He is tall, skinny and has a secret tattoo of a Mandarin word that he doesn't actually know the meaning of, on his bicep. Rumour has it, it means 'chicken noodles'. He really likes Chicken and Mushroom Pot Noodle, so that worked out quite well.

He smells strongly of Davidoff Cool Water and his curly hair has so much product in, it feels like running your hands along a tyre. Altogether – minus the dramatic break-ups followed in quick succession by a passionate rekindling, all in the space of a lunchtime break – we date for four years, and Chris is my first true love.

In the tropical summer of 2003, Black-Eyed Peas are top of the charts with 'Where is the Love'. We've hit a heatwave at thirty-two degrees, and no one is doing any work. In an idyllic corner of the West Country, my tribe of Year 11 girlfriends and I – skirts rolled up, socks rolled down, lie sunning ourselves on the grassy mound by the Sixth Form Centre, waiting to be let into the School Talent Show.

Teachers stand in groups chatting to each other, paying no attention to the Year 7 boys making a game out of pulling each other's trousers down. I'm sure Freud would have something to say about that.

The School Talent Show is an annual event, much like prom and the last day of term, where normal rules are overlooked and there's an air of recklessness that someone always takes too far. I've known for a few weeks that Chris was performing, although I didn't know what – he said it was a surprise. I'm already preening my feathers, ready to exude smugness in the direction of girls in the younger years, as they jealously roll their eyes at our romcom love story.

The school hall is packed, and my friends and I squeeze ourselves onto the front row bench – school pecking order means we have first dibs. It's stuffy, and I use the chewed blazer sleeve tied around my waist to subtly dab at the sweat that rolls down my forehead. A strip light blinks above, and the students' babble immediately ceases as the heady sound of a rap beat palpitates around the badly soundproofed space. I hear faint titters as Chris walks on, dressed in a skater hoodie, a baseball cap, a worn pair of Etnies and baggy jeans with a silver chain from the back pocket to the front. I never understood the purpose of those.

Before he's drawn breath, I'm hit with the horrific realization of what's coming. I imagine this is what happens when a gun is pointed at your head. My secondary school life flashes before my eyes. I'm plagued by nightmarish premonitions of being pushed into lockers, having my ponytail snipped off and willingly taking detentions to try and regain my credibility. Chris takes to the stage with (and I have to give it to him) a little swag, but I could never have prepared myself for the humiliation that is about to take place.

There's something jarring about a skinny, white teenager with a country accent and no sense of rhythm spitting bars. It's like thinking sleeping with your boss will get you a promotion – it's a nice idea but when it comes together it'll be a right mess.

Unfortunately, after the third verse (of seven) I weirdly, urgently need the loo, so I can only tell you a few of the lyrics Chris had written. Of course I remember them, they are inked onto my memory like chicken noodles. The first verse opened with:

'Her name is Madeline, she is so fine, I wanna make her mine, I'll always be on time. Yo, Madeline, I'll wait in line, you are so fine (f-f-f-fine, fine, fine, fine), will you be mine, Madeline?' (Dance break.)

By the end of the dance break, I had ducked out – and it was a very long duck, past forty-five rows of benches of grinning, nudging schoolchildren. I'm now leaning over the chipped ceramic Armitage Shanks sink, staring at my teenage crimson reflection in the lip-gloss-smeared mirror of the girls' toilets.

I try to steady myself by focusing on the slow drip of a leaky tap falling onto a screwed-up soggy piece of toilet paper. Chris's rap echoes through the hall, finding its way to me. I feel guilty, I want to show my appreciation, but I care far too much about what everyone else thinks of me. I console myself with the idea that I will explain I had period pains. I'll even let him grab my fifteen-year-old boobs on his bunk bed at the weekend to make him feel better.

That hideously, sphincter-clenching display of affection was one of the most genuine shows of romantic love I would receive for a very long time. Perhaps I would have stayed until the end of his rap serenade if I'd known that. There was no insincerity, games or mind-play. Although I feigned tonsillitis for two weeks until I hoped everyone had forgotten, deep down I appreciated what he was trying to do. He was proud to be with me and wanted the entire school to know.

Chris was about 4 on the Psychometer – a sweet guy, certainly not a Controll. He had a good heart, although perhaps he should have been a little more realistic about being in the next 8 *Mile*.

You see my jagged relationship history hadn't started that badly. At eighteen years old, I was set free into the auspicious world of love and dating. But my disillusion grew with every relationship. I ambled on, knocking about from man to man, always hoping it would get better and I'd finally reach my destiny. I pretty much only ever had long-term relationships. I didn't know 'fling' was a word until my early thirties.

I lived with multiple men. After only weeks of dating I'd be convinced that moving in together would cement our relationship.

Add that to extortionate London rent and you've got a recipe for multiple failed tenancies and a lot of money lost in deposits. All this for the hope a housing contract would turn into a marriage licence and I'd meet my destiny.

I did everything in my power not to be single. The non-existent time between relationships was pointed out by friends but I always managed to brush it off: 'I don't look for these men, *they* find *me*,' I'd retort as I stepped off the tube after my three-hour circling of Canary Wharf to lure an eligible bachelor on Crumble.

Very plainly: I was terrified of being alone. I did not want to be left behind and I thought life would be lonely, boring and repetitive. How wrong I was. By the way, this is nothing to do with me having abandonment issues. It's not like I was going around saying, 'Hey, if you're looking for a girl with abandonment issues, then look no father' . . . sorry, further. Further.

It wasn't just being single that I had issue with – it was the breaking-up part I couldn't hack. Even if I was certain the relationship was wrong for me, I was not able to end it. Not only had I convinced myself I couldn't deal with all the heightened emotions that surround the ending of a partnership, but I really, really, really did not like upsetting people. I can't believe what I put myself through so I wouldn't hurt anyone. I lived with an ex who peed in the bathroom sink with the door open. One time we went to a bar and a pair of his dirty boxers fell out of his jeans leg, he sniffed them and said, 'Still some wear in these,' and put them in his pocket. Worst of all, and this is horrific, he used a Sports Direct mug as his *first* choice of crockery. What was I thinking?

The shortest relationship I landed was with a deeply religious

Canadian guy called Logan. Logan came about from need rather than necessity, in one of my panics at being alone. He wasn't really a terrible man, but I knew we weren't a good fit after a few weeks together. He was book-smart and liked the quiet life; he described me as 'a complete whirlwind' and would 'sshh' me under his breath when he thought I was talking too loudly. I worked and re-worked my dumping letter to him in the notes section of my phone like I was trying to be the new Brontë:

> Dearest Logan, my heart, my love,
> It has fallen upon me at this deathly hour to inform you that I do not think we should be as one. It brings me great sorrow for thou art a good man with noble courage and religious morals. My mother will be greatly saddened to hear of this, ~~yet I cannot betray my heart~~
> ~~I cannot do it any more~~
> Lest you're an annoying shit of a man
> Logan. This isn't working you keep telling me I'm too loud, it's really fucking patronizing.

But I couldn't bring myself to even text dump him. I stayed with him for a bit longer, eventually resorting to giving myself migraines from being so deliberately shouty and annoying. It worked, and he finally caved, saying he couldn't deal with my excessive energy any more. I lay in a quiet room for exactly 7.2 days then popped off to find the next man.

The older I got, the more Controlls I attracted. I could change my hair, clothes, music taste, it didn't matter – a Controll was just around the corner ready to mould (and then devour) me. But in that time, I never stopped, grounded myself and asked . . . why? Why does this keep happening? Why am I so appealing to Controlls? Now seems a good time.

A CONTROLL'S COGNITION

We should switch our viewpoint to that of a Controll if we're going to outsmart them. It's time to get the inside track on the Controll brain.

As Empaths and Codependents love to find broken people to heal, Controlls love to find broken people to hunt. It's almost a total reverse. To circumvent them, we need to work out how a Controll can possibly know:

1. Who would be their best victim, the most vulnerable to their advances?

2. Which set of tactics should they implement to ensnare you?

3. When can they 'turn off' these tactics, knowing their victim is under their thrall?

Let's work through those:

FINDING THEIR VICTIM

How do Controlls know exactly the person to have some fun with until they're over it and onto the next? Well, victim identification is second nature to Controlls. The more narcissistic and/or psychopathic they are, that's to say the more traits they tick off, the easier it is for them to source their prey.

But how? Two words: non-verbal cues.

Non-verbal cues are the way we walk, hold ourselves, our body language, our eyeline. A study titled 'Psychopathic traits and perceptions of victim vulnerability' detailed a group of male university students who were shown videos of twelve people and asked to comment on the ease with which they thought they could be mugged.[1] The students who ticked off more psychopathic traits were better at picking out the most vulnerable and spotting those who had already been victimized. This was down to the victims displaying perceivably 'weak' body language like dropped shoulders, uneasy, awkward hand gestures, and even how high they lifted their feet when they walked. These non-verbal cues indicated that these victims would be easy prey, already physically and possibly psychologically feeble and totally susceptible.

The suggestion then being that if we display even 'mock confidence' – maintain eye contact, broaden our shoulders, and walk with our heads held high we'll be less exposed to Controlls.

But is it that simple? Hold up, I thought . . . That night at the bougie bar in East London, I didn't remember being particularly meek. Fine, yeah, I was worried I had a VPL, but I wasn't avoiding eye contact or dragging my feet. And yes, I know I had just come out of another domineering relationship and my defences were down, but I've always been a positive, confident character. *So why me?* What vibe was I giving out?

Well, there's more to it than being a victim just because we have slumped shoulders or fidgety hands. The idea that people are targeted because they have previously been victimized or lack confidence leads us very rapidly towards a victim-blaming mentality. This is when we hear things like:

'If they weren't so weak and weedy, they wouldn't be as defenceless to being abused.' Now wait there, cowboy, it's not only these 'vulnerable' characteristics that elicit the Controll cunning.

Dr Liane Leedom, a psychiatrist who herself has been a victim of an abusive relationship, often discusses what Controlls are looking for in their prey:

1. **High in empathy and compassion**: able to be gulled into feeling sorry for their perps (tick)

2. **Adventurous**: those seeking excitement who enjoy thrills (tick)

3. **Invested in relationship**: people's people, those who like the company of others (tick)

Controlls *also* seek those who have strong character traits that they may lack so they can learn to emulate them, then conquer the other person. They will groom their victims – which is when they begin to gain their victims' trust. If the Controll's sighted prey fits the bill, let the games begin.

If Controlls easily source vulnerable people plus all those listed above, then how in the sweet hell do we avoid being their next course? First and foremost, we use gut instinct, and we watch out for those that aggressively turn on the charm. No need to point your finger at every showy ballbag, but when you see or hear something that may indicate a Controll's behaviour, you step back, observe and distance yourself. This could be, for example, in the form of love-bombing – a potential Controll loading the compliments thick and fast, very early on into meeting you: 'You're incredible, everything I've been looking for. Let's move to Highgate, get married and have lots of Boden catalogue children', etc.

Controlls are incredibly glib, meaning they are smooth talkers whilst gliding over any fact or depth. A politician can glibly address a crowd, telling them all about his well-thought-through plan to increase tax so that all children can have free school meals without actually going into any detail. They win us over with perceptibly perfect patter masking shallowness and insincerity. It all seems great on the surface, but it's just that – surface.

WHICH TACTICS
WILL THEY ADMINISTER?

Let's say you couldn't pick up the clues and now the Controll has invited you into his web; you're earmarked as possible prey. Yum, yum. How does he, she or they know which tactics to use to best trap you? Let's remember they've already spent some time assessing your weaknesses so they're building their case against you. There's a folder with your name on.

Controlls are the best listeners, and they will be guided primarily by you and what you think and say about yourself. Perhaps you have body hang-ups, you're self-conscious about the way you look, you think you're overweight. On one level this is incomprehensible to them, they are the ultra-egotist, why pick flaws in yourself? But they've heard you do it, so they'll start the relationship discerning that you need to be built up over your looks.

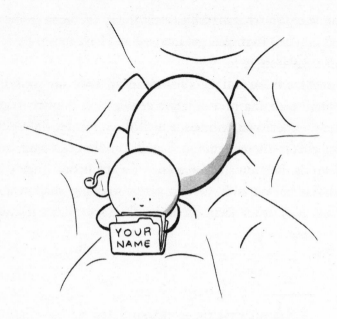

They'll tell you you're beautiful, there's nothing wrong with you, but that's not enough, they'll give you so much praise about your appearance that you will want more, more, more – you've never felt so good. You're on Cloud Eleven. Alongside this, they will imitate you: 'I also have these hang-ups, we're the same,' they'll say. Gradually, very gradually, it'll be you and them against the world. No one else gets you like they do. They have mirrored you. Ironically, at first it's actually *you* that's leading, not them.

Now you're really fucked, the Psycho Spider has started turning you round and round in his sticky web and it's very difficult to get out. It's all been superficial; you've been so swept up.

Not only have they wined and dined you,
they've also mined you.

They know *exactly* what makes you feel good and they reproduce it. Knocked. Off. Your. Feet.

It's near impossible for you to struggle your way out of this. They've set the scene and you've been lulled; so when they start taking away their charm, validation and 'love', you justify their behaviour because you think back to those early days when you were unbreakable together. You're sure you can get it back . . . right? Wrong. But you stay, especially if you're a Codependent, because this person is the only one who's ever made you feel that good, plus you're terrified of being alone. (Hi, three days between relationships.)

But wait. There's more.

NEEDLESS NEGGING

There's another tactic they use too. That tactic is called '**negging**'. This toxic term was made famous in the nineties by pickup artists. The majority of these being incels (involuntary celibates), who don't have enough genuine personality, amiability and charisma to find a suitable match and so learn 'tricks' to gull unfortunate women into their beds.

'Negging' is emotional manipulation, plain and simple. It starts extremely subtly, sometimes so shrewdly we hardly even notice it. If we do, and we call it out, it's easy enough to dismiss. The Controll has showered you with swathes of compliments, affection and supposed love; you're ripe for a knockdown.

Negging fuses notes of validation with smacks of insult. If you're the rock, they very slowly start taking a chisel to you by negging. You'll feel on shaky ground, not sure where you stand;

and when you're low in self-esteem you'll no longer have the courage to escape.

I had an ex that started to correct things I said or tell me I was grammatically incorrect in text messages I wrote to him. On its own, it seems like an arrogant, dick move, but eventually, over months and years, I started to question my intellect. 'Oh, I thought I was good with words. Wow, he's much smarter than I am, how are my literacy skills this bad?' It's dangerous when, as a writer, you lose faith in your aptitude for words.

It's vital to spot negging as soon as possible because it's indicative that the person serving it is trying to take you down a peg or two. It doesn't necessarily mean they are a true Psychopath. Maybe they're just intimidated by you, but that's not your problem – get out, it'll only get worse.

If you do bring attention to it, watch for the typical response: 'I'm joking!' Maybe they were joking, and you want to let them off, but if it happens again, catch it and be decisive. Ask why this person is seeking to weaken your confidence. I can guarantee, 9.9/10 it'll be because they want to control you.

Of course, it's possible for all of us to say things that can be deemed a bit 'neggy', but the difference is that negging is never accidental.

It's a systematic plan to rid you of self-belief.

Negging could look like:

- **'Constructive' criticism:** 'You write really well but it's like you use a thesaurus all the time. Do you know what half these words mean?'

- **Job advice:** 'I'm sure you'll be great at that sports journalist job, it's just weird they've chosen you – you know nothing about sport!'
- **Backhanded compliments:** 'Wow, that dress is really gorgeous but so different to what you'd normally wear. I thought you didn't like your arms? I'm just trying to help you.'
- **The ex comparison:** 'Phew. I'm glad you haven't put too much make-up on today. My ex used to shovel it on, and I hated it. Natural is so much more attractive.'

Negging is a disgustingly crafty way to make you desperate for approval. Why wouldn't you want it? They've just spent x amount of time weaving you into their web with compliments, so you truly believe they're a nice person. You'll start to think you can change yourself to fit their ever-shifting mould. As the days go on, you lose yourself piece by piece until you are weak and so lacking in self-confidence that you are fully under their control.

When your self-worth has been depleted enough by their negging, they'll add a few final flourishes with lines like: 'You'll never find a man like me', or 'No one else will want you.'

WHEN DO THEY KNOW
TO TURN THE TACTICS OFF?

Now they're ready to start pulling back and moving towards turning off their tactics. The dial from 'charm' to 'choke' has been fully switched.

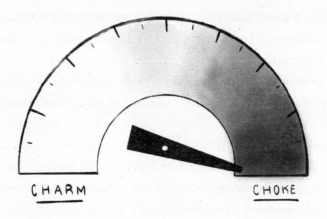

CHARM   CHOKE

The ever-observant Controll will not yank it to 'choke' overnight. No, that would be too obvious, it may shock you into action, like escaping. They need to be 100 per cent certain you are trapped in their web first. They will test the water, perhaps saying a few things that leave you with a sour taste in your mouth. It's all very subtle. They need you as exposed as possible before they turn that dial. A tactic that accompanies negging is isolation.

ISOLATION: VULNERABILITY IN NO NUMBERS

When you're isolated you're at your most vulnerable. Ideally, the Controll wants you alienated from all your friends and family because then you are trapped exactly where they want you, with no external support network to help pull you out. When they start sensing you're losing faith in yourself, they will make moves to ensure you're going to be as segregated as possible. They may say things like:

'Your mum is lovely but she's so interfering. Doesn't she think you can live your own life?' Or, 'Your dad doesn't like me because he's controlling and wants to choose a partner for you. Can't you make your own decisions?' Or, 'It's strange to have a best friend that is so critical of your life choices. Can't you make them on your own?'

Without realizing it, when it's said enough times, in as many ways as possible, you start to believe the Controll's words and cut off the 'domineering' mum, the 'manipulative' dad, the 'interfering' best friend. Trust me on this one, you may be closer than ever to your family – I was and now, thankfully, I am again – but said on repeat, you will believe these undermining lies.

When you start cutting yourself off from close friends and family, you start to feel you would be totally alone if you left your partner, so you can't do that. You're exposed, and so the dial is swung.

All I knew, being at the receiving end of these tactics from a Controll, was that the longer I stayed in the relationship, the more terrified I was of being alone. The more terrified I was of being alone, the quicker I jumped into the next relationship with a Controll when the previous one ended. By my third Controll I might as well have dressed as a sexy fly and trampolined upside down into their web, willing and ready to be devoured.

Boing.

The next chapter is a bit uncomfortable. In fact, it may make you slam the book shut a few times, perhaps even dislike me – and that's OK. I had to bite my lip and hear some truths like you're about to, too. But eventually, when I understood what I'm about to tell you, the cycle started cracking.

CHAPTER SIX

MISS CODEPENDENT

The Ins and Outs of Codependency

I need more from Damien. I'm 26 and 30 is raising her judgemental head. Damien and I have been together coming up two years and I can see I'm fading from him by the day. One anxious, restless night the solution to all my problems comes to me. After a lot of badgering, Damien finally agrees.

In my estimation, him moving in with me will be like a 'band-aid baby'. You know, when dysfunctional couples have a baby in an attempt to save their relationship. But for us it's sharing a damp studio apartment in Seven Sisters. It's going to solve everything. I'd lived with many people before Damien, I lived with many after, but nothing could prepare me for what was about to come.

OK fine. I'll hold my hands up and confess it perhaps wasn't my strongest idea. When Damien does agree to move in it magnifies the pre-existing peril. Our lives are aggressively smushed together as messily as two colours of Play-Doh.

But it's not all bad all the time; it's far more complex than that. There are times we're an Instagrammable stereotype of #relationshipgoals. When he's in the mood, Damien and I create make-believe worlds, rolling around laughing, entangled in limbs, wrestling between lust and ecstasy. We make a game of 'cohabiting'. In those moments he lets me slot into his existence. It's these flashes which make me understand why I love him so much it hurts.

I have this visualization of a couple getting their city flat. They meet up after work and eat home-cooked meals as they stare over chimney tops, head on shoulder – one unified silhouette – watching the city skyline sink into darkness. Damien and I never reach that, but there are fleeting moments we're close.

One of the reasons I'd chosen my studio flat was the road it's on. It's lined with beech trees, which look majestic until you see the contamination of litter and fag butts at their base. The flat is nestled right in the middle of the street. It's one of those places listings describe as 'ample', 'cosy' and 'deceptively spacious', AKA not enough space to air a fart. The living room is open-plan with a kitchen area on one wall, and a sofa jammed up against the other. To walk between one end of the sofa and the kitchen surface you have to pivot on your side and suck in your stomach. It serves as an unwanted weight-gain barometer.

My flat is on the sixth floor of a tall Georgian house, there's no lift and the stairway is narrow.

'Heat rises so we save loads on energy bills,' I optimistically chatter as I puff up the stairs the day he moved in. A sweating, pissed-off Damien shakes his head, grits his teeth and starts the descent for more boxes.

I've always been a homemaker and as soon as I had moved

in I quickly made the small space as lovely as I could. I'm proud of my . . . our flat and I want to show from the start I am a domestic goddess that he is going to love living with. I call my apartment 'ours' as soon as Damien reluctantly agrees to share.

The flat is furnished with a hodgepodge of memories from my previous abodes. Above the TV there's a black and white photo of Brooklyn Bridge that I've strung with fairy lights. I found that in a back closet of a dilapidated house-share in Barnes. I swapped the photo for my cheap IKEA print of Klimt's The Kiss (a staple for every twenty-something that wants to be seen as a bit 'arty').

In the bathroom, a slightly sad-looking aloe vera sits thirstily lapping condensation. I found that at one of my first houses in London, where I lived with five male students. One of these men had a habit of 'losing his way' and I woke with a start several times as he was drunkenly getting into my bed. I left that place after six months and took the aloe vera as part-perve-payment.

In the bedroom is one of my favourite acquisitions – Parisian shutters that I'd painstakingly removed from my previous apartment. I'd negotiated with my landlady that I would leave the tenancy early so she could sell, in return for the shutters. If I get myself into the right state of mind when sitting in front of them, I can half close my eyes and imagine I am in my own country manor in Provence.

Our first night together is nowhere near the head on shoulder, city skyline silhouette. There are irritated barks at each other from separate rooms as I try to perfect every tiny nook whilst he sits watching videos about cage fighting. The *only gazing is me staring at the back of his head, thrusting Lady Gut Instinct back down into the pit of my stomach. I haven't listened to her in such a long time, she is now only a whisper, but I can still hear her nipping up with a hushed tone saying: 'Well, sis, you've really fucked up here.'*

Damien has subtle self-esteem issues which grow more prevalent the longer I am with him. He used to care about portraying himself as a package of stability and security but he's letting that facade slip fast. I like to console myself by thinking he's showing me more of himself because he's comfortable. The reality is, I'm sure he knows these 'issues' are what bind me to him.

Often, I want to hold him tight, tell him everything is going to be OK. Even if my world is falling apart, I'm more concerned with his. He can make me feel useful and significant. He can also make me feel the polar opposite. The power always lies with him.

Damien tempts me with these glimpses of vulnerability and I slide into the regular role of being his caregiver, confidante and counsellor. I take to my position of Rescuer like a Psychopath takes to coercion.

When I was at school my nickname was 'Mummy Maddy'; always the mother of the group, making sure everyone got back from clubs safely, consoling on break-ups and rubbing backs of binge-drinkers. With Damien and my other Controlls, it's no different: I happily cast myself as 'Mother'.

When I fix one broken man, I don't have to wait too long for another to come along. I may as well fit a revolving door at my front porch to make the transition seamless.

But they don't come more broken than Damien.

THE LEAD ROLE OF 'FIXER'

What I didn't factor in back then is that some people can't, or don't want to, be fixed. It's also almost impossible to do so. Just because you appoint yourself 'Fixer' doesn't mean you're cut out for the role. The desire to be healed must come from that person and that person only. Additionally, if you're trying to rescue someone who falls on the higher end of the Psychometer, it'll be you who needs the repairing for many, many, many years to come.

It's wiser (and often realized with much hindsight) to appreciate that the reason we are attracted to fixing those on the higher end of the scale of the Psychometer is because of our own brokenness. 'I'm better at sorting other people's problems than fixing my own.' Gulp. I told you it was about to get uncomfortable. Stay with me.

It took me a long time, a lot of therapy and self-reflection to see I had been Codependent – desperate to be offered the title position of 'Fixer' because then 'maybe they'll love me'. I didn't think I was enough. Years later it hit me:

**You don't need to offer repair
in return for love.**

AM I CODEPENDENT?

Let's look at some clear and basic traits of codependency:

- **People-pleasing.** Listen, it's cool if you'd prefer people liked you rather than didn't – welcome to being human – but this is way beyond that. Being a people-pleaser means you act, think, speak with the intention of keeping other people happy first, *before* yourself.
- **Lack of boundaries.** This goes for both respecting other people's boundaries and feeling confident enough to lay down yours. As with people-pleasing, you're trying your best to make others eternally content and most likely struggle with the word 'no'.
- **Poor self-esteem.** Carrying around the general feeling that you're not good enough. This can manifest in many ways and has hugely negative implications. You may feel inadequate, unlovable or not worthy of respect.
- **Caregiving.** A desperate desire to help others. Everyone's needs come first and you're quick to jump up and nurture anybody else, when in reality it's you that needs the care.
- **Struggle with gifts.** You find receiving anything that recognizes your worth uncomfortable, be that compliments, grand gestures or gifts. This stems from feeling deep down like you don't deserve them.
- **Poor communication.** You'd rather say nothing than rock the boat. You can be heard repeating phrases such as: 'I'm not confrontational' or 'I hate arguments', which also means, 'I'll keep quiet, so I don't upset anyone.'

You've lost touch with your own needs and desires and
the ability to express them.

- **Lack of self-image.** We all feel a bit crap about ourselves
  sometimes but when it affects us daily it needs attention.
  Lack of self-image could look like constantly insulting
  yourself, either in your head or maybe out loud with the
  intention someone will negate it and fill the emptiness.
- **Dependency.** You've either convinced yourself you can't
  live without someone or they can't live without you and
  they become your raison d'être.
- **Relationship addiction.** Often Codependents are totally
  addicted to relationships. They cannot be alone.
  Uh-hum. Sound familiar? They look to their spouse as
  their safety; alone they feel upset and unable to cope.

If you identify with most or all of those points then you, my friend,
could fall, or have already fallen into the codependency trap. We
Codependents confuse 'pity' with 'love'. We seek out broken people
(people more obviously broken than we are) and use all the
resources we have (and sometimes those we may not) to fix them.

When we are carrying out our repairs, we finally feel useful
and significant; it's a sheer high – 'Look at me, I've found
someone I can help, and, boy, do they need and appreciate me.
I am SUCH a good person! Give me recognition, give me validation, give me love!'

But when Codependents have given everything and realize
they are not getting their expected approval, they will feel irritated, upset and walked all over. If it's someone from 6–10 on
the Psychometer that you are trying to reconstruct, then please
wait patiently for the incoming tornado that's about to rip you

from your comfortable, genial life. Because when Controlls meet Codependents, that's when the real toxicity happens.

Controlls are the world's best fraudsters. To them, Codependents smell like bacon on a Sunday morning: deeeelicious. They have no qualms about using and abusing all your general do-gooding and will take you for a wild ride that may be financially, sexually, physically, emotionally or mentally ruinous.

They will daub vulnerability onto themselves like face paint, and the Codependent will rush to get a warm, soapy cloth and lovingly and gently remove it. By that point, it'll be too late. You're already sucked into the cycle.

Together with codependency can come self-abandonment. Codependents will often forgo caring for themselves to nurture others. You may be reading this smugly thinking 'that's not me', but the truth is most women at some point in their lives have a tendency toward codependency. That's not to say people aside from women can't be codependent – no, no, of course not, but women are *brought up* to be caregivers. It's often little girls playing 'Mummy' at the tea party, making sure everyone else is comfortable – even the teddies get cared for above her. You can see why it's relatively easy to put ourselves second.

THE VALIDATION VENUS FLYTRAP

When you first begin dating, those on the 6+ side of the scale may feed you titbits of affirmation; it will feel like *finally* someone appreciates you, but, very gradually, your efforts will be ignored. The odd acknowledgement for your work will be dangled in front of you – making you salivate for more, giving you faith you're being seen. You'll keep trying, thirsty for their praise, going out of your way to guess what will make them happy. You'll offer advice, do chores, cook, clean, wipe their ass, but it will never be enough.

You will never be enough for a Controll.
You will never be enough for a Narcissist.
You will never be enough for a Psychopath.
Ever.

They'll get very tired of you, and you won't understand why so you'll work harder, do more, be better, but you'll never get that same buzz from the first few weeks or months of being together. Controlls prey on your need to be validated. What then if we started out with a genuine acknowledgement that we're already enough? What if we were happy with ourselves as we are? What if we took the time to get to know who we were as an independent individual? Well, then we begin to disempower the Controll and we're heading in the right direction. And ain't that a beautiful thing?

THE CYCLE

This is the cycle of a relationship with a Controll: **Distinguish – Devalue – Discard**.

Distinguish
Initially you are everything that your partner has been looking for, and more. They will idealize and glorify you; you can do

no wrong. This will feel like fairy-tale, romantic love. They'll sweep you off your feet and make you feel distinguished, different from anybody else. Often, they'll compare you to their nutty exes: 'If only I'd met you first.' Sigh. 'I'm here now, my darling – I'll save you!' It's the first hit of heroin, highly addictive and euphoric.

You are both in this state of limerence – infatuated with each other, it's equally reciprocated. That crack got you hooked, boy.

I couldn't believe Damien had chosen me and I wanted to do my utmost to show him gratitude and prove I *was* everything he had been looking for. Every single act – cooking, cleaning, being at his beck and call, doing everything he wanted sexually – was rewarded with recognition, love, company, and endless affection.

Devalue

Slowly, though, he began to get bored, and I felt it. Hard. He knew I was addicted to his attention, and he no longer needed to maintain the pretence that he idolized me. I was under his thrall, hypnotized. But the chase had already been won and I was no longer box-fresh.

At the start of a relationship with a Controll you represent their number-one kick. They need to 'get' you and it's exhilarating. But soon your consistent, caring nature becomes monotonous. You'll get pushed down the list to second, third, fourth supply and someone else will take your place. In fact, some Controlls think even less of you for staying whilst you're getting mistreated. You see, Controlls are coping with a deep emptiness – their fragile high self-esteem – and it's never enough to have just one person worshipping them.

The devalue stage doesn't happen overnight; your partner won't wake up one morning with a phone notification: '08:00. Reminder: Devalue stage begins.' It's a mysterious process that is difficult to put your finger on until you look back and realize there has been a noticeable change. The devaluing stage can last from a few months, to years, to decades.

Discard

Eventually, they will discard you, stamp you out, you just don't know when. It's like the shittest version of whack-a-mole ever.

Think of it as a cat playing with a mouse. The more the cat toys with the mouse the floppier and weaker the mouse becomes, gradually having less and less strength to escape. Sooner or later, the cat will get bored and find something else to play with, and the mouse is left desperately whimpering for a piece of cheese and some TLC.

CODEPENDENCY OUTSIDE
OF YOUR LOVE LIFE

It's important to be aware of inclinations towards codependency because they can affect all areas of our life.

At work

A lack of boundaries and low self-esteem could appear as taking on far too much in your career – people-pleasing, fear of being fired, never feeling enough. A Controll boss would love a host of codependent workers, all doing their best to seek validation and never receiving it. What a prolific workforce that would be!

In a family

In a family system codependency can emerge where one person likes to pry into other people's problems, trying to make them their own, unaware of the need for emotional space. This behaviour could force other members of the family to hide their lives, shunning help and feeling suffocated.

With friends

Having a codependent friend is exhausting. It'll almost feel like you're in a romantic relationship. They'll demand constant updates on your life, have an unending need to 'talk things out' and will reiterate how much they miss you even though you only just ate a Rocky Road with them thirty minutes ago. They could even emulate everything you do, almost like they hero-worship you. It'll make the recipient feel uncomfortable and smothered. Perhaps you are that codependent friend, constantly requiring reminders of your friend's love and appreciation. It may be framed as 'caring', but you'll know deep down that a normal amount of attentiveness is out the window. The truth is, you're relying on them to keep you happy and validated. It's draining to say the least.

WHY AM I CODEPENDENT?

The causes of codependency are vast and varying. Childhood trauma, and growing up in a dysfunctional family where a child is overly burdened with the need to create the stability that is lacking, can be a root cause.

Abandonment

It could be that a parent departed early on in a key developmental stage of childhood, leaving a gaping hole and fear of
abandonment. It's natural then (but not unfixable) for that child,
when they grow up, to feel the desperate need to cling to a
partner, *even* if they're no good for them. Perhaps, without even
realizing it, they are doing all they can not to be alone and
re-living that fear of abandonment.

*Even if the relationship may be eating them from the inside
out, the thought of being deserted again represents a scarier, more
deeply rooted pain.*

Addiction

Another example of a relationship which could spark codependency is the relationship between an addict and the person
looking after them. This doesn't necessarily mean drugs, it could
be an addiction to gambling, shopping, Instagram . . . anything.
The person attending to the addict assumes the caregiver role,
offering more and more support and love, desperate to heal the
addict; often getting little in return.

As a child, if you grew up in a house where addiction was
present, it's likely you had to grow up too fast, becoming an
adult when you were only a kid yourself. The child would have
to acclimatize to being caregiver – whether that was to other
siblings, the parents, or themselves. They may have even been
praised or rewarded for having the initiative to take on this role.
You can see how it would be natural for the child to develop
this behaviour into adulthood – 'Wow, I'm the top fixer!' Even
better if they could find another addict to care for – they've had
years of experience, they know exactly what they're doing.

*

I found it difficult to come to terms with where my codependency started because I did not have a turbulent childhood. Sure, once my twin brother hacked the hair off My Little Pony and buried her in the garden, but after years of counselling I'm proud to say I'm finally over it. You too may not have had a traumatic childhood, but that doesn't discount you from having co-dependent tendencies.

If you have deep-seated abandonment issues that stem from an abusive childhood, then this is something that needs to be addressed with therapy rather than hoping it'll get better in time.

Inherited

As I delved into the root cause of my codependency it dawned on me that it's possible I had inherited codependency. In the mid-1950s, American psychiatrist Murray Bowen developed a theory on family systems. He believed there is a level of inter-dependence within the emotional framework of a family unit, and that we can inherit problems that are generations deep.

Codependency can also be 'inherited' through observation. If you grew up watching your parents or guardians play out the caregiver or rescuer role, always being the ones to over-offer, then, as a child you would have normalized this behaviour. The child puts this learned behaviour into practice as quickly as they can and becomes far more prone to take this codependency into adulthood.

CODEPENDENCY UNCOVERED

There's another way to look at codependency, because being a Codependent does not mean you are some saintly figure perched up on your fluffy cloud waiting to rain love, affection and domesticity down. No, being codependent is actually not pure selflessness.

**Codependents can be rather
controlling themselves.**

That doesn't feel very nice, does it? Hold on – we want to break the cycle, right? You see, there is manipulation to co-dependency. You actively rely on others to give you that injection of gratitude, praise and approval, then, when you don't get it, you project your hurt onto them.

Let me say that another way: you need other people to make you feel good and worthy and when they don't offer that, you get upset. That is control. A different kind, but control all the same.

THE DANCE BETWEEN CONTROLLS
AND CODEPENDENTS

Controlls and Codependents feed off each other. It's not a one-way street. Ross Rosenberg describes the toxic relationship between a Codependent and Controll partner as 'the dance'.[1] He writes:

When Codependents and Narcissists pair up, the
dancing experience sizzles with excitement – at least
in the beginning. After many 'songs', the enthralling
and thrilling dance experience predictably transforms
into drama, conflict, feelings of neglect and being
trapped. Even with chaos and conflict, neither of
the two spellbound dancers dares to end their
partnership.

Both 'dance partners' are gaining – the Controll gets domination, and the Codependent gets subservience. It doesn't mean
there is harmony, it just means this is what they are used to,
and therefore what plays out. They remain in an exhaustive loop
of control and relinquishment. The longer the dance goes on,
the more tiring it becomes for the Codependent, but remember,
when the relationship started they chose to give up power,
perhaps without even meaning to. It is not and never will be
the Codependent's *fault* that they have become entrapped in
this dance, but there is power in taking accountability.

FAULT VS ACCOUNTABILITY

There is a difference between fault and accountability. It is not
the Codependent's fault they exhausted themselves in this dance,
but they can take some accountability for not allowing the time
to analyse themselves and grow, as a precursor to entering this
relationship.

Accountability was something I struggled with. I was quick
to blame and berate myself for remaining with Controlls – 'Why

do I think I'm not good enough?' 'I should have escaped sooner.'
'Why did I put up with all that bullshit?' 'Why did I ignore all
the red flags?' But when I looked at the situation again through
the gauze of compassion, I realized I could grow and ultimately
heal if I exonerated myself and understood I was doing the best
with what I had at the time. I took accountability whilst forgiving
myself.

Before we go any further, I need to make something very
clear:

**It is not your fault you wound up
in a toxic, abusive relationship
with a Controll.**

It did not happen because you are:

- Gullible
- Codependent
- Naive
- Empathetic

Coercive control can happen to *anyone*. Full stop.

However, what we can do to protect ourselves in the future is:

**Take accountability for creating and
cementing boundaries, learn who we are
and use awareness as our armour.**

Of course, there is great value in showing support for your partner. It's when support becomes meddling and caring becomes obsessing that the line is crossed. If your mood is dependent on how your partner is feeling, then you may have ram-raided the heavy steel door of codependency.

One of the most frightening sentences I've ever heard come out of my mouth was to Damien towards the end of our relationship, when I said the cataclysmic words:

'I will only be happy when you're happy.'

COME AGAIN? There I was offering up my entire outlook, mood and life perspective to him on a silver platter. Can I get you some bread and a sprinkle of subordination with that, sir?

A healthy, loving relationship should have a foundation of freedom and equality. That's both of you having your own independence and being happy and trusting about it. A constant need for contact by one of the partners can make the other feel suffocated and, inevitably, they will soon push the other away.

HOW DO I STOP BEING CODEPENDENT?

Codependency is not permanent. Allowing space between relationships is essential. You use that alone time to re-find you and refocus your values.

Content creator Helena Honey Selassie coined the phrase 'Healing Girl Summer' and I'm here for it. It's incredibly empowering to take the time to extricate musty old belief systems from those that are working for you. Being single is not a handicap, you don't get a disabled parking badge every time you're dumped, because that would be all right, wouldn't it? Maybe more people would do it.

Let's remove the stigma of being single; be as boastful as you like that you have chosen to seize control and take time for you. I don't care what age you are, periods of being single in your life are not a hardship, they are a necessity.

I'd rather be single and happy than in a shitty relationship and miserable.

Without rightfully giving ourselves time to recuperate and heal alone after a toxic relationship we are putting ourselves in a very vulnerable position. We have to check and then act on our codependent tendencies.

Taking the time to develop your self-esteem and aggrandize your self-worth is fundamental to ending the cycle of controlling relationships.

If a person has low self-esteem, they will find a partner who treats them exactly how they *feel* they *deserve* to be treated. It's certainly not as easy as saying, 'I don't deserve to be treated this way,' and then expectantly waiting for all the dickheads to be detoxed from your life.

It's fine to feel a bit needy. It's OK to be a people-pleaser on occasion. It's all right to require validation for hard work. We can accept these as parts of ourselves, but instead of trying to siphon that love, affirmation and understanding from others, turn inward first. Be proud of yourself. When was the last time you patted yourself on the back? Do it now. I mean it, right now. Pat, pat, pat. Nice, isn't it?

Sometimes, giving yourself the space to understand what you need can be aided by therapeutic help. A great therapist will enable you to find ways to appreciate and love yourself.

What else can we do to short-circuit codependency? Well, after (or during) dating a Controll it's likely you've forgotten what *you* want, desire, love and loathe. Now it's time to relearn. This goes far beyond relationship goals, I'm talking about your life, career, health, family.

Ask:

- What makes me feel good?
- What do I want to do with my time for me?
- Who do I want to become?

BOUNDARY-SETTING BABES

It's time to set some boundaries – wahoo! I knew many of my codependent habits sat in cooking, cleaning and generally domestic-goddessing for the men in my life. They went beyond acts of service when I understood I was doing them for recognition. I made a pact that when entering a new relationship, I would not cook for my potential partner until at least five dates had passed. I did not need to 'win that person over' by immediately showing them how banging my lasagne was. That's not a euphemism.

Start valuing yourself and stop doing things for other people all the time. It's you who's worthy of your time, not them. If you must set a day that's 'just yours', then do. Cook a nice meal, look after yourself.

Worry about other people when you're safe, secure and stable.

You do you.

Once you have begun to process the link between codependency and the propensity to fall into a relationship with a Controll, you'll be far better placed to ensure it doesn't happen again. Awareness is the key. If you identify with the hallmarks of codependency then seek help, research it, and make it your sole priority to heal before entering *any* relationship.

Think of it like this: the classic dangling carrot. If we don't address our codependent issues and work on self-esteem, we'll find ourselves consistently crawling towards the carrot held by the Controll. The carrot represents their validation and 'love', which they can tempt you with as they please.

Acknowledging and sorting out our pre-existing codependency and/or self-esteem issues is giving ourselves time to grow our own carrots. And what mighty carrots they are. So, when the Controll pops up dangling a carrot in front of us we're like, 'Mate, I've got a whole luscious garden of carrots, yours is skinny and kinda unhealthy-looking, why would I want yours?'

CHAPTER SEVEN
SYNCHRONIZED SWIMMING

Enmeshment

After Chris with the Noodle tattoo I was desperate to 'settle down'. That's right, at the grand age of 19, nearly 20, whilst my mates were getting their stomachs pumped on a Saturday night, I was scouring for my ever-after.

When I met Ollie, he was helping a friend move house in a posh part of London. The two heavy-shouldered men could have been brothers as they passed boxes and took it in turns as lookout for the traffic warden. I deliberately crossed the road feigning the 'I've forgotten something and it's this way' look and gracefully but very deliberately tripped over a cheese plant balanced atop a vintage trunk. It was all very Notting Hill. *Three hours later and Ollie was measuring wardrobe space in his bachelor pad for my belongings.*

Three months later and we were as good as married . . .

'You really didn't need to take me to the door, Ol. I'm happy to get the bus.' Ollie, lit by the blue haze of the car's centre console, takes off his seatbelt and turns to me like I'm a

disobedient child. 'Maddy, sweetheart,' he says, with a sigh. 'I don't let girls go home alone.' I'm 20 years old. 'I prefer to drive you, so I know where you are, then I won't worry.'

'OK, thanks,' I say, fetching my weathered handbag from the footwell. 'For dinner, too. I had a lovely time.'

'Now we just need to get you out of this shithole,' he says, vaguely motioning to everything outside. 'It's OK,' I reply, feeling a rush of defensiveness for the beaten backstreets of Elephant and Castle. It's exactly at that moment a drained mother with too many shopping bags chooses to stop outside his black Jaguar XJ, pull her 4-year-old child's Teenage Mutant Ninja Turtle pants down and hover him over the pavement to wee.

'Soon we'll get a house in the countryside with big gates and CCTV.'

I don't want to live in a house in the countryside with big gates and CCTV. I love the hustle of London: cultural fusions, dwarfed by highrises, kaleidoscopic colours, jaw-dropping tourist attractions you never actually go to if you live here, and the fact you can get a whole Turkish feast at 3 a.m. followed by a sushi platter next door. Who wouldn't want that?

'I'll take you out around here one time,' I say. 'We can dance till dawn, then eat a dirty burger on the benches in Burgess Park.'

Ollie swallows like he's partially vomited bile into his mouth.

'You tell me all the repulsive things your flatmates do then expect me to be happy you live here.'

It's true, I had taken glee in recounting some of the larger-than-life tales of my fellow housemates. Like the time Samantha had moved out and we'd found six months' worth of used tampons under the bed. And her room was next to the bathroom. But it's home. There's always someone to talk to, milk to steal and a party to crash.

'Anyway, we'll discuss it anon. I'm going to miss you. Please keep in contact,' Ollie says insistently, placing his hand over mine. This man is unbelievably good-looking. Dark curls fall in front of his cocoa eyes.

My twin used to have a plastic Superman toy when we were younger with a kiss-curl just like Ollie's. I'm sure it was part of my first pubescent fantasy.

'I'll miss you too. But you're back in like . . . four days, right?'

Ollie looks hurt. 'We'll have a lovely time when you're home,' I say, trying to retract my brush-off.

'Can you update your calendar if things change? You know I like plans to stick,' he says.

Ollie made me share my diary with him only weeks into our relationship.

I know what you're thinking – clingier than a restaurant-size cellophane. But it's fine, I'm OK with it. He needs to know what's happening, that's all.

'Sure,' I say, leaning forward to give him a kiss. He smiles and looks at me with those deep, oil-pit eyes. I've never met a man more serious than Ollie.

A few days later, Ollie has flown to the States and I have a day off. Having checked the forecast the night before, my polka-dot rucksack is already packed with a towel, sun cream, book, sandwiches and a Diet Coke. I will not be wasting a second of the four-day summer we've been blessed with. At 8 a.m. I unchain my rusty, second-hand Raleigh and I'm on the road, weaving in and out of rush hour traffic, cycling the half hour to Tooting Bec Lido.

When I get there, there's already at least twenty people in the queue. I lock up my bike, clip my green helmet to it and join them. The sun beats down through the oak trees. My open-toed sandals have collected dirt from the cycle, and I'm dismayed to see the sweat has made my toes look grubby. Embarrassed, I plop my rucksack on my feet as I wait.

When I finally get inside, I see the endless water is as azure as a Hockney. I'm so hot from standing in line I'd happily throw myself in fully clothed. As soon as I've earmarked my spot, I pull off denim shorts and my Bowie T-shirt to reveal my neon-yellow bikini.

I use the open showers, watching the collected grime funnel down the serrated plughole and then I make my way to the rungs. Lowering myself down, I suck in my stomach against the colder-than-it-looks water. After doing a few laps I try and float horizontally, perfectly still. I must have been in there for well over two hours. The temptation of my cheese and pickle sandwich pulls me out and I sit, sopping wet, no second thought about tummy rolls or pancake thighs, in total bliss. Then I lie back on my towel and quickly fall asleep.

By the time I wake the Lido has three times the number of people in it. I look up blearily, now bone dry, to be greeted by the face of a young child with two snail trails of snot extending from her nose to her mouth. She grins at me. I hate falling asleep in public places; I feel unsettled, like someone has given me a Sharpie moustache.

I reach into my backpack, mouth as dry as the Sahara, drink

my whole, now-warm bottle of water down and casually check my phone.

23 missed FaceTime Audio calls: Ollie

Huh? I had missed one only seconds ago. I sit upright and call back. Snail Trail pulls herself onto the concrete bench next to me and stares at me in that horror movie way that only children know how.

Ollie picks up in less than half a ring. He sounds panicked and breathless: 'Maddy?'

'Hi, babe. You OK?'

'Am I OK? Not really! I thought you'd been in an accident!'

I laugh, looking at Snail Trail, who is still gaping. 'No! I'm fine. Just at the Lido catching some ra—'

He cuts me off. 'I'm glad you find it funny, Maddy.'

'Wait. What? I–I don't find it funny, I'm sorry. I was in the water and then I fell asleep. I was tired. I got woken up by my flatmates at 3 a.m. Sorry. I didn't mean to make you worry. I thought you had meetings all day?'

'I missed them, Maddy. Because of you.'

'I'm–I'm sorry. You should have texted me.'

'I did. I texted and called, numerous times. Unbelievably careless.' I place him on speaker to scroll down countless messages from him, getting more and more agitated as they go. I feel bad. Maybe I had been careless. This was my first serious relationship since Chris at secondary school. I had zero practice. Perhaps I should take it more seriously.

I hadn't even got to Shiv yet. Let alone Damien. God save us all.

Snail Trail peers into my phone. I take him off speaker, giving her a cross face.

Ollie inhales deeply at the end of the line. 'It can't be like this, Maddy.'

I can hear him sniffing. I don't ask if he's crying but I'm certain he is.

'If we're going to settle down together, we can't do this every time I have a business trip.'

I say nothing, feeling like I've been put on the naughty step. I watch Snail Trail give up and waddle over to the water.

He starts again: 'I didn't want to say this but, Maddy, when I'm back, I think we need relationship counselling.'

Even though at the time I think his request is utterly stark bollock batty, I go. In fact, it was worth it to see the look on the relationship counsellor's face when she asked us, 'How long have you been together?' and Ollie and I both say in harmony: 'Three months.'

I make allowances for Ollie. He wouldn't care so much about where I was and what I was doing if he didn't really love me, right? In fact, to begin with, I enjoy it. It's nice to be wanted. He's sincerely interested in my life. OK, his need for constant reassurances that I love him have started to get mildly suffocating but I've put that down to his ex cheating; something he'd told me thirty minutes into our first date.

Ollie never gets angry. He doesn't shout or swear; I don't think in the three years we stayed together he even raised his voice. But after a while, I found myself shrinking. He asked me why I talked lots; I had to learn when it was 'quiet time' and there was no singing in the shower. That last one was nearly impossible – I'm very close to winning a Bathroom Grammy.

He tells me in order for relationships to work, partners need to be an open book – that means expressing any and every concern, worry and thought. 'It's like synchronized swimming,' he says. 'We're a team, we have to be in unison, forever watching each other. We're in this together – I feel how you feel.'

Ollie is convinced I'm being deceptive and, last week, when he found out I'd bumped into a cousin and gone for lunch, he was silent for days. After this incident I try to play the game. I become as transparent as he needs, even though it's knackering. I'm an award-winning people-pleaser and I want to crack the case.

I discuss an idea I have for starting my own business where I will go into companies and run team-building exercises with a difference. Instead of those cringe-worthy 'trust games', I will demonstrate confidence hacks. This in itself is hilarious seeing as my spirit will zap to zero over the next decade. But I'm none the wiser at this point.

I spend hours writing copy, coming up with images and researching competition. Ollie insists it's pivotal to the idea's success that I let him read over my work, seeing as he's the one with the business brain. 'Synchronized swimmers, remember?' he says. Hours later, he emails me the document back with 'a special surprise'.

The surprise is that he's added his name to every single page of the document, he's inserted his biography and a smiling photo of the two of us. I'm taken aback . . . this is my work; I want to do it alone. When I question him, he's distraught: 'I was only trying to be nice. I need you to let me help you. I want to be loyal not only to you but everything you represent.'

I feel sick. If Ollie crawled up under my skin, it wouldn't be close enough for him.

As with all Controlls, it's never all bad all the time. Otherwise, we'd leave. Ollie and I had picture-perfect memories together and we both so desperately wanted one thing: to be loved. But his idea of love was worlds away from mine.

MIRROR MOODS

Ollie tightly enswathed himself in my life. It's not as if he didn't have one of his own, no, he was a busy guy. Somehow, though, he found time to guarantee he knew everything I was doing, at all times. I began to notice something strange . . . Whatever mood I was in, Ollie mirrored it. If I was anxious, he was anxious. If I was depressed, he was too. Even if I was tired, he'd start nodding off. I equated this with his debilitating and unfulfillable desire for constant intimacy. And I'm not only talking sex. The guy manufactured it so he experienced what I experienced. It was nothing to do with an infectious laugh or catching a yawn, nope – this was some Freaky Friday shit. Many years later, I discovered what had been going on, and it was called **Enmeshment**.

The term 'Enmeshment' was first coined by Salvador Minuchin, who was a family therapist. In 1974 he used 'Enmeshment' to describe the tightly woven relationships that develop from malleable and unclear boundaries, where partners or family members have high levels of communication and little distance between themselves.

Enmeshment usually happens on an emotional level. It could be that a daughter is feeling irate, and the mother would take this on and express the same emotion, without giving her daughter the space to express herself. These weak boundaries between parents and children result in over-involvement with their lives and do not allow children to grow independently. Enmeshment can happen at all ages, all stages, and in romantic relationships too. Eventually, Enmeshment compromises and then corrodes an individual's autonomy.

When Enmeshment goes too far, those at its core will struggle to tell their feelings apart from their partner's or loved ones'. They become so intertwined in the life and emotions of the other person, they lose sight of themselves as a separate being. It was difficult to see Ollie had become enmeshed with me; I took his over-concern for anxiety and his emulation of my emotions for empathy. Enmeshment is a form of control – when your needs are so tightly wound up in someone else's, then you require them to be happy so that you can be too.

ENMESHMENT: FAMILY STYLE

Let's look at the most common place to find Enmeshment – manifesting in familial bonds. The mother that can't let her child grow up, the father that insists on providing financially for his daughter in her thirties. In parent–child relationships Enmeshment can present as the parent's yearning to always be close to their child.

Of course, this is normal through the early years, but there comes a point when giving your child the space they need to evolve as an individual is necessary to produce a healthy, well-rounded adult.

Enmeshment could be caused by the parent being neglected as a child, or perhaps an accident happening to their child which they feel deeply responsible for. A child might have suffered an illness when they were a baby and the overly caring, highly attentive nurturing given at that time might never have adapted when the child became better.

Enmeshment could lead a parent to treat the child as an equal, relying on them for emotional support and guidance, perhaps placing all onus on them to steer their mood. This could be the case if substance abuse is at play, but that doesn't always need to be present.

A close-knit family is not necessarily an enmeshed family, however. Within a healthy family unit there should be clear roles laid out. In an enmeshed family it's unclear who is the parent and who the child. There's also a severe lack of privacy.

When children get to a certain age, normally around the teenage years, it is imperative that parents pull back on how much they know about their child's life. Boundaries must shift as the family grows. Of course, it's necessary to be open and ready to listen and nurture the child, but in an enmeshed family there will be a huge burden put on children to share every single detail of their lives. Children will be left feeling lost, not having had the opportunity to individuate, losing a sense of who they are.

ENMESHMENT: ROMANTIC STYLE

Let's move this to romantic relationships. Enmeshment may be confusing because it can feel like an extraordinarily close bond, but there's one way to tell if it's stepped into the toxic and that is . . .

Dependence

When a partner becomes reliant on the other for their own mental wellbeing, in order to keep them 'up' and to prevent them from feeling lonely, there is an extraordinary weight put on the shoulders of the other person. This does not breed healthy love.

This is why I take issue with the phrase 'my other half'. My other half suggests you were not whole in the first place and, as we've hopefully learnt by now, if you aren't whole, you're certainly not ready for any kind of relationship. 'My other half' compels the other person to fill the gaps and replace what's missing. What was happening there with Ollie was a whole load of messy, lack-of-boundary-filled dependence. I was definitely his 'other half'.

Enmeshment in both familial and romantic settings can lead to:

- Anxiety
- Fear of abandonment
- Dependence issues, such as not learning to deal with your own problems
- Not developing autonomy

Does Enmeshment remind you of anything? The overwhelming fear of being without your partner or family member, the desperate need to take care of them, wanting to be in every nook and cranny of their lives? Huh? What's that, do I smell a little codependency? Ten points to you if you got the link. Enmeshment and codependency are very tightly knit (excuse the pun), and in therapy the two terms are sometimes used interchangeably.

SO, WHAT'S THE DIFFERENCE?

Enmeshment refers to behaviours and the way a partner communicates. Within an enmeshed relationship, it's difficult for someone to differentiate between their problems and those of their partner or family member.

Codependency denotes someone who takes on a rescuer or caregiver role, lacking in self-esteem, desperate for approval. In both cases, you lose yourself in a relationship due to messy and unclear boundaries.

**Both Enmeshment and Codependency
involve dependence on someone else.**

With Ollie I was under constant stress to keep my mood level, so his would stay the same. I could have given him an all-access pass to my life, but it would have been insufficient. The guy needed VIP, front-row guest passes with a blue band on entry and a permanent-ink hand stamp.

WAYS TO HEAL FROM ENMESHMENT AND DEVELOP HEALTHY BONDS

Learning to say 'no'

When you learn the art of saying 'no' you are gifting yourself personal power and time that is rightfully yours. If you aren't used to this it could feel selfish, but it's not. It's all about prioritizing your needs.

Take your life back

When your ideas and dreams are placed in someone else's hands – in the family sense, if you feel you must achieve only to please parents, or in a romantic sense, everything you do is to make your partner happy – then it's time to take your life back. Start journaling events, locations, career opportunities that bring you joy and work your way towards ticking them off.

Set boundaries

Such as saying 'no'. When you set clear boundaries you are working the relationship on your terms; your partner or family member should do the same. Your boundaries could be things like: 'I want you to trust me enough that I don't need to share all my passwords with you' or 'I need alone time each day.'

Healthy language

Check the way you're speaking with your partner or family member. Are you putting everything on them to make you happy, or vice versa? If so, call it out. Here's some examples of switching to healthy language:

ENMESHED RELATIONSHIP	HEALTHY RELATIONSHIP
I need you to make me feel better.	It's everyone's job to make themselves happy.
Can you let me know your plans over the next few weeks? I need to work out what I'm doing.	Next week I'm going to see my friends, but I'd love for us to spend time together on Sunday, if you're free?
Are you feeling low? I feel very depressed too.	I'm feeling a bit low today, I'd love to talk it out with you.
I don't think working as a lawyer would suit you, it would take up too much of your time and I'd never see you.	I totally support you becoming a lawyer, that's an awesome choice for you!
I need you to be here for me over the next three weeks. I feel anxious, please keep time free.	I've got a lot going on at the moment and I feel anxious. I'm going to take some time for myself to work through it.
I've spent so much time alone recently it would be great if you'd take some ownership of that and come and see me.	I love being by myself as much as I love being with you!

Control is multi-pronged and laden with nuances; there are innumerable ways a Controll could dominate your life. When we cover terms like Enmeshment you can see how easy it would be for them to be swept into a pile of 'just a little needy' or 'no, they love me, they're just a bit clingy!' And, as we saw with codependency, 'caring too much' and a need to fix others lead us swiftly down a tunnel of toxicity.

OK, we're becoming experts on this whole harmless vs hazardous bond thing, aren't we? Then I think it's about time we revisited Damien and I'll let you be the judge of how things are progressing.

CHAPTER EIGHT
THE SHAME GAME

Controlls and Shaming

Yes, fine, you were right. Damien and I need to get out of this flat. It was a bad idea him moving in for a while.

When we open the windows, swarms of flies buzz in and circle the big light because we live right above the communal bins. It's worse on Mondays – the day before rubbish day. I can't help thinking it's a euphemism for the turd that is our relationship. But it's fine. All can be remedied. We need a sunny resort, Lay's Cheese and Onion and watered-down vodka to inject new love into this partnership.

There are a number of reasons it's taken so long for the idea of a holiday to come up. The first being that Damien never has the time for a break. 'Career comes first,' he says. He's just been promoted to VP (I had to look it up, it means Vice President) of the tech company and I am nervous to even imply a week off might be conducive to productivity. The second is money, or lack of.

Although I work a part-time arts admin job, I nanny and

I'm trying to pursue a career in comedy . . . I am flat broke. I spend three-quarters of my salary on rent and money management is not my strong point. Years ago, Shiv used to try and 'help' me with my finances; he said he'd take over my accounts so he could see what was going in and coming out. Damien doesn't seem as bothered but he's made a few offhand comments about my inability to budget and how I can never afford anything. Maybe they're both right, I am useless with money.

I'm used to the hand-to-mouth regime. I'm about to receive a few hundred quid for an article I've written, and that pay cheque represents a holiday. Clearing my overdraft is far less enticing than the thought of white sands, margaritas at dawn and blazing sunshine.

Damien and I are going through a calm patch; I know to seize these moments and make the most of them. Dating him is like playing Minesweeper – remember that nineties computer game that you, like me, gave many hours to in IT classes? You're minding your own business, going through a good bit and then . . . BOOM! You accidentally hit a bomb and it's game over.

I numb myself to the lows and live for the highs and I don't think it can get much better than a week together in the sun. I suggest a place in Greece; it's not too expensive, and it doesn't appear to be the kind of resort that many EDL tourists turn up complaining no one speaks English.

I eagerly present Damien with photos, stats and resort ideas; but he's apathetic, to say the least.

This will bring us closer than ever, I think, imagining us lying together on the beach, listening to the lulling waves, feeling that sticky heat, drinking badly mixed cocktails from midday. I am determined to be in the best shape of my life and immediately begin a ruthless workout programme. Damien has been getting less and less interested in me and I want to show him I can be whatever he wants me to be.

I love the build-up of holidays as much as the holiday itself. Doing 'wishlist shopping' – adding £60 diamantéed, cut-out bikinis that you know will only give you bad tan lines and a yeast infection to an ASOS cart you're never going to check out. I plan, pre-plan and pre-pre-plan where Damien and I can go once we arrive, find restaurants with good reviews, add the destination to my weather app and look at it fifteen times a day.

I book us onto an early flight from Gatwick. 'We'll be on the beach by midday,' I cheep. He's unimpressed at being pulled out of bed so early.

Finally, we arrive. There's no better feeling than stepping off an airless plane to a holiday destination and being confronted by that rush of balmy air. Closing your eyes for a few seconds, acclimatizing to the new atmosphere as the heat seeps into your bones.

The airport is one of those tiny ones where half the passengers are in a queue outside the terminal waiting to go through border control and half have moved quickly and are already inside. Personally, I think it's sacrilegious to rush or clock-watch from the moment the holiday begins when you board the plane. I can tell, however, that Damien is irritable as we stand in the full 11 a.m. sun.

'You OK? Should be in soon.' I smile, taking his hand. He grits his teeth, plucks his hand from mine, and says

nothing. There's that familiar squeeze of anxiety in my stomach.

'Shall I go and get you a drink?' I say, doing my best to douse what is already a smouldering situation.

'Where are you going to get a drink? We're standing in the middle of a runway,' he says, with a quiet rage.

'Yeah.' A little prickle of tears in my eyes. I subtly look to the couple behind us; the woman is jokingly pulling her partner's cap over his eyes and he's laughing.

That could be us. But you're a Psychopath.

I have done my best to study the Guidebook of Damien, but it's forever updating and consequently near impossible to keep up with. There are some elements I am clear on: when he's displaying anger or in what he would deem as a 'tense' situation, avoid conversation. Stand away and do not, under any circumstances, keep asking if he's OK.

'Sure you're OK?' I say, forgetting the Guidebook completely.

'Maddy.' His eyes flash. Shit. 'I am standing in the fucking scorching sun, so, no, I am not all right.' I swallow. I want to go home.

Damien is extremely smart. If he's incensed and I am in his proximity he will never, ever shout or scream so someone else can hear. He won't even put his fury into a text message or email; I assume a foresight in case I ever show anyone. That would be too easy, wouldn't it? That would make him look bad and why would he want that? No, he only ever uses direct, hushed rage that blisters like the 11 a.m. European sun.

Eventually we're through border control and out the other side. I've booked us onto a coach and, as we walk to find the right bay, I am fuelled with determination to recapture the holiday spirit we abandoned on the runway.

When we find our coach, we're smacked with cool air conditioning as we climb the carpeted steps; I could jump for joy. Not for me, of course, for Damien. It's a signpost that everything has the capacity to cool off and calm down.

After an hour of driving through the arid landscape on bumpy, single-track roads, I can sense the re-emergence of irritability from Damien. We were meant to have arrived an hour ago. With Damien, minuscule problems grow into colossal transgressions in a heartbeat.

I reach down to the floor for my canvas bag and pull out the purple folder I have carefully colour-coordinated, with labels: TRAVEL, HOTEL, RESTAURANTS, NIGHTLIFE, BEACHES, ACTIVITIES. I thumb to TRAVEL. Damien shifts in the seat beside me.

That's when I realize. I don't know how it happened, I was so organized, I've been planning this for weeks; my heart whacks into my stomach. Of course, in reality it's not a huge deal but this is it for me. The holiday is ruined. I've messed up the times, the coach travel is a lot longer than I anticipated. Hours more to go. I'm not concerned about the duration of time I have to sit on this coach, crammed with loud, pale tourists, I'm fine. But Damien is not, he's going to hate this. Blood flushes to my face before I can think how to carefully break the news. I know what you're thinking . . . Is that it? Yes. That's it. Now – I'm with you. Then – it felt like I'd been caught sleeping with his dad.

'What?' he says, somehow turning his body away even more.

'Um . . .'

It's mildly annoying, at best. We could play cards, listen to music, God forbid, even have a conversation. It will add a few hours to the trip, but that's really all. I know Damien well enough to understand that really isn't all. After I gently break the devastating update he stares at me a little longer than comfortable. His entire face and disposition have changed. He doesn't look like he did moments before. He has a vacant yet needling stare. A blank look. Unreachable behind his still, pointed rage.

Damien always makes it extremely clear when the line has been crossed, and this is one of those moments. Sometimes he'd seethe with anger over the smallest things, and it was wise to give up wondering why such a seemingly immaterial thing had set him off. In all honesty, it could have been anything. The point is, he was pissed off anyway, anything I did minutely wrong would have set him off. I could have accidentally nudged him, spilled my water on his lap, or flashed the bus driver. They'd all be a catalyst for chaos.

The stonewalling is worse than the fighting. At least when he argues I have something to cling to or fashion into armour. But the silence is like trying to climb a crumbling rockface.

Tears tumble down my cheeks as I look out over the scenery zipping by. Partly unjustified frustration for not getting every single thing right and also deep sadness that this is the state of our relationship. I know it doesn't have to be like this.

Damien hates it when I cry, he thinks I'm putting it on, which only makes me cry more. I turn my face 90 degrees to be absolutely sure he can't see me; it will only exasperate him further. I never used to cry this much. Never used to be this weak.

I change my perspective from the dry landscape to my wet, teary reflection. Suddenly, in an excruciating beat, I realize the woman sitting behind – who is the cap-puller from the queue – is watching my image in the window. We catch each other's eye, and she quickly turns away.

The couple are in the same hotel as us and, when we eventually step off the coach, two hours later, Damien laughs and jokes with them. Slapping her boyfriend's shoulder like they are old pals. Then he gives her a peck on the cheek and a hug as they head to their room, hand in hand. I'm left standing there, knackered from the turbulent emotions of the trip.

This 'incident' is brought up for the rest of the holiday and continues, weeks later, when I forget to pick up some shopping. Damien questions if I 'genuinely have memory problems'. I am shamed for minor mistakes, reprimanded for not following unfollowable rules. I am told so many times I could be forgetful due to worrying neurological issues that I'm convinced I'm losing my mind.

Maybe I am.

A Controll uses shame as a darkly manipulative tool. They cast shame to feel superior and elite. Damien shamed me for expressing any emotional reaction to his behaviour. He would store away occurrences when I had spoken out, reacted sensitively or, God forbid, talked back. These would be used to discount future occasions where his actions were being called into question; often twisting his account of the events wildly, making it difficult for me to remember the real version:

'You're always overreacting and fabricating stories in your head. Remember when you completely lost your shit at the festival when I smiled at a woman I worked with. You need to sort your paranoia out.'

'Are you on your period? You're acting totally histrionically! You're embarrassing yourself.'

Gaslighting with a robust foundation of shame. It doesn't come more unbreakable than that. The two are the parasitism of coercion.

ANYTHING IS A SHAME SITUATION

Alongside a fear of their next outburst, you live with the dread of 'stepping out of line'. (Basically, doing anything which your Controll can use against you to shame you.) The thing is, no one is an angel 100 per cent of the time. I know for certain there were many instances when I spoke or acted out in frustration or did things to spite exes, but the difference is, my intent was never to disgrace or control.

Controlls do not like to be humiliated; in fact, it's one of their biggest fears. They despise being shown up. They would far rather call you out for something you may not have even done than address or critique their own behaviour. Shaming is their middle name.

**If they can discredit and embarrass you,
they're winning.**

DRUNK DILEMMA

When I was dating Shiv I'd gone out for drinks with friends, which was an extremely rare occurrence. Seeing my old friends and being back in that comfortable, sympathetic bubble with people who genuinely loved me was intoxicating, and so were the five bottles of Prosecco the three of us got through that evening.

As the night drew to a close, even in my inebriated state I began to feel panicky – I couldn't go back to Shiv hammered, but then I'd get in trouble for staying at one of my friends' houses and have to deal with the repercussions in the morning. What should I do? Either way I was going to be persecuted. Eventually, after an hour of dithering, I decided to go home to him. My friends looked confused when I told them my dilemma.

Many, many years later, when I was free of Controlls, my pals and I recalled that night and they spoke about how they wanted to step in but felt like I was 'dealing with it'. They were right, I'd normalized that anxiety, that sheer terror as I flash-forwarded the fights that would come from my supposed carelessness. My returning home drunk on that one occasion was brought up relentlessly with Shiv. He savoured shaming me with it. I was dubbed the 'reckless alcoholic'.

A Controll will use the smallest of misdemeanours against you, even if you haven't necessarily committed them, and they will be overplayed. They are trying to elevate themselves, and highlighting your faults through shaming is a sure-fire way to achieve this goal.

Shaming someone is a means to obtain dominance over them.

Hannah Kaplenko and Jennifer Loveland produced a study which explored the role of shame as potentially affecting men's need to exercise pathological control over their intimate partners.[1] Men who confessed to high levels of shaming others also reported endorsing beliefs about using imbalanced decision-making power within their intimate relationships.

Their findings are broadly supportive of much research that indicates that shame may be an important factor in why men, in particular, use coercion to counter their intense negative self-image.

This research falls exactly in line with what we know about NPD – Narcissists will hold up a mirror to others to distract from looking at any flaws in themselves. Underneath it, they are trying to hide a weak, imbalanced and hypercritical personal view which is completely at odds with the image they portray.

GASLIGHTA'S PARADISE

Another tactic a Controll uses to shame you for having feelings, reacting, questioning . . . well, pretty much anything, is **gaslighting**.

Gaslighting isn't a twenty-first-century fad. It's likely been around since the beginning of time. It was first referenced in the 1938 stage play *Gas Light*, by Patrick Hamilton. This followed the psychological abuse of Bella Manningham by her womanizing, manipulative husband Jack. He was unrelenting with his quest to convince his wife she was going insane.

The famous 'gaslighting' scene follows Jack asserting that the gas lights in the house are not dimming, even though Bella sees that they are and it's him that's causing them to do so. She very slowly starts to lose her mind.

Bella ultimately realizes her husband is at the root of her torment, but for most of us the awareness does not come that quickly, if at all. Gaslighting is a form of manipulation whereby the culprit sows seeds of doubt in the mind or minds of those at the receiving end.

When you are gaslit, over time you lose your self-esteem, question yourself and start disbelieving your gut instinct.

Gaslighters seek confusion in their victims. They mix memories, deliberately trip up your recollections, and make-believe a whole new version of events – remember, they're the best actors so it's near-impossible to disbelieve them.

Damien was superglued to his phone and whenever I would walk into the room, he would hide it. On the very odd occasion he was even a few centimetres away from it, he would turn it face down on a surface. I began to get increasingly insecure about his activity. I asked him a few times what he was doing and would get the angry reply, 'Jeez, you're so paranoid.'

Eventually, I succumbed to the gaslighting and blamed myself. I thought I must be unreasonably suspicious or overly jealous. I tried everything I could to shake the feeling that something was going on behind my back. I was worn down over time, so that when more blatant signs of cheating showed up, I questioned my judgement. This is the epitome of gaslighting.

Sanity, or compos mentis – from the Latin, 'compos': having mastery of, 'mentis': meaning mind – is synonymous with rationality. Being of sound mind to make safe, balanced decisions and trusting your inner thoughts. When you are made to believe you are losing your grip on reality, you'll be more inclined to trust someone else, rather than listening to your own thoughts and feelings.

> **Because it's the Controll convincing you that you are mad, you'll shift an ever-increasing amount of your power over to them.**

Gaslighting is insidious. It won't start by the Controll moving your car in front of you and telling you you're seeing things. Bit by bit they systematically strip your footing on reality. You lose faith in your mental state; convinced you're going insane, you decide to stay quiet. *The abuse will only get worse.*

Gaslighting has been recognized as a serious crime under the Domestic Abuse legislation since 2015 in the UK, and in the US gaslighting is also classed as a form of emotional abuse and is therefore covered under domestic violence law. It is a violation of both civil and criminal law and has lasting consequences on the victim. It should be taken extremely seriously.

HOW TO PROTECT YOURSELF
WHEN YOU ARE BEING GASLIT

Here are some ways to cling on and stabilize yourself whilst being gaslit:

Remember your truth
Hundreds of times truth has fallen right out of my hands. Perhaps because the situation exhausted me, I wanted peace, or I had become so confused myself. This is when the gaslighter

is victorious, and their flame burns brightly. They have made you question your own experiences and that's a scary, scary place to be.

I think of it like being on an eighties kids' show when suddenly the characters are in a new world and the editors would use that (now rubbish, then incredible) warp effect, making the screen all wibbly. That's what happens when you are gaslit for long enough over time: you lose your balance and step into their made-up, completely falsified world.

Write your truth, the real version of events, down in a journal so you can reference it. Some Controlls have a photographic memory – I know mine did. Or it could be that I was so tired and wired I figured my memory was a myth. Combine this with gaslighting and the other domination tactics and you've really got to put the work in for your team to stay steady.

Find and maintain your clarity and calm

Controlls use gaslighting to manipulate you with chaos – 'You're wrong. Your version of events is incorrect. You're losing it. Do you know how crazy you sound?' You get swirled and whirled into their den of dubiety until eventually there's no second-guessing, you accept their version of reality.

Before this happens, where at all possible, instead of defending yourself or trying to save face, escape. It may just be a three-minute trip to the loo, it doesn't matter. Anywhere that you can breathe and step away from their lies and manipulation. Do not get sucked in.

I often tried to protect my self-image: 'No wait, that's not what happened. I didn't do that. It's just not like that. Please don't think of me in that way.'

It. Doesn't. Matter. What. They. Think. Of. You.

What is your version of events? That's what's important. Hold onto your clarity and maintain your calm. You are not the bad/crazy/insane/overdramatic person they are making you out to be.

Affirm: I will never win

I know that sounds defeatist; bear with me. The sooner you make peace with the fact that they will 'win', the better.

At the very end of my ordeal, I limped out, battered, bruised and a shell of the woman I once was. I called my twin brother – one of the closest people in the world to me, my absolute hero – and I said, 'He's won. I wave the white flag.' There was a beat and my twin replied, 'Maddy, these people never win. No one wins.' And he was right, no one wins. Their life is monochromatic, spent trying to control others, and, if you stay, they will ruin you.

There will never be accountability on their part, there won't be an apology, so step back, breathe, and detach yourself as you watch them flounder for control.

Gaslighting is just one of the terms that is in the Controll dictionary. I think we should read some more:

The Cocksford English Dictionary of Controlls

Boundaries

Boundaries are limits or expectations you set yourself so that you are very clear when one has been overstepped. When someone else's actions or words have inflicted psychological, emotional or physical harm, our boundaries have been crossed.

In a sentence: *When I started a new relationship we sat down for lunch and set our boundaries early so we knew what was expected of each other. When one got encroached, we could calmly point it out.*

Breadcrumbing

The deceptive act of leading someone on with false promises and lies. This could be the possibility of holidays, dates, or future events that won't ever happen. People can also send you a message every now and again to keep you interested, i.e., dropping breadcrumbs for you to follow.

In a sentence: *I dated this woman I really liked but slowly saw the pattern of her messaging me every few weeks, promising me the world then disappointing me. I blocked her and booked myself a spa day.*

Gaslighting

The emotionally manipulative act of making someone disbelieve their own thoughts, gut instinct or sanity by casting seeds of doubt in their mind. A slow-burning, devious process that will screw with the victim's reality.

In a sentence: *They told me they were working today but I saw them in a bar with their ex. They said I needed my eyes tested. They were gaslighting me, so I told their boss they were pulling a sickie then left their sorry ass.*

Gut instinct
Your intuition, inner reasoning and voice of consciousness, based on your experience, that you absolutely, totally must not ignore. An instinctive feeling that will guide you in the right direction.

In a sentence: *I knew from the second I met my cousin's boyfriend something wasn't right, his whole energy was off. Later, he started touching me inappropriately in the lift, so I told my cuz and we charged a bottle of champagne to his tab and got a cab.*

Hoovering
A term used to describe what the Narcissist or Psychopath does to seduce someone back into a relationship with them; they perform the 'Hoover Manoeuvre' in order to return to prior people who have in some way gratified their ego.

In a sentence: *As soon as I saw his message, I could tell he was Hoovering. It was all 'I miss you', 'we had something', 'let's try us again'. I blocked him immediately and happily went back to my cheese on toast with a dash of Worcestershire sauce.*

Love-bombing
The actions someone takes of deliberately showering hugely over-the-top amounts of love and affection in a bid to blindside, influence and ultimately control their victim.

In a sentence: *My best friend told me that he was on a first date and, after one drink, the guy told him he was the best thing that ever happened to him, he wanted to marry him and have his children. He knew he was being love-bombed so climbed out the loo window.*

Negging

The process of burying negative comments in flirtatious ones and calling it 'banter'. A precursor to abusive behaviour whereby a person deliberately undermines the confidence of the victim, consistently lowering their self-esteem and increasing the desire for their abuser's praise.

In a sentence: *After embarrassing me again in front of the class, my lecturer told me I was 'going red' and was 'way too sensitive', then, later, I had 'no sense of humour'. I wrote down all the incidents and took them to the Deacon. Anyway, I love our brand-new professor.*

Normalizing

Normalizing in a relationship is the process in which abusive behaviours and actions are made to feel normal and natural, eventually accepted as everyday life. Over time, when abuse happens we seek to play it down in an attempt to survive.

In a sentence: *He'd been away for a few weeks, and I got some clarity on the situation and my friends helped me realize I'd normalized his womanizing behaviour. I changed the locks, chucked his shit clothes out the window and dumped him. I've never been happier.*

Scapegoating

When someone is assigned all the blame for every fault. A Controll will scapegoat their victim even if it's something they themselves have done wrong.

In a sentence: *I was the family scapegoat – always made to take the fall for other people's problems. It was really damaging and I've worked through it in therapy.*

Self-esteem
This refers to our own individual self-worth, essentially how much we love, approve and favour ourselves. The higher our self-esteem, the greater we treat ourselves and the better the people we attract into our lives.

In a sentence: *I have spent so many years working on my self-esteem that I can see that woman is about to zap the joy out of my life. I'm worth more. I'm off to get a burrito, see ya.*

Stonewalling, also Silent Treatment (The)
When someone refuses to communicate or behave in a pragmatic way. They use the silent treatment as a form of punishment towards the other person for petty manipulation.

In a sentence: *Every time we have the smallest of arguments, she stonewalls me and refuses to listen to my point of view or communicate. I deserve more than that, I'm gone and I'm taking my favourite bowl.*

Thrall (Under their)
The psychological state of utter bondsmanship and entrapment. In an abusive relationship, when someone is 'under their thrall' they are hypnotized, enslaved and entirely subservient to their controlling partner.

In a sentence: *I look back now and see I was entirely under his thrall, thank God I read* How to Leave Your Psychopath *when I did and managed to find my way out.*

You'll find that once you start learning the terms it'll help you recognize what's happening and, consequentially, call this shit out and wave goodbye. Anyway, I'm feeling rather tired. Mind if I have a lie-down?

CHAPTER NINE

SLEEPLESS IN SEVEN SISTERS

Biderman's Chart of Coercion

Some weeks after the holiday things are starting to return to normal. I'm more alienated than ever at home but at least it's calm. You know when you can sense you're an annoyance but you're not sure what to do about it? Yeah, that. I had to delete a tab on my 'Frequently Visited' web browser page yesterday. Seems I've searched 'what happens when love gets lonely?' too many times. I know every word of that Oprah article.

Damien's been busy. Friends, work . . . other things. I don't ask. What I've learnt is if I keep my head down things are OK. He still comes home to me. And that's all I want. The flat is clean, the sheets are washed, I keep on top of my appearance. I don't know there's much more I can do.

Please don't make that face, dear reader. Of course I hate this. I'm embarrassed by it. My dad tells me if I'm with the wrong person I'll never find the right one. They don't know the half of it. No one does. Anyway, Damien is the right person, it's just a rough patch.

On my daily scroll this morning I saw:

Don't Give Up!
This is the sign your waiting for!!!!!
@Lawofattraction247

You're. That was directly targeted at me. A sign from The Universe. Don't give up on this relationship, don't give up on Damien. I won't, Universe.

Look, it's easy for you to sit there and cast aspersions but you're not in this. It may appear he's the marionette master and I'm crumpled on the floor, my strings lax, but that's not it. When I get his undivided attention, we'll be great again. Actually, that time is imminent.

There's an event marked in my calendar that's days away. It's called the 'Imagination Weekender: The Home of Creative Champions' and Damien is guesting. We laughed so much at the name when he got the invite. I smile and feel a little weight float off my shoulders with the memory.

I didn't even know these things existed. It's basically Edinburgh Fringe and TED's unwanted love child.

Heads of huge publishing houses sit on high stools with Voss bottles next to them as they chat to their celebrity authors. In an adjacent tent, Hollywood art directors livestream their discussion: 'The Future of Concept and Language in Cinema'. CMOs of forward-thinking creative conglomerates with thick black non-prescription glasses, itchy tartan suits and neckerchiefs hold sessions on 'Practicality, Progress and TOV'.

Acronyms are popped like ecstasy. IMO. It's very middle-class and very creative. Crowds smile, titter, and nod as if they understand what the fresh hell anyone is talking about. It's the Emperor's New Clothes of The Arts.

This is exactly the kind of place Damien hates, and these are exactly the people that love Damien. We're already starting on the back foot because the organizers have messed up and told Damien last minute he needs to camp as all the local hotels are full. I think this is the only reason he reluctantly nodded for my attendance – to help set up the tent and keep him sane. Good luck me.

Once Damien's finished his talk, he wants to network, which I receive loud and clear as my cue to leave. I wander off and get a drink. It's actually a pleasant change. Being around new faces is wonderful. That Oprah article is past pixel.

It's after 9.30 p.m. and the sun has lingered for longer than usual before it sets into a navy marble across the sky. Pimm's in hand, I meander through an area sectioned off for speakers. I look up and a splodge of summer rain plops onto the centre of my forehead. It's followed by a few more heavy drops and then the heavens open. People screech and laugh, we all run for the trees. I shelter with a young couple. They bring me into their circle immediately, offering me a tin of citrus gin and tonic and a cheese straw from their Patagonia backpack. I told you it was middle-class. But even so, I can't remember a time I've felt this content. I look toward the grounds of the event and see Damien, hood on, stooped stance, making his way over. He does not like the rain.

The grey cloud that hangs above him is bigger than any in the sky. 'Fuck this,' he wheezes as he reaches me. The couple I've befriended laugh. He ignores them. 'Not camping in this. I'm driving back.'

'It's late!' I say, high on the mood of the evening. 'Then fucking stay,' Damien snaps. He knows I have no way of getting back. He must be seething; he's never spoken to me like that in front of anyone. His words are Narcan. I'm immediately sober. I don't move. He mistakes my fear and confusion for inertia, gives me a death stare, then walks off. I canter after him, cheese straw in hand, not even a 'goodbye' to my new friends.

Damien jams the muddy tent into the boot, and we speed away from the site. A suffocating silence toxifies the air and I grip the sides of my seat with every bend. It's a four-hour drive. As we approach 1 a.m. I can no longer resist the pull of fatigue, I close my eyes. It's been a long day. Suddenly I'm jolted awake by the loud bass of the radio. I open my eyes quickly and look at Damien.

'If I'm not sleeping, you're not sleeping,' he says with a definite sneer to his voice. And that's how the journey goes. Anytime I'm betrayed by my heavy eyes, the volume is jammed up.

That sleep deprivation had me shaky, dropping things and tripping over words for days.

Sleep is pivotal not only to give our bodies the chance to rest and reboot but to give our minds the space to unwind and disconnect from our physical form.

I hadn't realized how vital it is to find a harmonious sleep pattern when sharing a bed until a few years ago. In fact, I would argue there should be a Potential Partner Checklist (PPC) – we'll write ours at the end of the book – and on that list, clearly stated: are you a night owl or early bird? I am very much an early bird but Damien . . . oh no, Damien was a creature of the night.

Throughout our relationship our sleep preferences became less of a clash and more of a catastrophe. I would never have dared to accuse but I was certain he found glee in keeping me awake to suit his lifestyle:

I'll be back in about an hour. You better not be sleeping!

he'd text as I squinted in the half-light to read his message. The times I was too exhausted to get up, make myself look present-able and sit in the living room waiting for him, I would be reprimanded:

'I always make an effort to see you, but you never bother, so what's the point?'

I'd gently suggest that we could find time at the weekends to spend together rather than midnight on a weeknight. To which I'd get snippy responses like: 'Here we are again, everything on your clock.' He argued he worked late and this was 'called compromise'. I knew deep down that many of those nights he certainly wasn't working. 'Don't rock the boat. Be pleased he wants to spend time with you,' I repeated as I willed myself awake. When he finally turned up, he'd watch TV and I had to sit beside him to 'keep him company' like a dutiful dog.

The closer we got to the night of the Red Wine Angel (more on that later, I'm not ready yet), the more sleep eluded me. I was descending into madness. Slowly succumbing to sleepless-ness. My lack of sleep wasn't always a direct result of Damien. Sometimes my own thoughts, recounting his vicious words, would keep me awake. I'd try and piece together events, find the root cause of arguments, but that was like attempting to solve Pythagoras's theorem on ketamine.

BIDERMAN'S CHART OF COERCION

In the 1950s sociologist Albert Biderman was sent by the US Air Force to discover why so many patriotic American airmen who had undergone brutal torture and become prisoners of war chose to defect to Communist China after the Korean War. There was public outcry as these POW soldiers not only sided with the enemy, but also backed them.

The rumours were that a form of brainwashing had taken place, but Biderman suspected there was something far darker at play. He was right.

Biderman discovered that in order to break the will of these men, the Communists surmised that violence would not be enough. Violence may break down the physical body, but the torturers required a way to capture their minds. The Chinese Communists had developed an intrinsic, yet relatively simplistic set of steps which Biderman detailed as 'The Chart of Coercion'. Biderman's Chart of Coercion is made up of eight practices that psychological torturers will use. The umbrella for these techniques is: **Debility, Dependency and Dread**.

Ergun Cakal, legal adviser at the Danish Institute Against Torture (DIGNITY), states in his paper: 'Psychological torture is deployed to break and obliterate human resistance, spirit and personality . . .'[1]

To break and obliterate human resistance, spirit and personality.
Sound familiar?

In 1973 Amnesty International published a 'Report on Torture' where they stated: 'The most effective way to gain . . . cooperation is through subversive manipulation of the mind and feelings of the victim, who then becomes a psychological, as well as a physical prisoner.'

Amnesty used Biderman's Chart of Coercion as the standard for psychological torture techniques. Diana Russell's revolutionary book *Rape in Marriage* laid Biderman's Chart of Coercion alongside the consistent techniques that perpetrators of domestic abuse use. The correlation was extraordinary. Let's look through Biderman's Chart of Coercion ourselves; the second column is adapted from the Amnesty International version (1994). I've added a third column to give you examples of these tactics in practice:

METHOD	EFFECTS AND PURPOSES	EXAMPLES
Isolation	• Deprives victim of social support for the ability to resist. • Allows victim to be present at all times. • Makes victim dependent upon perpetrator. • Develops an intense concern with self.	Perps use many tactics to isolate the victim from their friends and family. This ensures they are not open to external influence on the perp's behaviours.

METHOD	EFFECTS AND PURPOSES	EXAMPLES
Control of perception	• Fixes victim's attention upon immediate predicament. • Punishes independence and/or resistance. • Perpetrator manipulates using charm and then becomes volatile when demands are not met.	Walking on red-hot coals. When you're hyper-aware that you may set off your partner's anger, you are not focused on yourself. This heightened state means you are constantly tense.
Humiliation and Degradation	• Weakens victim's ability to defend themselves. • Increases feelings of worthlessness and incompetence. • Pushes exhaustion to the limit.	This can start as negging. Can also be denials of privacy – walking in when you are showering or using the bathroom, for example. Perhaps forcing you to let them look through your phone. This can go all the way up to constantly attacking your appearance, refusal of personal hygiene, administering demeaning punishments and sexually degrading you.

METHOD	EFFECTS AND PURPOSES	EXAMPLES
Exhaustion and Confusion	• Weakens mental and physical ability to resist. • Means the victim does not have the time to assess what is happening to them. • Puts victim in a constant state of fear from being so tired they won't 'fall in line'.	The expectation that you must be busy and catering to your perp day or night. Forever on their schedule. An assumption that if they can't sleep, you can't sleep. This constant state of exhaustion gives you little to no time to check in with your feelings, look after yourself and eventually escape.
Threats	• These threats are held over the victim to keep them in a depressive state. • They are scare tactics used to keep the victim compliant. • Without perhaps even realizing it, these threats keep the victim in a state of terror. They ensure they won't 'step out of line'.	These threats can come in all forms and are by no means just the far end of the scale, i.e., threats to kill you. They could be a threat to kill themselves or your children if you do leave or if you complain to someone about what is happening. These threats could also come in the form of what would occur if you left: 'no one would want you', 'you'll always be alone.'

METHOD	EFFECTS AND PURPOSES	EXAMPLES
Occasional indulgences	• Provides positive motivation for accepting and conforming to the perp's abuse. • Works to sow seeds of doubt in the victim's mind: 'Maybe it wasn't as bad as I thought. Maybe they can change?' • It puts the victim on unstable ground, doubting their own perception of events – 'they must love me really, look at this new coat they bought me.'	If the perp senses that what they have done has pushed you too close to leaving, they will sprinkle an occasional indulgence over you, and it'll be quickly forgotten. It could be affection where there was none before, a surprise fancy dinner or an unexpected gift. Eventually the victim will start working towards these indulgences, as if they are things to be earned.
Demonstrating omnipotence or superiority	• Creates a feeling of helplessness. • Suggests futility of resistance.	This is displayed as an 'it's my way, or the highway' attitude. They choose when you eat, what you eat, when you sleep, etc. They may tell you you're mentally ill, delusional or paranoid.

METHOD	EFFECTS AND PURPOSES	EXAMPLES
Forcing trivial demands	• This reinforces who has the power. • Ensures that the victim will learn to obey the perp. • Adds to the exhaustion of the victim – it's impossible to get anything 'right'.	The perp will ensure that they are someone to be obeyed. You will be punished for not conforming. The demands are often impossible, trivial and contradictory. 'I told you to message me when you were on the way home, not before and not after.'

Adapted from Biderman's Chart of Coercion (as published by Amnesty International, 1994)

You may have felt exhaustion from reading this table. If you've been in, or are currently in, a relationship with a Controll, take a moment to steady yourself. Take a deep breath and drop your shoulders, feel the floor under your feet. The first time I came across this chart I burst into tears. I could associate with every one of those techniques of psychological torture and, in a way, it affirmed for me that what I'd been through was real. It was a hug of belief. There it was in black and white – tick, tick, tick.

Biderman's Chart of Coercion is not only true for POWs or victims of Controlls. Any tormentor wishing to score the highest level of dominance over their victim will use tactics like these – kidnappers, cult or gang leaders, and so on. Anyone that seeks to systematically tyrannize the minds, hearts and souls of others.

These tactics can be used to a greater or lesser extent. As with all force administered by a Controll, it happens methodically.

Some of the techniques you can ignore, pass them off as 'their little ways', but gradually you'll realize you're stuck fast. Damien's consistent methods of sleep deprivation – whether he thought it through or not – helped him ensure that I was far too exhausted to argue. Or escape.

GUILT SHOES

Another of Biderman's tactics I clearly remember was 'Occasional Indulgences'. I'm not saying that if your partner books you an expensive dinner, surprises you with a gift or even buys you a helicopter ride you should run screaming for the hills (unless you're scared of heights). It will, however, be extremely clear when an 'indulgence' is used as a means to pacify and control.

With Damien the phenomenon of Guilt Shoes was born. Ironically, when I received the guilt shoes, I didn't call them such. It was many years later when I was with my best friend Harveen cleansing my belongings, and I had five pristine, designer pairs of heels laid in front of me, that I sat down and reminisced on how each pair had come about.

I don't wear heels. I say I'm 5' 7" when I'm at an audition with a short man playing my husband, but in reality, I'm 5' 9". The only time I wear heels is if I'm paid to, or I can't find a ladder. Anyway, I began to notice patterns in my relationship with Damien; it was cyclical – two good months, explosion, two bad weeks. When we'd hit the landmines, I could predict how they'd manifest but this didn't make me any more prepared.

The bigger the explosion the more likely the Occasional Indulgence. And you guessed it – they came in the form of

Guilt Shoes. It's wrong of me to even associate the word 'guilt' with them because I know they weren't given from remorse; they were given to placate and therefore coerce:

'I did something wrong/yelled/cheated/abused but I refuse to apologize. Instead, here is an extravagant present. Now you can't come back at me or you're ungrateful and spoilt.'

All those years later when I sat on the bed with these beautiful (and I have to admit they were), totally unworn, designer shoes laid out, this is what we crowned them. Meaningless, assuaging tokens of control.

Little did I know, the very act of me accepting the Guilt Shoes meant a neon sign flashed above my head: YOUR BEHAVIOUR IS TOTALLY FINE. I'd had enough time and space to start on the road to becoming aware. We'll get to that – we have to get through it first.

BID GOODBYE TO BIDERMAN

What do you do if you think that tactics from Biderman's Chart of Coercion are being used against you?

1. **Give yourself a celebratory squeeze.** Go on, wrap your arms around yourself and show some love because you have opened the door of awareness. It doesn't matter if you're not ready to act, you've started wising up. This is great.

2. **Don't do anything rash that will put you in danger.** If the Controll is choosing to exhaust you with lack of

sleep, forcing trivial demands or similar, don't call them out on it if you think it will compromise your safety. Note it and work around it at this stage.

3. **Tell someone.** If you realize you have become isolated, and it's possible to do so, send a message or start a line of communication with someone that you trust and would be willing to help you at a later stage.

4. **Don't expect too much of yourself.** The techniques used in Biderman's Chart of Coercion are a continuous set of behaviours used over time. They have not appeared one day, out of the blue. The tactics are systematic. It is likely your spirit has been crushed, as mine was; be patient, allow healing and energy to cut the ties and carefully remove yourself from this situation.

5. **Believe yourself.** You have been taught to ignore your gut instinct, perhaps think you are a bad person – paranoid, delusional, jealous, egotistical and worse. You're not. Even if you can say a few positive words to yourself each day you will start rebuilding the faith you need to have in yourself to eventually leave. Remember – if highly trained soldiers can fall victim to coercion, so can you.

As you read this book, you may not associate with *all* the Controll's techniques. Coercive control, emotional abuse, intimate terrorism happen on a sliding scale, but please be super clear about one thing: **IT IS ALL ABUSIVE.**

Don't pardon them because yours 'isn't as bad as that'. The

bottom line is none of it should be happening and *all* of it is toxic.

Later in the book I am going to give you clear steps to take if you think you or someone you know is trapped in a relationship with a Controll. For now, stay alert, grounded and calm. We will get you or them out. Awareness will be your shield.

But first, there's another tactic of control I haven't touched on yet. Quick question – what's the worst gift a partner has ever given you? Mine has got to be an Excel spreadsheet. Let me tell you, you get some weird looks when you try and regift that paltry present.

CHAPTER TEN

MONEY, POWER, RESPECT

Financial Control

Christmas is the worst time to be single. I don't care how much of an empowered feminist, independent, fuck-everyone, go-getter you are, it's true. Watching couples Christmas shopping, glove-in-glove, condensation kisses in cafes over coffee. Heart-wrenching to watch when you're alone. But this Christmas is different. And I'm not just trying to make myself feel better. Pre-Damien, post-Shiv, I'm sandwiched in singledom, and it is glorious.

The glue that once cemented my phone to hand, in case I missed a text or call from Shiv and had to explain myself, has dissolved. Tension in my shoulders has evaporated and, for the first time in what feels like years: I'm present. Right here in this moment, allowing myself to be swaddled by steady familial love.

Weather warnings have been issued and it's bitterly cold but as yet there's no snow. Multiple generations of my family have travelled from all corners of the globe to be together. The juniper wreath sprinkled with gold and red berries hangs on the freshly painted powder-blue front door. Mistletoe has been strung in the low-ceilinged entrance hall. If anyone was to look through the fogged-up bow windows right now, they'd see sickening festive perfection.

Memories of my dad lugging a seven-foot Christmas tree up the stairs because he got it 'on the cheap, direct-from-ground' are now a distant aberration as the log burner crackles and the underfloor heating lulls my family into a cosified stupor. I'm sitting next to my mum on the turmeric-coloured sofa, reindeer blanket on lap. My young nieces and nephew are playing 'cleaning' – a good game to invent for under-4s when no one can be arsed to hoover.

It's after 5 p.m., almost totally dark outside. Presents have been opened and a cardboard box stuffed with discarded wrapping paper stands next to folded, crinkled sheets that will definitely never be reused, but are 'too nice to recycle'. We're waiting for The Snowman *to christen our TV for the first time this Christmas, with its warm, glowy animation and opportunity to wail: 'we're walking in the aaaaaaaiiiirrrrr'.*

The remaining Quality Streets are passed for the third time, everyone still navigating their way around the purple ones. Shallow pools of red wine in smeary glasses sit next to half-cups of tepid tea. A glass-collect is inevitable.

I decide to take on the task – I don't think I've stood up in over three hours. Heaving myself off the sofa, I begin to gather glasses and mugs, to the meek protestations of my family. Once I've stacked the dishwasher and done the mandatory peruse of the fridge, I make my way to my seat. My phone lights up with a second nudge of a text:

SHIV

One of the first things I did when Shiv and I broke up was change the privacy settings of my messages so the full text isn't shown on screen when I get a notification. In a role reversal of what is to come with Damien, Shiv had been convinced I was hiding something (I wasn't). My phone always had to be visible. (Note denials of privacy and enforcing trivial demands from Biderman's Chart.)

Even though I haven't read his message, his name on my screen takes me right back to an acute suffocation – standing in his kitchen, him berating me for spreading my germs whilst I cleaned with a cold. Yes, that to the woman with a bottle of bleach in her hands.

My reaction is more discernible than I realize. 'You OK, Mad?' my dad says, turning his head from The Snowman *and snapping me out of the flashback.*

'Er. Yeah,' I say, taking a seat.

I grab my phone and pull it close; taking a well-practised, steadying breath, I open his message. Put the phone back on my lap. Shake my head. Pick it up and read it again. I can't bridle the sharp exhale of air that escapes the side of my mouth. My mum looks at me, cocking her head with a look of inquisition.

'S'nothing,' I say in a muted voice, aware the youngest members of the family are currently soaring over snowy rooftops and do not want to be disturbed.

Although at first my reaction is incredulous, I can't ignore the gnawing anxiety rising from the pit of my stomach. 'He can't be serious!' turns to: 'Fuck. How am I going to handle

*this?' And then: 'Prick! It's Christmas Day! What an
arsecracker!'*

He messages again:

Let me know if you have any questions.

*Any questions? Yes. Yes, I do. My question is: were you born
a tiny-dicked control freak or did you evolve into one? I'm
not going to write that. I scroll back over his first message,
hoping for a moment I've suffered a minor stroke. Nope, it's
there:*

Hi, Maddy. Attached you'll see a spreadsheet of the expenses
you incurred over the time we were together. I will be
understanding about payment dates and open for discussion if
you want to set up an instalment plan. N.

ATTACHMENT
Maddysexpenses.xlsx

Detail	Amount
Lunch @ Dukes	£22.50
Zip-up boots. Happy to pay half.	£80.00
Weekend in Bristol – petrol	£30.00
Dinner @ Frank Bellucci	£32.00
Trip to Newcastle – petrol	£43.00
Coffee at Regency	£16.50
Dinner @ Sketch	£64.00

It goes on.
And on.
And on.

In total it comes to over £600. The petrol – his car he had filled, I just happened to be in it. The zip-up boots – 'a gift' he had chosen and presented me with. The meals out – at his insistence. The rest of that Christmas was a blur. I checked inactive bank accounts to find any 'hidden' money, I did sums upon sums (a reminder – not my strong point) to work out what I could do to pay him off. I came up with nothing.

From a Christmas that began boosted by hope I stumbled into a new year shrouded in dread.

How the hell am I going to solve this one?

I think it wise here to explain my financial situation. I was very used to being in debt. I dealt with debt like men deal with health problems: acknowledge it's uncomfortable, complain, but do very little about it.

I had been over 15K in debt for a decade and no matter how hard I tried I couldn't shift it. Shiv knew this. Shiv knew one of my greatest fears was to fall further in. Shiv, or rather Shiv's family, was wealthy beyond belief, and he had never known that breath-zapping feeling of being strangled by arrears.

In the most spiritual of senses, like attracts like; what you think, you become, as the saying goes. Well, I was shit scared of money and I attracted a severe scarcity of it. You could say, I actively repelled it.

Throughout our relationship Shiv had used money as a rope around my neck and this Excel spreadsheet on Christmas Day was the final tug. He booked restaurants I couldn't afford, made me feel uncomfortable surprising me with lavishly expensive gifts, and took me on pricey weekends away. 'Lovely!' you may be thinking.

It's all in the giving.

If someone takes you to an upscale restaurant then makes a show of pondering whether to split the bill, knowing you can't pay and therefore can't leave, it's the opposite of 'lovely'.

There were certainly times my guilt was at fault. I felt guilty I couldn't pay. I felt guilty he was not with someone who was on an equal paygrade. I felt guilty I couldn't reciprocate the nice gifts. But in general Shiv relished being financially superior to me. He used money as a means to hold control.

What Shiv was doing with his Christmas Day Excel was administering the final bit of control. In that relationship it was me who initiated the conversation about breaking up, and he hated it. He despised how small it made him feel and chose to skew my escaping him as a 'final act of rebellion' for which I should be punished.

Ultimately, I shouldn't have paid Shiv a single penny, but I did. I did because I didn't want to hand him a smidge more power. I did because I was scared. I did because money was so intertwined with fear it had coiled around me and I was unable to move an inch. I ended up borrowing what I could from a dear friend, dumping it in his bank account and blocking him.

AM I BEING FINANCIALLY CONTROLLED?

When **financial abuse** is at play, you'll hear things like:

'All your clothes are cheap. I spent £150 on that dress and you never wear it. You totally take me for granted.'

'I've treated you to an expensive meal out and you're honestly telling me you're tired and don't want sex?!'

'I paid for this weekend away so don't bitch and moan, the least you can do is be happy.'

'You're awful with money; show me exactly what you earn and what you spend it on. I'll support you.'

Later this can turn into:

'I need access to your accounts; you obviously can't help yourself.'

Financial control can come in all guises. At the very top we have total financial dependence on the perpetrator, and this is not the fault of the victim. As with all elements of the Controll's desire for total power – it happens gradually.

When buying houses with Controlls, they can convince you the deeds need to be in their name. They could even make their victims lose their jobs or tell them they will cover costs, so they don't need to work. You could have children with the Controll, so not only is your life in their hands, but your children's lives are too.

The Controll could decide when to pay bills, buy food and pay the rent or mortgage. If they're late and you're stressed, they'll dismiss it, perhaps even find your state amusing. Maybe your bank account and mortgage is in their name and you have little to no ability to earn your own money.

In the Citizens Advice Bureau's report 'Controlling money, controlling lives'[1] they state:

A broad range of behaviours have been documented in relation to financial abuse. These include:

- Interfering with employment and/or education
- Stealing
- Destroying property
- Stopping and/or controlling access to finances including benefits/savings/wages
- Forcing victim to take out credit
- Forcing victim to commit fraud

This list is certainly not finite. Financial abuse is incredibly nuanced. A Christmas Day Excel may look pretty pathetic but lined up against years' worth of putting someone in uncomfortable, demeaning and sometimes dangerous situations, having them 'at your beck and call' due to being financially obligated to you, is downright abusive.

THE 'I'M ONLY HELPING' CARD

Sometimes Controlls may be onerous, bullying and intimidating when it comes to the monetary demands they place on the victim. Other times it can be subtle. They're 'helping you out', 'getting you out of a sticky spot', but the end goal is always the same: Control.

The number of instances of financial abuse is huge: according to Refuge's study with the Co-operative Bank, one in five people in the UK have experienced financial abuse in an intimate relationship.[2]

WHY DO THEY DO IT?

If victims of financial abuse flee a relationship with a Controll, often their credit histories are pockmarked, they may struggle to get loans in the future and they will have lost confidence in their ability to handle money.

Controlls abuse their victims economically because it:

1. Limits the chances of the victim being able to leave.

2. Reduces any confidence the victim has in being able to survive without their perpetrator.

3. Presents further danger to the victim of being looped into financial misdemeanours caused by the perpetrator. Money and stress are two additional factors that keep the victim tied to a relationship with a Controll.

When you give away your money, or it is taken from you, there is an overwhelming sense of insecurity. Those of you who have been in situations where you do not have enough money, if any, to pay for basics like food or shelter will understand the stark feeling of vulnerability. You are totally exposed. Exactly where the Controll wants you.

There are certain states the Controll likes you to experience:

- Inadequacy
- Vulnerability
- Intimidation

- Instability
- Isolation
- Self-doubt
- Low self-esteem

If your access to money is either solely in the hands of your Controll, or they determine exactly how you spend your money, you will resonate with every one of those feelings.

In whatever way it happens, financial abuse will not get better on its own.

It is more likely to escalate.

HOW DO I STOP BEING FINANCIALLY CONTROLLED?

It took me a long time to learn this critical life rule:

MONEY = POWER

When you have financial stability, or at the very least something to fall back on, you gain confidence that you have your own back. There is a justified feeling of power, and with that – stability, comfort and reassurance. This was an alien state to me. Every other area of my life was so swamped with tension that being financially unstable didn't come top of my 'to action' list.

You are not alone, and you are certainly not reckless, useless, stupid, or any of the other names thrown at you. You did not let this happen – it happened to you.

Here are some key steps to take if you think you are a victim of financial abuse:

- The first thing to do is try and keep track of the situation. Gather receipts, documents and statements that may be used in evidence later on. You need to gauge what is going out and what is coming in.
- There are helplines you can call such as the National Domestic Violence Helpline. These are trained professionals that can give you solid advice on what to do next. You'll find a comprehensive list of numbers at the back of the book.
- Speak to a trusted friend or family member about your concerns and let them help you make a plan of action.
- If you are in a position to, set as much money as possible aside, even if this happens incrementally, perhaps in a separate account or with someone you trust.
- Where it is safe to do so, cancel joint bank accounts and put spending caps on accounts and loans.
- Once you have escaped the relationship there are banks that can assist you, such as the Co-operative Bank who partnered with Refuge on the 'My Money, My Life' campaign: 'A campaign to shine a spotlight on this often-overlooked form of domestic abuse and call for industry-wide agreement to support people who experience financial abuse in their relationships.'

WHAT HAPPENS IF YOU HAVE
A HOUSE AND KIDS TOGETHER?

Victims of Controlls who are tied into houses, have children, or perhaps don't even own a bank account – I got you. I understand that the idea of putting away a small amount a month is impossible. There may be victims who are over twenty years into a relationship with a Controll. It's like being released from jail with no money, family, or hope. Just the thought of leaving your relationship or marriage in this situation will feel mind-numbingly unbearable. Take it step by step. Utilize the resources section at the back; there are plenty of people and organizations that can help – you are not alone.

The fact you've survived shows you have more strength than you know.

LET'S TALK ABOUT IT

I never thought I would be able to deal with my debt; I was sick of people telling me I should 'have a rainy-day fund' and be 'money smart'. Trust me, Samantha, if I could, I would. I'm not taking financial advice from you, anyway. You live at home with your mum and dad who still pay your phone bill.

Speaking about money matters is taboo – people hate to discuss how little they have (but will more than happily parade a leased Mercedes on their Instagram). Be ready to start opening up to those close to you if you're in difficulty.

The day I paid off my debt was underwhelming to say the least. I expected a brass band, maybe some fake monkeys with cymbals, a confetti cannon, but it didn't happen. I decided to put away a little a month into a locked savings account – sometimes it was only £10. Over the course of three years that grew, and with that, seeds of my power started to return and sprout.

Don't get me wrong – I still shudder if that text comes through: You have exceeded your agreed overdraft limit. Bleurgh. But I am in a position to be able to deal with it, and if I can't – I ask for help. Communication is key.

Next, it's time to get really shady. There's a side to dating a Controll I've carefully glided over . . . until now. Family, friends, anyone closely related to me, please look away. Everyone else, steel your nerves. This next chapter is recommended after mealtimes, no more than once a day.

CHAPTER ELEVEN
SEX WITH A PSYCHOPATH

Sexual Coercion

The sheets in a hotel always feel different to your sheets at home, don't they? They manage to get them all crispy and starched. I guess that's because they've been washed so many times. At least, I hope that's what it is.

The air con is drying out my contact lenses, but I don't want to put my glasses on, and I can't take them out or I'll be blind. I reach to the plywood side table and take the full tumbler of strong gin and tonic, finishing it in one.

Very few hotels get away with not looking seedy. The expensive ones manage, but the chain hotels are carbon copies of each other. Worn green carpet, uninviting ancient armchair, limescale-sheathed shower head. I especially hate those coloured bits of fabric they lay on the end of the bed. I learnt the other day they are called bed scarves. So stupid. Why does a bed need a scarf? Unless Paddington's on a stopover. They never wash them, apparently. The remote control is filthy too. If I use it, I put a tissue over it. I'd like to have one of those UV black lights to see the stains before I sit anywhere. Maybe it's best not to think about it.

Damien has been in the bathroom on his phone for nearly forty minutes. Ordinarily I'd feel stupid lying out here, alone in this, the uncomfortable black lace stocking suit he's bought me, but I'm used to it. I don't bother looking at my phone, there'll be nothing on it, no messages or calls. If there is anything it'll be from my family and I especially don't want to read that now, so I stay staring up at the Styrofoam tiled ceiling. There's some kind of red stain in the far corner by the bolted window. I hope it's ketchup.

The toilet flushes.

He comes out in his grey Calvin Klein boxers. Before I go any further, I want you to know this isn't some Fifty Shades shit. Nor is it erotic fiction. Don't get cosy. Right? Good.

He sits on the end of the bed, takes his boxers off then slides next to me. I hate lying on my back with no proper underwiring, it makes my boobs flow under my armpits like a slow-motion paint spill. He grabs my right breast. I use the word 'grab' deliberately.

Damien and I don't make love. We've never made love. He has sex with me. Recently he's started inviting me to lots of his work seminars, which makes me optimistic about our future. I ignore the fact my only purpose on these trips is to stay in the hotel and be ready for him to have sex with.

We're on the grim edge of suburbia. You can always tell you're in suburbia when the train stations start to hyphenate: Ross-On-Wye, Sutton-Cum-Lound, Wells-Under-Shitterton.

Not that I've seen much of the outside.

As he places my hand on his erection, I start thinking about the woman who got hauled off the train earlier for not having a ticket. I empathized with her. She was only young. The inspector was a prick.

Damien has pulled me up so now he lies on the bed, and I'm knelt, knees each side of his legs. I give him three seconds to . . . yes, here it is, the hair grab. He wraps my ponytail around his hand and forces my mouth onto him.

That poor girl. She didn't look like she was deliberately avoiding the fare, just that she had to desperately get somewhere and couldn't pay. I should have offered to buy her a ticket. Not that I have much money myself.

Damien enjoys it when he makes me gag. He likes to feel powerful. I'm very well trained at thinking up stories and even running over to-do lists whilst he has sex with me. I feel him rummaging around, look up and see he's filming. This isn't a new thing. He wants to be omnipotent. I don't question it any more. I dread to think in five years what it'll take for him to get his sexual kicks.

A long time has passed, my jaw aches. He's decided he wants to have penetrative sex. I lie on my back and he pushes heavily on my chest as he enters me. It hurts both inside and on my chest because I'm already bruised from times before. It doesn't matter. Soon he'll move . . . there we go, around my throat. There've been times I've thought I might pass out. I can't speak, he keeps going. It's especially bad if I have a blocked nose. I've moved his hands away before, but he gets mad and moves them back. God forbid I say I'm not in the mood. Been there, done that, got the trauma.

I wonder how old that girl was? Maybe only 14. All by herself. She was still in school uniform and had a faded green bomber jacket that looked like it would do nothing to keep her from the bitter cold. The inspector humiliated her. He made such a show of it. Condescending fuckbucket. Someone should have stuck up for her. I should have.

I'm exemplary at making the right noises and faces. I suppose anyone from the outside would think I was enjoying myself. I'm not. But I know if I make the correct sounds, it'll encourage him, and all this will be done. He calls me a slut and a whore as he's thrusting into me. I especially hate it when he . . . there we go, spits at me. He does it into my mouth; I retched last time which isn't great when there's hands round your neck.

I said goodbye to my dignity years ago.

I've lost so much weight my clavicles protrude. They're completely unprotected from his heavy, rough hands. I've used make-up before to cover the purple marks, I'm not sure I have the right stuff with me. Will see later.

He's finished. I was fortunate this time. Sometimes he likes to ejaculate over me as I'm on my knees as a final 'fuck you'. He feels mighty when he does that, I can see the fulfilment in his eyes. A signifier I am his property and he'll do what he wants.

Tonight wasn't so bad. I worry about the videos and photos, but whatever to make him happy.

He pulls the sheet over himself. I head to the bathroom to clean myself up. Funny, when I look back at snapshots of myself from this time, I can see how thin and worn down I was but now, in this hotel bathroom, looking in the mirror, I pinch the non-existent fat on my stomach, punishing myself for not gyming enough that week.

I sit on the toilet for a long time, staring into space. Maybe *he's already asleep. I'm pro at getting into bed without waking him.*

After I've showered in the most unsatisfying cubicle there is, pissing lukewarm water out, using the hotel shower gel, which is exactly the same as the shampoo, I wrap myself in a thin, scratchy towel and inch the door open. He's sitting up, on his phone. Puny bedside lights on. He looks at me, expressionless face, and pats the bed next to him. I smile.

Maybe all he wants is a cuddle.

Sex should bring people closer, it's the greatest act of intimacy and love that there is. Yes, sex can be fun, filthy and forgettable but never, ever should sex be gained through coercion.

What you may have noted from my anecdote above is that not once did I say 'no'. That must mean it was consensual, right? There wasn't a moment I clearly stated anything close to: 'I don't want this', so Damien was well within his rights to continue. Correct?

Nope. The Controll, in this case Damien, through recurrent displays of belligerence, sulking and getting snarky when I had previously said 'no', had conditioned and coerced me into giving in, backing down and choosing the less resistant route. This, of course, being to let him have sex with me, however he chose to.

Previous occurrences where I'd stood by my 'no' he'd act affronted, withholding affection. Desperate for any form of love, he primed me into understanding that this only came when attached to sex.

CONSENT MATTERS

When a Controll implements **sexual coercion**, they are deciding:

- When, where and for how long you have sex.
- What the sex will entail, what they will do to you and what you will do to them.
- How you should behave when they are having sex with you.

Some tactics used in sexual coercion are:

—Guilt tripping you into making you think you owe them sex

—Giving you substances to loosen you up

—Pressurizing you because you're in a relationship or married to them and 'that's what loving couples do'

—Becoming resentful or angry when you say no and continuing to harass you for sex

Caving in to sex with anyone under these conditions means there is not consent.

Consent must always be given with free will.
Otherwise, it is not consent.

Both or all parties must agree to whatever sexual activities are about to take place, through having the freedom and ability to make that choice.

Consent cannot be given if:

- The person is incapacitated through drugs, alcohol or being asleep.
- The person is unable to communicate their lack of consent due to a disability.
- The person was subjected to threats, violence or abuse in order to coerce consent from them.

For some reason, there are people who seem to find the idea of consent rather confusing. Let me help them out.

Any form of sexual contact – kissing, stroking, touching, licking, fingering, fucking etc. – *without* direct and voluntary permission **IS NOT CONSENT.** This includes your long-term partner. The fact you are in a relationship with them does not give you an ongoing consent card.

Let's say you are with your partner and you've had a few wines, you're feeling frisky, and you get naked and indulge in a little foreplay. Then you decide: 'Actually, I don't want to have sex.' Your partner is all turned on, ready to rumble, and you say: 'I'm not feeling this. No, I don't want to have sex.' The only valid thing that should come out of their mouth is something along the lines of: 'OK, I understand, that's cool.' No bitterness, no resentment, no frustration. That's it.

If your partner gets stroppy, storms out the room, pesters you to change your mind, refuses to talk to you and then, *because* of their sullen, disrespectful behaviour, you have sex with them to appease – **THIS IS NOT CONSENT.**

You should never feel forced, guilted or harassed into a sexual situation with a partner. Ever. I would like to make clear that even if you do not think your partner may be narcissistic or psychopathic, they can *still* use sexual coercion.

You are not beholden to have sex with anyone. Not your partner, boyfriend, girlfriend, husband, wife, or anyone else. It is not a means of bargaining. No matter how much debt you are in, how irritated you've seemingly made them, or whatever supposed obligations or implications they are holding over you – *you do not owe them sex.*

THE ROUGH SEX DEFENCE

There's something else going on in my not-so-sexy hotel stay. Did you spy it? Through instances of forceful, sadistic, rough sex, Damien had chosen to weaponize degradation. This is not uncommon for Controlls. The worse you feel about yourself, the more disrespected and debased, the more power they have to do whatever they want.

This degradation could come in many forms. It may be masking non-consensual throttling, asphyxiation, spitting, restraining etc., as 'rough sex'. That gives them the caveat to bypass any repercussions – 'What? It's rough sex. I thought you were into that?' They could use shame to deliver the final blow, with lines like: 'I like kinky girls. You're so vanilla.'

The new Domestic Abuse Bill 2020 includes provisions against the 'rough sex defence'. The 'rough sex defence' was increasingly used in cases where victims were either seriously hurt or killed by their abusive partners to justify why the violence had happened. Small steps are being taken in the right direction.

In a research study for BBC Radio 5 Live, it was found that

more than a third of UK women under the age of 40 have experienced unwanted slapping, choking, gagging or spitting during consensual sex. Of which, 20 per cent had been upset or frightened.

**If their behaviour comes
without warning or consent,
then this is sexual assault.**

There should be no second chances.

Listen, it's more than OK if rough sex is your bag. If that's what turns you on and this derives from a place of consent and freedom, then all power to you, sis. Spend some dollar on a collar, revamp with a clamp, get kinky with a Slinky. You're all good. No. I'm discussing something quite different here. I am talking about **Intimate Partner Sexual Violence**.

INTIMATE PARTNER SEXUAL VIOLENCE

Intimate Partner Sexual Violence (IPSV) covers sexual assault and rape that takes place within an intimate relationship. Sexual violence is used to dominate and hold power over the victim. It could include, but is not limited to:

- Physical assault and violence during sex, which could be touted as 'rough sex'. Strangling, slapping, choking, punching, spitting, etc.
- Forcing the victim to take part in sexual activities with others or with someone else observing.

- Using bullying, vitriolic insults towards the victim like 'whore' or 'slut' when they are unwanted.
- Taking photos or videos of the victim without their consent.
- Forcing them to watch pornography.
- Unwanted touching or kissing, oral, anal or vaginal intercourse.

Let's look at forcing victims to participate in making or watching pornography for the benefit of the Controll. Sometimes the victim is unaware this is happening. Sometimes they call it out, and when this happens, the Controll becomes hostile. This is Intimate Partner Sexual Violence.

Sexual assault, harassment and rape

Grand. Time for some swotting up on sexual illegalities. What is the difference between sexual assault, sexual harassment and rape?

According to the London Metropolitan Police:

> The law defines **rape** as non-consensual penetration of someone's vagina, anus or mouth by another person's penis. This signifies a male on female or male on male rape, of course female on male rape exists but rape is a significantly gendered crime. The Sexual Offences Act 2003 made the victim of rape gender neutral so there is no longer differentiation of 'rape' and 'male rape'.
>
> **Sexual assault** is any physical, emotional or psychological violation in the form of a sexual act without consent.

And the Citizens Advice Bureau tells us:

> **Sexual harassment** is behaviour which is meant to, or has the effect of defying your dignity, or creating an intimidating, hostile, degrading, humiliating or offensive environment. This could be sending you explicit photos, making sexual comments, or remarking in a sexual way about your body.

That dick pic sent without consent? Yep. That's sexual harassment.

Revenge porn

I hope we've all heard of revenge porn. Revenge porn is the act of someone, usually an ex-partner, 'leaking' and sharing sexually explicit photos or videos, nude or semi-nude photos or videos of you without your consent.

According to data shared with BBC Three, in 2020 the Revenge Porn Helpline saw an 87 per cent increase in the number of adults needing help and advice for intimate image abuse. An overwhelming 3,136 new cases were opened, which is the highest number the helpline had ever seen. Over half of these people needed to access mental health services and 45 stated feeling suicidal as a result of the intimate image abuse they suffered.

The end goal with revenge porn is always the same: to degrade, debilitate and destroy. Victims often comment they feel 'all eyes on them' when out in public, with alarming numbers suffering such bad anxiety from the abuse they struggle to leave the house at all.

This violation of trust can have lifelong consequences. When the images and videos taken are of a victim who has withstood a Controll's months, years or decades of abuse, the outcome of revenge porn can lead to suicide.

In a perfect world we would trust our partners to keep intimate photos private. Unfortunately, no one knows what the future holds, you can't be certain there won't be a messy break-up or a leak to photos or images on the cloud.

The advice is to never send compromising photos or videos to a partner, ever.

Even if they beg you. If they try to persuade you after you've said no – this is coercion.

Your choice not to send an explicit photo or video for the smart reasoning you are protecting your future self is by no means an indicator you have no faith in the relationship; it's being savvy and switched on. Think of it as self-defence.

If you still want to send explicit images solely because you have the free will to make that choice, then doctor the images and make sure your face is not in them. That way you're protecting yourself later down the line should anything ever go awry.

Listen, don't panic. If you're uneasy reading this because you have sent intimate photos of yourself to someone, keep calm. The chances are the images won't be shared, but in the future, don't run the risk. If you still speak with the person you sent them to, ask them to kindly delete. Any half-decent person would totally understand and would do so immediately.

On 13 April 2015, Section 33 of the Criminal Justice and Courts Act 2015 came into effect. This was an updated law that made sharing these private sexual photos and videos a specific offence, covering all social media platforms and electronic communications like WhatsApp and Snapchat.

Revenge porn is a crime, and offenders can face up to two years in prison. This is called image-based sexual abuse and it is not your fault, *even* if you consented to the images or sent them in the first place. There is a dedicated phone line to call if you think you have been a victim of revenge porn: 0845 6000 459. This is the Revenge Porn Helpline, or visit: www.revengepornhelpline.org.uk.

Fine, so what about photos and videos taken of you whilst you were in a toxic relationship? Those that perhaps you weren't necessarily in a strong mental state to say no to? Well, we're getting into a grey area. Again, I would suggest – where safe to – asking the recipient to delete. If you are worried the images are being circulated please call the Revenge Porn Helpline for more advice on dealing with this and having any shared images online removed.

When a victim is exposed and debased, they lose their self-worth and often come to the conclusion 'it's easier if I let them do what they want'. **This is not consent.** This is downright exhaustion and terrorization from repeated conditioning, sexual coercion and abuse.

Porn and its effect on sex

Let's assess another side of IPSV and consent. Within seconds, degrading, rough and violent porn – in the majority, against women – is at our fingertips. This standard of barbaric sex as one of the first things you access on porn sites represents across LGBTQ2+ communities too.

Thing is, the inquisitive minds searching for sexual 'education' via porn sites are not going anywhere. That's OK. But what is not OK is the bombardment of degrading porn that primarily targets women.

Porn sells violence against women as a fantasy.

According to a study, 88 per cent of popular porn scenes contained violence – choking, slapping, spitting, etc. – and 49 per cent contained verbal assaults, the majority of those, 87 per cent, against women.[1] But there's more to it than that: 95 per cent of these women were seen reacting *positively* to the violence and verbal abuse. Therefore, not only is porn conditioning men to think IPSV is fine, it's also telling women this is something they should accept and even enjoy.

We need to move towards porn that pushes the kerazy concept that sex should be enjoyed by all parties and not seen only through the male gaze. Although extremely limited, there is some porn seen through the female gaze. Swedish-born erotic film director and screenwriter Erika Lust has been instrumental in promoting a host of equal, feminist pornography.

All in all, with violent pornography so readily available, the line between consent and coercion is heavily marred. This is still not an excuse.

But, but, but WAIT. I smell a scapegoat. Let's take this further. It would be so easy for us to use rough sex in porn as the excuse for why there is a rise in IPSV; that way we have someone to blame, don't we? How about this for a clanger:

Men have the autonomy to
not be violent at all.

Ohmagerd. What? Yes, rough sex in porn or not, men have the free will to choose if they want to dominate and abuse women. I know, right? Sure, the amount of violence against women in porn is disgusting, but the result of that is not the root of IPSV. It doesn't help, but it is not the sole reason. It is a symptom, not the cause.

SEXUAL COERCION BINGO

The Crime Survey for England and Wales estimated that 20 per cent of women and 4 per cent of men have experienced some type of sexual assault since the age of 16, equivalent to an estimated 3.4 million female victims and 631,000 male victims.

The sad thing is, I could put money on the fact that every single person reading this book has been sexually coerced in some way.

In fact, let's see how many you can get. Let's play . . .

SEXUAL COERCION BINGO

We're in a relationship. You owe me.	I lent you money, it's the least you can do.	I thought you wanted that pay rise / promotion?	You said you wanted to spend more time together.	My mate has sex with his gf / wife / partner four times a week
It'll be good exercise!	It won't mean anything.	You're such a prude!	I thought you were kinky.	So you don't find me attractive?
It's Valentine's Day / Christmas / my birthday!	Come on, it won't take long!	FREE SPACE	We've been on three dates already.	I don't care if you're on your period, let's go!
Your friend would give it up way easier than you.	Don't you fancy me?	You had sex with me last night but now you won't? That doesn't make sense.	You sent me a topless pic earlier and now you don't want sex? You're a prick-tease.	I have a high sex drive. If you want to be with me, you've got to match it.
It's the least you could do!	I'll tell everyone we slept together.	I'll share those pics / video I have of you.	I thought you loved me?	You're so ungrateful.
Then I'll go and find someone who will.	It was your fault, make it up to me.	Oh come on, you'll like it!	Just the tip, I promise.	You've led me on this far, I'm not stopping now!

How many did you score? Eye-opening, isn't it? We all need to check ourselves and set boundaries. No means no. If you say 'no' firmly and clearly and the other person continues, they are about to commit sexual assault or rape, and by all means tell them that. It may shock them into submission. If they continue or make a joke of it, you can explain a prison sentence is no laughing matter. Get yourself safely and quickly out of the situation and call a friend or family member to communicate what has happened.

If your partner(s) respects and loves you, they will make sure sex is consensual. It doesn't need to be a damn two-hour press conference – a little check-in is all that's needed: 'Is this OK?' 'Are you happy with me doing this?' 'Let me know if this is good for you.' If the answer is something like: 'Actually, I'm a bit tired,' or 'I'd rather stop now,' or 'I'm not really up for this,' then it's very fucking simple . . . Just. Stop.

SPEAK UP,
WE'RE HERE TO LISTEN

If you have been the victim of sexual coercion, harassment, assault or rape, you must speak to someone. That person doesn't need to be the police if you don't feel ready. You can speak to Sexual Assault Referral Centre (SARC): type them into your search engine and check centres within your location. These are trained professionals you can chat to, in confidence, about what's happened. They will assist you in getting the help you need.

Rape Crisis also offers a free live chat helpline. Visit them at www.rapecrisis.org.uk.

It doesn't matter how long ago the assault or rape took place; the person responsible should be held liable. Start the conversation; there's always someone that is ready and willing to help, protect and guide you.

Look into therapy. In many areas of the UK, councils provide free Talking Therapy if you can't afford it. The aftermath of assault and rape can stick with you for a lifetime, but it doesn't need to. A good therapist will help you process what's happened and implement coping strategies to help you heal.

Your trust has been broken, but you are entitled to have faith in others. If you don't work through trauma like sexual coercion, harassment, assault or rape, it's like walking around with a heavy backpack of stones on: you'll feel weighed down and wearied by it. Therapy and counselling help you slowly remove your trauma, rock by rock.

THE FIGHTBACK

There are millions across the world doing their bit too. Me Too is a global social movement. The first use of #MeToo was coined in 2007 by activist and survivor Tarana Burke. It gained traction in 2017, when the sexual abuse perpetrated by Harvey Wankstain was outed. The Me Too movement paves the way to 'disrupt Rape Culture'; their aim is to empower people to speak out about the abuses they have suffered, offering solidarity and strength in numbers. To get support and read more on their ground-breaking work, visit: www.metoomvmt.org.

This whole consent and coercion thing all seems much simpler now, doesn't it? I hope you're feeling some of that lovely, justified rage. Talking of rage, have you heard the one about your mum and dad not meaning to fuck you up?[2]

CHAPTER TWELVE
LIKE FATHER, LIKE SON
Interparental Coercive Control

I forgot how soothing a horizon is. I'm so used to being surrounded by bricks and tall buildings; I'd virtually forgotten there was a world outside.

The heavy fog mars the line between sea and sky. It's like soft focus. I pull my long, black woollen coat tighter. Damien stands beside me, hood and collar up, tapping away on his phone. Missing it all.

You'd never think we were only an hour out of London. I'm sure I manifested this trip; I've been dreaming of Brighton. I even have a fridge magnet. We're not staying over, which is a shame. I'd love to explore the cobbled backstreets, have my chips nicked by a seagull, buy a blue suede pug ornament in Brighton Flea Market.

I don't want to jinx it, but Damien mentioned engagement the other day. I had a fantastical dream he may do it here, at the Hove Bandstand. Maybe it's a little further off. We're very much in love right now. I can't get enough of him. We've been killing ourselves laughing, doing things as a couple, united. I know what we can be. See, I told you that sign from The Universe that I saw on Instagram was for me – Don't give up!!!!!

Although I am well versed at what's to come, in this second, standing below the illuminated rainbow letters marking Brighton Pier, watching a murmuration of starlings, I can fantasize all I like that this is forever.

We've been together nearly three years. Last year, when I made a special anniversary meal, Damien punched a wall and needed hospital treatment. He was furious: he said I'd cooked to show him up because he'd forgotten the date.

I don't think I'll do anything to mark it this year. The hospital trip or our anniversary.

Very soon I'll be introduced to his family for the first time. I should have met them before, but it's never been the right time. That's what Damien said, anyway. It doesn't matter, it's happening now, and I couldn't be more thrilled. I'm good with parents. Let's hope they love me, then if he ever leaves, they'll convince him not to. Unlikely but, hey, ever the optimist.

It's his nephew's Bar Mitzvah. I've never been to a Bar Mitzvah, I'm not Jewish, but my grandad was. Maybe it'll send some Mazal my way. Damien isn't remotely Jewish either, he's been emotionally blackmailed into going by a family member, which I'm pretty sure is also not very Jewish.

Damien has navigated it so that we turn up when his uncle is giving the Prayer of Thanks, right at the end of the service. I would have liked to watch the ceremony, but at least I have extra time to prep for the parent schmooze.

We're on the concrete steps outside the synagogue, a gold

Star of David hangs above. Damien sparks a cigarette adjacent to a 'No Smoking' sign. Never one to follow the rules.

I hear cheers and applause from inside, it must be over. The colossal navy doors swing open abruptly. This is it.

Some families have genes as strong as Michael Phelps; with the array of chiselled jaws and cleft chins parading out of the synagogue doors, I can see Damien's family is no different.

A perfectly made-up woman in her fifties, bearing the same cleft chin, approaches Damien and me. Is this his mum? I haven't seen photos of her. I've furrowed deep caverns in my palm where I've dug my nails in. I can feel a dribble of sweat tear down my back and make the cheap navy lace dress I'm wearing stick to my skin. I wish I hadn't read that life hack to wear a pair of pants over the top of your tights to stop them falling down. I feel like I'm in a girdle.

'Damien!' she says, in a high-pitched Dudley accent. 'And who's this?' I leave it a beat, waiting for Damien to explain. He doesn't. I extend my hand with a smile. 'I'm Maddy.'

'Always were a lucky chap, eh? Give your aunty a kiss.' Damien doesn't move.

She spots yet another of the Cleft Chin Crew (The CCCs) and hollers, 'Esther! Over 'ere. Don't break yeh ankle!' Then turns back to us, and says, 'Told her not to wear those ridiculous shoes but your ma never was one to listen, eh, Damien?'

Damien has still not exuded a smidge of warmness or conversation in her direction, but she doesn't seem to have noticed.

Here we go. I get to meet Damien's mum. She's a slender, short woman, beautiful but unassuming. Her eyeline sticks to *the concrete, head bowed. Although unsmiling, she seems warm; wrinkles soften her sharp cheekbones. She lifts her head momentarily and I see the whisper of a greeting.*

'Mum, where's the party? I have to go back to London soon. I'm not hanging around.' Not even a 'hello', and I know he hasn't seen or spoken to her in months. Maybe they had a falling out?

'It's Ralli Hall. I think. Is it, Sarah?' Sarah, the first lady, rolls her eyes animatedly at Damien's mum. 'Yes, Esther. Memory like a sieve, honestly.'

Damien's mum has a forlorn energy. I want to wrap my arms around her. I do the next best thing – 'Hello, it's so lovely to finally meet you. I'm Maddy, Damien's girlfriend.'

Damien's mum raises her head. 'Maddy! Yes! I've been asking to meet you—' Damien cuts her off. 'Come on then. I've parked round the corner and there's no ticket on the car. See you at the party.' Damien strides down the steps and I follow, leaving Esther and Sarah with a smile and a wave. I don't think I've won them, but it's a start.

When we arrive at Ralli Hall, many of his family are already inside. There are round tables lining the sides of the wooden-floored community centre. A food station at the far end is split into sweet and savoury. Doughy rugelach, sticky, braided honey challah and pastries piled high. Then there's flaky Maina meat pies, salads and dips. It looks delicious; I haven't eaten since yesterday lunchtime so I would very much like to hover, but I have work to do. Still no sign of Damien's dad but, as Damien nips out for another cigarette, I spot his mum, Esther, and make my way over.

The family are talking, dancing, laughing. One man in

*particular is in very high spirits. He sees Esther and me and
staggers over.*

*'Sight for sore eyes!' The man leers towards me; Esther's body
tenses.*

*'This is Damien's father, Maddy. Samuel, this is Damien's
new girlfriend.'*

New? Whatever, let it go.

*'Hello! So lovely to meet you!' I extend my hand; it remains
unshaken. Samuel mimics me with a bad impression of
Camilla Parker Bowles: 'Ohhhh, sooo lovely to meeeet yoh!'
I'm not sure whether to fake laugh, I don't think it even
merits that.*

*'Samuel,' Esther says, lightly dusting his arm. I can tell she's
mortified.*

*Later that night, Samuel sinks another couple of bottles of
wine and is getting rowdier by the Hora. Esther looks half the
size from earlier. Damien is fifty times more immersed in his
phone. I don't quite understand how, but his family – primarily
his mum and dad – have short-circuited our passionate
rekindling. The crazy love from the last few weeks has fizzled
prematurely; and I am pissed off. We were due a little more
hedonistic head-over-heels, but looking at Damien now, eyes lit
by screen, I know our time is up.*

*Esther excuses herself for the bathroom. Samuel spies the
now-free seat next to me and lopes over. Quick as a flash,
feigning not seeing him, I pick up Esther's small navy clutch
and place it on her chair. It doesn't deter him. Samuel's eyes are
wild, he's rambling and swaying. Damien doesn't look up; he
must be very used to this.*

'Watch this!' Samuel says with glee, and places Esther's bag

inside his jacket, then trots back to the dance floor. What just happened? I turn to Damien, but he's so lost in his phone he wouldn't hear a nuclear bomb.

Esther returns. She smiles at me and I gulp. Will she think I stole it? Here's Samuel again. ''Right, Est?' he says. Esther senses her clutch bag is missing. I look at Samuel and he pantomime winks at me like I'm in on it. I'm not. I think he's discarded it somewhere else.

'Yes, I'm OK.' She's still searching. What do I do?

'Lost summink?' Samuel says, now poker-faced.

'No, it's nothing. I must have taken it to the loo. Only my handbag.'

'Not this again.' Samuel is side-eyeing me like he's one of the Two bloody Ronnies. 'She drinks too much then loses her things,' he slurs.

'I only had a glass of wine, that was hours ago,' she says. I watch her get progressively more panicked. I'm not going to be part of this.

'He took it,' I say, pointing at Samuel. I don't care how accusatory I sound. Damien looks up sharply.

Samuel shakes his head and walks away. Damien glares at me, digs his cigarette box out from his jacket pocket and walks outside.

I don't know what it is, but I feel a compelling unity with this woman.

Have you heard the saying: 'How a man treats his mother is a good indicator of how he will treat you'? There is some truth to that. If, for example, a guy speaks to his mother like she's a piece of shit when she's purely asking if he'd like a cup of tea,

I'd consider dropkicking him off the nearest tall building. There's a chance this person will be speaking to you in the same way very soon.

HAPPY SPOUSE, HAPPY HOUSE

If someone is brought up in a stable, loving home, you'd expect them to comprehend what healthy love looks like. They received the security of familial love as they matured and will be open to seeking this security with a partner in adulthood.

Of course, there is no hard and fast rule. You could find someone who was mistreated by their mother as a child and is determined not to make the same mistakes.

What's more pertinent than looking at how a man treats his mother is *observing how the father treats the mother.*

Now, this little section may not be valid for everyone. You could have been raised by a single parent, two mothers, or two fathers. I am speaking here really about the longest-term relationship between your parental figures, whoever they were. How did they interact? What did an adult relationship look like to you? The union between the child's guardians is naturally the relationship the child evolves to emulate. The child has been conditioned to uphold this as a 'normal' partnership. Which certainly does not mean it's the optimum.

DO THE CONTROLLED
BECOME THE CONTROLLERS?

When we looked at codependency, we observed how, when growing up in an addicted household – whether that be surrounded by substance abuse, alcoholism, or something else – the child may learn to become the caregiver, the rescuer. It's expected they will continue this role to adulthood.

With this in mind, if a child is raised in a household where either one of the parents is throttled by control, the child is conditioned in one of two ways. They surmise:

It's OK to control, this is the only way to get on top.

It's normal to be controlled, it's easier to keep our head down.

It's fight or flight: if a child sees their mother controlled by their father, continually criticized, coerced, destroyed, do they side with the mother or the father? It's not the child's responsibility to protect a parent, although this may be what they attempt to do. Equally, they could grow to believe a false rhetoric that their mother is weak, even deserving of the abuse, and thus, it's safer to emulate the abuser.

Let's look at it another way. If a woman is being demeaned and subjected to abuse, how well is she expected to parent? Now, it may sound like I am trying to force blame onto the mother; I'm not. We're looking at facts. The victim – the mother, in this case – is constantly navigating around violent mood swings, lack of sleep and ingrained fear . . . how could she possibly show her child the love they deserve?

It's likely the mother will do her best to shield the child from the abuse, she will try to manage the needs of the child, but parenting in this sense is like attempting to run an ultra-marathon on your hands and knees with a tumble-dryer strapped on your back. Unreservedly gruelling and excruciating.

How does seeing this maltreatment impact the child?

When a child is witness to intimate partner violence, they become a victim themselves.

Research indicates that, for children, witnessing domestic violence is at least as impactful as being directly abused themselves.[1] The NSPCC considers witnessing domestic abuse to be child abuse itself.

The child observing this abuse normalizes fear, instability and terror. They will either externalize or internalize this. Externalizing could present itself as:

- Antisocial behaviours
- 'Acting out' to get the attention they lack in the home environment
- Behavioural difficulties, inability to stay quiet in classrooms, restlessness or becoming violent with other children

Internalizing the abuse could appear as:

- Anxiety
- Low self-esteem
- Depression and/or suicidal thoughts

There are no two ways about it: a child that witnesses any degree of coercive control and abuse within the home will be faced with significant negative outcomes which may last their entire lives. The developmental stages of their lives are tainted by fear, their mental, physical and emotional health diminished, and their ability to form healthy bonds with others reduced to almost zero. The abuse will affect the child or children in a terrifying multitude of ways.

A CHILD AS A TOOL

There's another side to a child witnessing, and thus falling prey to coercive control, and that is that they may be used as a tool. It is often the case that the controlling, abusive parent will weaponize the child to add further harm to the victim. They could use them to attack the victim's parenting, use the child to relay intimidating messages, say that they will take the child away, attempt to turn the child against the victim, threaten to harm or even kill the child.

When we put all of these together, we foresee a horrific and perilous life for the child. Ultimately, the child . . .

Develops a tolerance for chaos.

There is the risk that the child who is so accustomed to verbal and/or physical and/or sexual abuse, who normalizes terror in their formative years, will either become a codependent adult or progress to become an abuser themselves.

A study researched a group of prisoners in Wisconsin (since prison is *one* of the more likely places to find Psychopaths) and found that prisoners who had witnessed abuse whilst growing up were more likely to score highly on the scale of psychopathic traits that we saw earlier from Dr Robert Hare.[2]

This doesn't necessarily mean, though, that psychopathy is directly *caused* by witnessing abuse as a child, however the link remains that a child brought up in such an abusive environment would be far more likely to learn psychopathic, controlling tactics.

If you think about it in respect of learning a language, do you think it would be easier to master a language on an app, sitting alone in your bedroom, or in the native country, being surrounded by that language every day? It's evidently the latter. If a child's 'native land' is a place of control, manipulation and coercion, they will be far more adept at picking up damaging behavioural patterns like cheating, stealing, lying and bullying. Effectively, the child's woeful choice becomes: learn these behaviours or desperately try and avoid them.

Even if a mother attempts to protect her child from witnessing the abuse, the sad truth is the child will be living in a similar state of terror to the mother – walking on red-hot coals.

Every child and every adult has a basic right to feel safe in their own homes.

Fundamentally, the view for children who witness and become victims of coercive control themselves is bleak. But that only makes it worse for the victim. They are trapped by yet another layer of shame and guilt: 'How could I allow my child to grow up in such an environment?' The child may feel guilty too, for being defenceless and unable to protect their parent.

HAVING A CONTROLL AS A PARENT

When researching this book, not only was I astounded by how many people, predominantly women, had been victims of toxic relationships, but also the number of adults who were being controlled by a manipulative parent.

I heard cases of how grown-up children in their sixties were still being dominated by an authoritarian parent. Their entire lives subjugated by a crumbly old crone. How is this possible? Surely if there ever was an indicator of how deep coercive control runs it's this. This illustrates the sheer terror coercive control wreaks and it doesn't matter how small, puny and vulnerable the abuser may appear: they will still destroy your life.

Coercive control can happen in any intimate or familial relationship.

This means a parent controlling another parent or a parent dominating a child.

A Controll parent (or parents) could very well be psychopathic; they can be impulsive – uprooting the family at a whim, inviting in an array of sexual partners – they may have substance abuse issues and be violent. Oppressive patriarchal or matriarchal figures could use their children as trophies: 'I created you, you belong to me, I will use you in any way I please.' The parent that is truly psychopathic will not be able to love their child. They will have no maternal or paternal tendencies and no primal instinct to protect.

Children develop self-awareness as they grow up, so for a

young child, having an emotionally abusive parent is detrimental to their growth as an independent, compassionate and well-rounded adult. They will have no chance to understand boundaries and will effectively be used as a battering ram for the untold number of issues their Controll parent offloads onto them.

A GLADIATOR HOME LIFE

Sometimes, if there is more than one child, the toxic dynamic the Controll parent creates will shift. One may be chosen as the 'golden child' and pitted against another. The family home becomes the Colosseum. All under the watchful, gleeful eye of the self-appointed Emperor parent.

Children brought up in these horrific homes will become conditioned to chasing any validation they can get. As with a Controll partner, there is nothing they can ever do to merit praise from the Controll parent – but it's human nature for the child to try. They may take up hours of domestic chores, gardening, or attempt to fulfil any trivial demands the Controll parent heaps on them. After a time, the neglected, abused child may protect themselves in the only way they know how, by closing down, complying, pushing their emotions further back, their own needs becoming a distant memory.

It's not only the parent that could be coercive, but also conceivable that siblings could be narcissistic and/or psycho-pathic and make the lives of their brothers, sisters and parents hell.

HOW TO HEAL AS THE VICTIM
OF A CONTROLL PARENT

It is probable these children, grown-up or otherwise, are heavily weighted with a burden of guilt or shame either that they 'let this happen', or that it's somehow their fault their parent didn't love them. It's devastating for them to see other doting parents and realize they were not blessed with the steady, all-encompassing love a guardian should offer. But it is possible to heal and live full, positive, and love-packed lives, away from the coercive parent.

This was not your fault.

**You are worthy of love, respect and
validation no matter how old you are.**

The victim child was lacking in love and consistency, so it is of paramount importance for the grown-up child to find these in adult life. The easiest way to find love is to start where you can give it most, and where it is most needed – yourself.

If you have been victim to a Controll parent, you will have been made to believe you are nothing. Through therapy and healthy living practices both for body and mind, such as exercise and meditation, it is totally possible to claw back the love you deserved but never received.

Here are some steps you can take to help you on your journey of healing:

1. **Accept.** Accept that you were born or 'raised' by a controlling, coercive, Controll parent. You may have previously chosen to deny this was your reality because it was too hard to face, or you felt you owe/owed them loyalty as their child. You don't. They owed you a secure, loving, compassionate upbringing but they didn't give you that, so why are you beholden to anything? The sooner you call your childhood what it was, the sooner you can heal.

2. **Don't rose tint.** It is natural to refute what you went through. Of course there were good times; as with all Controlls there are extreme highs and extreme lows. We all want to reminisce on happy childhoods, it is normal to pull out the joyful times, just don't brush this glaze over your whole experience. You went through it, you survived it, you are a warrior. Be proud of yourself.

3. **Research.** It's wonderful that you're here, truly it is. You are reaching out for reason and affirmation that, in fact, you weren't an insolent, disobedient child, you were a victim of a coercive parent. The more you know about narcissism and psychopathy, the better. It will help you arm yourself against falling into future toxic relationships. Don't research to excuse their behaviour, though. Yes, it's sad for them that they live in such monochromatic, 2D worlds, but this isn't your problem. Look forward. You do you.

4. **Grieve.** I'm so sorry that you went through this. Childhood should be a magical time full of curiosity,

play and fun and it's likely yours was an extremely mixed bag, with some crippling low points. Allow yourself to grieve the childhood you should have had. Cry it out, wail, beat a pillow, whatever you need to do (I don't suggest using alcohol or drugs, though). When you've made space and gone through the stages of grief, which are:

Denial. Anger. Bargaining. Depression. Acceptance.

Then you can move towards focusing on the future, loosening, and eventually ridding yourself of the chains of the past.

5. **Love.** It's time to reinstate the love you are owed; this is a lifetime's journey. But don't worry, it will be fun. Make a conscious effort to check in with your self-talk. There are some exercises at the back of the book that will help with this.

Good. I'm glad we went through that together and our Awareness Armoury is getting built up to the rafters. Wait, talking of rafts, I'm starting to feel a bit seasick . . .

CHAPTER THIRTEEN
MEMORY FOAM

How to Win an Argument with a Psychopath

I'm on a moss-ridden, battle-scarred houseboat called Knot
Guilty, *on Regent's Canal in Hackney, East London. Have you
ever been on a houseboat? They say you can't feel it moving,
but that's a lie. Every time I stand up, I question whose crotch
I'm going to fall into.*

*We're at the party of one of Damien's colleagues. Monty, I
think he's called, or something equally pretentious. It's New
Year's Eve. I've never had a good NYE, there's such ridiculous
build-up to celebrating that another 365 days have vanished,
and your crow's feet are now crow's legs.*

*It's only 7.30 p.m. Four and a half hours to go. What the hell
am I going to do for that amount of time? Monty hasn't even
put crisps out. What a lame event. Could have chucked us a
bag of multipack Skips at the least.*

*I'm perilously perched on a tiny stool that my arse could
swallow at any second, leaning on the narrowest strip of cheap
pinewood I think is serving as a table. Apparently, all the*

people who own houseboats here are young creatives seeking a better life. All I can see are coked-up middle-aged men 'rah-ing' at each other. They're talking about 'the freedom of the untethered lifestyle'. Give me strength.

I lost Damien as soon as we arrived, which is surprising considering the square-footage. But I can now see his feet in the darkness, up on the canal path next to a pair of tanned legs in neon pink heels. He's in a foul mood so I don't think I'll check on him. I watch his Fred Perrys turn and head back down into the vessel.

It would be great if I was mid-conversation, throwing my head back, laughing away with some new friend so Damien had to wait to speak to me; but I'm not, I'm too tired to socialize. Damien had me up most of last night for some indiscretion or other.

He places himself on the small, cracked, red stool next to me and dramatically stares out of the rectangular, condensation-thick windows. His rage is palpable.

I can bear the silence no longer.

'What's up?' I say, testing, but still unwilling to poke too hard. That would be like wrapping your hand in Parma ham and placing it in a lion's open jaw.

'You are fucking unbelievable.'

Here we go. If someone offered me a million quid to admit the infraction I'd allegedly committed, I'd remain a pauper because I haven't got a flying fuck what it could be.

'You slate me for my social media presence and yet you post that shit on your timeline. You embarrass me at every opportunity, and I'm expected to sit here and take it like some pussy?'

I'm racking my brains. What did I post? It can't be the joke picture of me kissing a tree with the caption: 'Branching out for a New Year's snog. #shouldhaveputaringonit'. Can it? Really? I thought it was quite funny.

He's still ranting, speaking just quietly enough that I need to lean in and no one else can hear. He spits his words at the window; I wouldn't be that surprised if molten lava started gushing from his mouth.

'You don't think I see how fucking entitled you are? Brought up in some suburban, silver-spoon place, no fucking clue about the real world.'

Oh, by the way – don't look for the correlation between my posting a funny meme and an idealistic childhood. There isn't one. This is how these things go.

Woah! He's just swung a hard left:

'I bring you to these events because you have no friends of your own and you sit like some spoilt brat waiting to be served.'

Meme – suburbia – brat. Contemptible rage. Magma building. Pressure rising. Then he spews like Vesuvius, covering me in a cloud of infernal ash. I can't see or hear a thing, totally confused about where I am, what I did wrong, how he's this wound-up.

Tears trickle down my heavily made-up cheeks. I'll have two white lines down my face now. I suppose I'll match the coke on the sideboard. I'm so embarrassed. I can hear the Rah-ers inches behind me. Can they see what's happening?

He doesn't stop. It's torture. I have to sit and take it, desperately trying to contain my reaction.

My shoulders are shuddering and shaking. 'Stop,' I murmur. I don't know if he heard me, but he doesn't. It doesn't need to be like this. Mere weeks ago, we were cuddled on the sofa, it was euphoric. I'm addicted to him, to those times. I guess this is the equivalent of rattling. Desperate for my next fix of love.

One of the Rah-ers, wearing an unironic flat cap, reaches between us to carelessly dunk his pint glass on the ledge. He doesn't register there's two people here. Damien glowers at him but, judging by his jutting jaw, Flat Cap is too high to notice. It'll be me who takes the verbal beating for that disrespectful gesture.

'Damien, stop. Please, it's New Year's.' He's going on about my ego now.

How did I get here? Trying to hide my tears from these hollow halfwits on a houseboat?

I can't catch my breath.

'I need to get some air,' I say, turning to him. It's extraordinary, Vesuvius is still erupting but he's not even looking at me. It's a like a madman's monologue directed at the shoes of the partygoers outside.

'You leave. We're over.'

One of the Rah-ers jostles into me, knocking me forward. See, I told you these houseboats move. Damien scowls at him. Isn't it funny, in that split second my thought is not 'I don't deserve this', it's 'see, he does *care about me!'*

I stand, the stool falls into the Rah-ers behind me. One sees my puffy, wet face and openly grimaces. Up the narrow steps of the houseboat, supposedly to stable ground. I'm walking along the canal path now. Graffiti under the concrete bridge glows in the moonlight. I open my phone. I want to be rid of him. All-consumed.

I launch WhatsApp, slide my finger to the left over his message. Three dots. Delete chat.

Contacts – Damien – Edit – Delete Contact.

Waiting for the sudden rush of relief that he's been expunged from my life.

It never comes.

By 3 a.m. I'm back on the houseboat with him.

What a sorry state of affairs.

3 January: 9.50 a.m., Exchange Surgery. Maddy Anholt to see Dr Nanatucky.

A young Somali mother pulls The Hungry Caterpillar *from her bag for life in a bid to silence her youngest who is trying to Hulk out of his buggy. The receptionist, a man with impressive Lego hair, keeps casting exasperated looks over, then returning to his computer. I bet he's only playing Solitaire.*

'Mandeline Anne Halt?'

The doctor calls from the corridor extending from the waiting room.

'Mandeline?'

'Er, yes,' I say, standing, hoping to give the mother a reassuring look before I leave, but Hulk has broken free, she's too distracted.

I place my George at ASDA's finest duffel coat on the empty green plastic chair and sit at 90 degrees to the doctor.

'So . . . Mandeline. What seems to be the problem?'

The doctor has the most perfect moustache; he wears it well. Like Tom Selleck. I know he's part of the medical profession and all that, but I still feel uncomfortable talking to him about women's issues.

'Um. Well. I haven't had a period in three months and—'

'Pregnant?'

'No. Not pregnant.'

'Want to do a test?'

'No. I'm on the Pill. I'm not pregnant. I did a test.'

'Exercise?'

'. . . I do exercise, yes.'

'Could be from over-exercising. Any pain?'

Emotional or physical?

'No. No pain.'

'OK. Well, let's keep an eye on it. Could be hormonal imbalance. Ageing—'

'I'm only 27!'

'Premature menopause.'

It's like he's narrating Web MD. In a minute he'll tell me I'm about to spontaneously combust.

'Could be PCOS. Polycystic Ovary Syndrome. Maybe.'

Wait for it, Elephantiasis will be next.

'OK,' I say to a lack of any diagnosis. 'I also wondered if you had something for this . . .'

I pull up the sleeves on my deliberately chosen ultra-baggy pink sweater to reveal my crocodile skin arms. Large red patches of sore, dry, cracked skin. Some bleeding.

'Hmm. Psoriasis,' says Tom Selleck. 'Stressed?'

I smile a definitely too-wide grin. 'Not stressed, no,' I say, breezily.

I'm as frazzled as Trump and Melania's marriage counsellor.

I walk out the surgery doors with a prescription for steroid cream and a complex I have days to live. I should have been happy at my prognosis because, little do I know, almost exactly a year from now, I'll have a far more monstrous demon to conquer than psoriasis and a missing period.

A BOXING MATCH IN A TUMBLE-DRYER

Being in an argument with a Controll is like falling into a tumble-dryer. The Controll throws you from point to point, you come out confused, shaken and upset, barely remembering how or why it happened.

It was a strange experience recounting arguments I'd had with Controlls. On paper you can see how nutty they are, but in the moment, your focus is not on correlation, it's on defence. What will they bring up next? How do they remember that? That's not how it happened. You scrabble to shield yourself but the swipes swiftly stupefy.

A Controll's aim in an argument is to catch you off guard then get you on your knees with a few rapid verbal punches. In a boxing match one of the best tactics is to start strong, delivering a sharp blow to stun the opponent. Single punch knockouts are rare; the fighter needs to arm themselves with knowledge of weak spots, surprise their challenger and be prepared to be consistent with their attack. Precision, speed and power will win the match.

A Controll will catch you unawares; it's impossible to read what the severity of the fight will be. It's better to brace yourself for extremes. They will begin by delivering one sudden crack; whilst you're doing your best to defend that, they're ten steps ahead, about to KO you with a rain of blows.

**Their goal is always to demoralize,
destabilize and destroy.**

If they sense they are not winning or affecting you in the way they want, they'll gaslight you with supposed misdemeanours from the past. The knocks keep coming. You're losing your footing, not only fighting words but your emotions too. They aren't even close to finishing. You're not yet on your knees.

They'll patronize you and won't listen; it's all about them. It doesn't matter if you make a logical point or not – they aren't hearing it. As if you aren't already toast, they display sudden and radical changes in mood: they're furious, then vulnerable, irate, then calm.

Ding, ding, ding. It's a knockout.

You cannot outmanoeuvre a Controll.

Though it's *their* words that are totally unhinged, they want *you* to look crazy. When you recount the argument later, you'll misremember it as you flying off the handle; the Controll will placidly remind you that you became hysterical and lashed out. You feel like you're losing your mind. You used to be calm, poised and non-confrontational, but in this relationship – whether it be at work, romantic, with a family member – it's you who comes off wild, deranged and antagonistic.

The Controll will keep on baiting you, provoking for a reaction. They will not stop. It doesn't matter if you're a damn Tibetan monk, when they've finally shoved you far enough, you *will* react. That may be bursting into tears, shouting back, even attacking them. *This is exactly what they want*. Bingo, now you're the loony. They'll smirk, act affronted, appear offended. 'You're hormonal, obnoxious', even 'violent and scary', they'll say.

When the ash falls, you reflect – you can't believe you

responded like that. Maybe you *are* hysterical, hostile, histrionic. You blame yourself: perhaps it really is you aggressing them. The Controll will step in to play the lead role of victim – 'how could you do this?' 'I can't be in a relationship with someone so temperamental.' 'You need help.' 'No wonder you have no friends.' You beg them not to leave, you'll change your ways, work on communication. Perhaps they tell you they'll try too – ahh, look, you've finally found yourself in harmony.

Even though they are an individual, it's as if they have an army behind them. You are one, inferior person – how will you ever win? They recollect everything, twisting and warping it.

**It's like buying a knock-off
memory foam mattress.
They remember everything,
and you get very little sleep.**

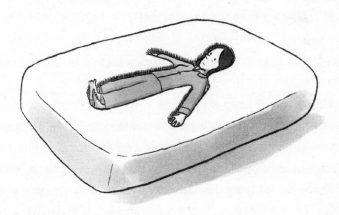

HEALTHY AND UNHEALTHY ARGUMENTS

Arguments and disagreements are a healthy part of a relationship. Conflict is not something to be feared – in fact, you should embrace it. It is merely a means to iron out differences and understand the other person that bit better.

Make sure each side is listened to, give each other space to talk. Clearly lay out at the beginning of the debate what you would like to achieve to resolve it. If you are uncomfortable, or hurt, wait for time to pass, meditate and breathe, then speak with the other person. Quarrels in the heat of the moment often lead to regretful words and actions.

Arguments with a Controll respect not one iota of this. Trust me, you'll know the difference when disputing with a Controll or a non-Controll.

RED FLAGS: ARGUMENT EDITION

Here are red flags to look for in arguments:

Ultimatums
Ultimatums are demands which if not met have drastic consequences, in particular the ending of a relationship. They could be things like: 'If you don't agree to this threesome, I'm leaving you.' Or 'Give me your social media passwords or I'm out the door.'

They are essentially 'do this, or else' threats and equal the hangman's noose for relationships. Sometimes ultimatums can be masked and you could hear things like, 'If you loved me, you'd let me do this to you.' Although not as overt as the examples above, they are equally as damaging and coercive.

Emotional blackmail

Emotional blackmail is putting the other person into a stranglehold. The perp uses feelings and emotions to manipulate the decisions you make, so they are not made consensually.

Often emotional blackmail will be masked by attentiveness: 'I'm only telling you not to see your friends because I want to spend time with you.' That's sweet, you may think. But watch your footing – that's a slippery slope.

In an argument, emotional blackmail can be used directly or indirectly.

Directly looks like: 'You can't learn to pick up the phone when I need you, so I'm going to stop calling you.'

Indirectly looks like: 'If you can't learn to pick up the phone when I need you, I can think of a few women who would.'

Emotional blackmail teaches the receiver that it's far easier to comply with the demands, which will only grow bigger.

Raised voices

It is absolutely 100 per cent possible to have a disagreement and not shout or scream. The purpose of raising a voice is to shock and humiliate. If you think of a psychopathic boss yelling at an employee in the office, it's so everyone else can hear and that employee comes out shaken and embarrassed.

I understand that sometimes there can be such a build-up of emotion and tension that shouting is a means to release it, but when it happens with every single disagreement there's a serious problem.

From the point of raising your voice, the argument should be over. It is no longer a discussion or debate, it is intimidation.

Swearing

Right, as I'm sure you've already gathered from reading my book, I fucking love a good swear. Swearing is like adding a gorgeous filter to a conversation. Really ups the saturation and brings out the colours. BUT. In an argument when swear words are hurled *at* the other person in ways like 'Fuck you!', 'Shut the fuck up', or 'You're a fucking idiot', they add an element of terrorization and aggression which is only serving one purpose: to belittle and scare the receiver.

Stonewalling aka the silent treatment

Everyone has been guilty of this at some point in their lives. It's 'I'm upset and pissed off, so I refuse to speak to you.' If it happens once, then, when it feels right, discuss it and communicate how it made you feel. Express how you were isolated and shut out by their actions. The other person should take on board what you say, and you can talk about it calmly, suggest other ways to deal with heightened emotions.

Constant stonewalling, when the other person refuses to speak to you for days or weeks after an argument, is not OK; it is a means to punish the other person – even if they don't see it that way.

Lack of empathy

Is the other person unable to put themselves in your shoes? Are they incapable of seeing things from your point of view? Do they lack emotional responses when you are upset? No matter how angry someone is, they should feel a sense of compassion for the other person, even if it comes later. Do they even seem to enjoy that you are shaken and upset? Does their quiet rage terrify you? If they are cold, unreachable and unemotional, is this really the kind of person you want to share your life with?

Name-calling

Calling someone a 'bitch', 'dickhead', 'dumb twat', or anything of the sort is a huge red flag, because it causes emotional damage. It is verbal abuse. Name-calling is playground bullying and is definitely not necessary when it comes to adult, mature disagreements. Name-calling often happens when there is really nowhere to go in the disagreement, all the toys have been thrown out and all that's left is the blankie. That indicates the people involved are not cool-headed enough to be in this situation. That means both parties should back away, take some time to breathe, before a compassionate and logical debate can happen.

Threats of violence

Any threats of violence are not only unacceptable they are criminal. Harassment is both a criminal offence and a civil action under the Protection from Harassment Act 1997 and in California, among other US states, under California Penal Code Section 422 PC, it is illegal to make criminal threats.

It is never, ever warranted for someone to terrorize you by saying things like, 'If you don't shut up, I will strangle you,' or even, 'Listen to me or I will make you listen to me.' Threats of violence are a sign of an abusive, dangerous person and they can *never* be excused. You do not deserve to be intimidated.

Breaking things

If someone breaks furniture, smashes a door, destroys your possessions, then you need to make a safe escape plan, quickly. Yes, they have an anger management problem, but this is *not* your issue to resolve. Destroying things is a sign of deep-rooted and uncontrollable aggression. They may gaslight you later by saying whatever they broke are 'just things that can be replaced', or 'you made me do it, I'll buy more'. This is not the point – their behaviour will only escalate. Get out. You don't have to live with it.

Physical abuse

Really short this one: never acceptable.

No pushing, shoving, slapping, hitting, punching, kicking. No physical harm whatsoever is the firm, unmoving boundary I would like you to have right now, if you don't already. It's a zero-tolerance approach. It doesn't matter how much they apologize, take time away, promise it'll never happen again. **It will.** It's a no, they cannot come back, the relationship is over.

Promise me? Thank you. Bottom line:

**You should never, ever
be scared by a partner.**

As long as toxic behaviours do not become a pattern and you're putting yourself, your needs and feelings first, there's no reason why an argument can't result in a step closer to the other person as opposed to away.

HOW TO 'WIN' AN ARGUMENT WITH A CONTROLL

When it comes to a heated discussion, argument, debate with a Controll, all normal rules go out the window.

There are three simple steps to take when you are pulled into an argument with a Controll:

1. Remove your emotions

Honey, you're talking to the woman that has to lie in a dark room for three days after watching *One Born Every Minute*; I am the most emotional person I know. But when it comes to a disagreement with a Controll – do not get into complicated emotional discussions, they do not understand them.

If at all possible, steel your feelings and do your best to close up. Preferably, leave before you get too upset.

2. Be very clear about what you want

You want this to end in as little carnage as possible. This can only happen if you don't fall victim to their lies. They *want* you to get wound up by their fabricated stories of all the ways you've disrespected/humiliated/insulted/annoyed them (delete as appropriate).

I like to think of them as a boiler that has high pressure: you need to bleed the radiators, so the hot air comes out.

You must be careful not to burn yourself. You can let the air out slowly and cautiously by allowing them to rant and rave, but be prepared to cut them off once the pressure is starting to normalize. However, be aware of this one critical fact:

You do not need to 'sit and take it'.
Doing this, in whatever way it comes, is self-harm.

3. **Get pragmatic**
It's time to be logical and realistic. Ask them clearly what the issue is, ask them to isolate one problem at a time. Do not aggress or patronize them. Repeat yourself:

> **You:** Let's deal with the one issue at hand, what is that?
> **Them:** You posted that photo on social media and—
> **You:** So the issue is I posted—
> **Them:** Fucking listen, you posted that on your social media, and you're an entitled—
> **You:** Let's deal with the one issue. I posted that on my social media. What did you not like about it?
> **Them:** You always do this, remember that time at the festival—
> **You:** One issue at a time. I posted on my social media . . .
> And so on.

But in all honesty . . .

The argument will only ever go one way – they will explode, you will get more distraught, confused and intimidated.

Whatever you say will fuel them until finally they get tired. Eventually. It will *never* end well for you. They won't see the error of their ways. They won't apologize, and if they do, they won't mean it.

Time to start backing off, my love. You're doing so well, I'm proud of you. The good news is, now we're off to a wedding! Who doesn't love a wedding?

Did you know the Old English name for a wedding was 'Bridelope' which means 'Bridal run'.

I suppose it depends in which direction.

CHAPTER FOURTEEN

GROUND CONTROLL TO MAJOR TOM

Learned Helplessness and Bad Boys

I flick away shards of dry leaves I've crunched between my fingers and watch the light breeze carry them further along the parched patio. I think my right side is in shade, I'll have to move in a second.

Somewhere inside the château I hear the pop of a cork and Holly yelping with her bridesmaids. I haven't looked at the schedule since I arrived. I think it's meant to be 'Al Fresco Brunch' followed by 'Photos in the Vineyard' but I'd rather lie here until the final strokes of the palpitating southern French sun have dissipated.

I'm not sure why I'm here at all. When the invitation was sent out almost a year ago, Holly and I spoke at least once a week. But over the previous six months we must have exchanged only a handful of messages, all mostly about her wedding. We're old work friends but, as happens, we've drifted apart. I barely know Holly any more, let alone her giggling gaggle of maids. I've strayed from most of my mates. None of them like Damien. I had to double-check the name of her groom before I left. I'm sure Holly sees me as an apparition from a past life. I'll make sure to stand at the back in her wedding photos.

Still no response from Damien. Maybe my phone's overheated? I reach over and place it by my side on the plastic sun lounger, dragging it into the now ample shade from the purple and cream magnolia overhead. There's definitely not a signal problem – the first thing I did when we all jumped off the sweaty people carriers that brought us from the airport was get the Wi-Fi password in case Damien wanted to get hold of me. I got several side-eyes from the wedding party when I did that but I chose to ignore them.

What I couldn't overlook was the shadow of dejection when Holly's cousin, Rhiannon, was told she'd be sharing a room with me. Well, Rhi, I didn't aspire to split airspace with a 16-year-old emo who cuts her own bangs. I should be celebrating love with my long-term boyfriend.

There's no way Damien didn't see the wedding invite. It was stuck under my BRIGHTON magnet on our fridge for months. I made sure to pick the most fluorescent, eye-catching one I could find and pin it front and centre so he couldn't miss it:

To Maddy and Damien
....

𝕳olly 𝕾elene 𝕭rown and
𝕵eremiah 𝖂illiam 𝕳ill

Cordially invite you to celebrate the
joyous union of their marriage at

Château 𝕭ranche 𝕯'olivier,
Trouillas, France

On 22nd July
RSVP

*I suggested to Damien that we use it as the first part of a break
away, then we could hire a car and have a week in the
Dordogne. He brushed it off the first few times I hinted at it
and I knew better than to keep pushing.*

*A week before we were due to leave, I found it difficult to
hide my unease. Why hadn't he mentioned packing? Did he
need new swimming trunks? Should I have looked into the car?
When he saw me pull out my huge purple suitcase that had
seen many better days, he stopped mid tooth-brush and stared
at me: 'raff are you drroing?' he said, brush-in-mouth.*

*'Starting to get organized for the wedding in France,' and
then, without missing a beat: 'Do you have anything that needs
washing for the trip?'*

*He glared, spat in the sink and looked up, white toothpaste
drool slipping from the corner of his mouth. 'Maddy, you can't*

*decide last minute to swan off to France and expect me to join
you. I have work. Unlike you.'*

*I'm not sure why I was shocked. There was no point asking
why he hadn't booked time off, no need to unpick and analyse
why he didn't want to come away with me. I know it all.
At the very least I hoped he would attempt to stop me
leaving. I'd even have taken a show of delight at my soon-to-be-
absence. Anything aside from apathy would have been
smashing.*

*That's how I've ended up here, surrounded by young couples
in the most sickeningly romantic of destinations. Candle-lit, oak
dining tables that extend endlessly towards the vineyards and
an aquamarine, glistening water feature to greet the guests.
Splat.*

*Sky-high stone walls extend up to a rustic staircase that
leads into endless low alcoves and bedrooms. It's all very 'Cask
of Amontillado'-ish. I was obsessed with that tale when we
learnt about it at school. Did you study it? It's a short story by
Edgar Allan Poe that follows a man who seeks revenge on his
friend, Fortunato (the Fortunate One), for insulting him.
Without knowing it, whilst Fortunato is drunk and inattentive,
he is taken deeper and darker into catacombs under the Italian
streets. Fortunato gets more and more disorientated before his
friend leaves and Fortunato is buried alive. Huh. Imagine that,
being so wrapped up you're blindsided to the fact you're
precariously close to asphyxiation . . .*

*Once I admit defeat to further tanning, I take my towel,
book (that works as prop to carry from one place to another)
and phone to the bedroom. I can hear Rhi shrieking from the
foot of the stone stairs. When I reach our door it's at fever*

pitch. Unsure whether to go in, I wait a moment, take a deep breath, then enter.

I see Rhi sitting on the luxurious Egyptian-cotton-covered double bed I'd already bagsied as mine, sobbing on the phone. She's moved my canvas bag to the floor that I had placed as a territory marker. Wonderful.

Rhi stops her conversation mid-howl and stares. 'Can I help?' she says, snottily.

'You're on my bed and I want a shower,' I say. She makes a noise somewhere between 'God' and 'gah' and stands, flopping heavily onto the single bed next to the door.

'Stop listening into my conversation, then,' she snaps.

'I think the whole château is being forced to listen, hun,' I say, unravelling a towel folded as a swan and marching into the bathroom.

I can still hear her through the rustic (read old and cracked) wooden door. She's banging on about some guy who's seen her message but not replied. He's called her needy and paranoid. She's found out a heap of lies he's told, like when he had to leave Rhi's house to go and do his homework but instead he went straight to another girl's and stayed over. When confronted, he shrugged his shoulders and showed zero concern. I get you. Unsettling, isn't it?

Still nothing from Damien. I've been told my limit on times I can text is three. I'm not clear if that includes unread messages or not. It's best not to tempt fate.

When I come out of the bathroom, shadowed by a cloud of steam, hair wrapped in towel, Rhi is lying quietly and staring at the ceiling. She turns away from me.

'You OK?' I say, feebly pretending to care. I have enough on my plate.

Rhi says nothing. I watch her trace circles in the thin summer duvet with her chewed fingernail. Silent tears roll down her cheeks. My heart pangs for her.

'Men are dicks, babe. The sooner you know, the better,' I muster.

'Yeah,' she says quickly, obviously desperately needing someone to talk to. I sit on my bed and unfurl my wet hair.

'I guess, I . . . I can't help myself. I love a bad boy,' she continues.

'Thing is to try and not attach too many feelings early on,' I say. It's all I can do not to burst out laughing. I think this is called giving advice by the bucket but taking it by the grain.

'Is that why you're single?' she says. 'Probably easier. I wish I'd never talked to mine.'

'Oh, I'm not single,' I say hastily.

'Where is he then?' She turns on her side and faces me.

'Working,' I say, trying to sound decisive. Neither of us believe me.

'What happened?' she probes. It's a loaded question. What happened that I can't convince my partner of three-plus years to come away with me? What happened to bring me here alone, sharing my troubles with a 16-year-old? What happened to bring me to a point of total addiction to a man I know is poisoning me from the inside?

'I–I don't know.' I'm seconds from confessing it all – the lies, the gaslighting, I want to tell her how tired I am, I barely speak to my family or friends any more. I'm so lonely. I'm in pain. I've lost three stone in under six months. I'm sure he's cheating. He has horrible, degrading sex with me. But she's 16.

At this point even I haven't made sense of it.

A phone pings. We both jump to check ours. Rhi sighs. It's Damien:

Cool. Enjoy!

You can't get more disengaged than that.

I'm in a state of learned helplessness. This is just the way it is. It's all become routine.

Rhi looks at me, lifts herself up and scoots to the edge of the bed, perching like a tormented teenage owl. She blows her badly dyed black fringe from her eyes, but it sticks to her forehead; it's hot in here.

'What did he say?' she asks.

'He wishes he was here, misses me, that kind of thing.'

'Sure,' she says. Then, sensing I'm rawer than I first seemed: 'Shall we leave our phones in the room and go and get drunk on expensive French wine?'

I nod and smile.

A small strand of sisterhood extends from me to her. It would be silly to tell her I'm so totally hooked on Damien, absorbed by the drama, conditioned by the abuse (not that I realize that's what it is), that I can go nowhere without my phone.

My phone is my life and deathline.

For a few hours Rhi reminds me of a sisterhood I'd long forgotten. That silly, invincible, love-fuelled bond that some women have. But it doesn't last long. Insipid worries of what Damien is up to yank me from the present. I should be immersing myself in the mesmeric French countryside, enjoying my twenties. But instead, I ferret into alcoves, sucking signal, scrutinizing his social media, checking if he's online.

Eventually, at gone midnight, I decide to phone, I don't care how much it'll cost. I'm taken aback he picks up at all. It's noisy where he is. It sounds like a club. I crouch in a corner of the now-cool courtyard, away from the guests.

'Hi! You OK?'

'Maddy. Yes. What?'

'Just wanted to say hi, I miss you. Where are you?'

'At home.'

He's not at home. I hear a female squeal in the background.

'Are you?'

'Fuck sakes. Pathetic, Maddy. You chose to spend money you don't have on that trip. Suck it up.'

The line goes dead.

A couple: him – shirt open, her – dusky pink dress flowing, swoop past me squatting in the darkness. My heart cracks open. Tears fall from my eyes onto the dry cobblestone below.

I see Rhi approach, she's drunk and has found an oversized and awful black butterfly clip which pins the fringe from her eyes. She looks happy.

'Mads! You OK? Oh no! You're crying. Don't cry!' She stands over me protectively and pats my head. I don't think my life could get more depressing than this.

A day later I sit on my bed in the beautiful château, watching the sun stream in, catching the dust, counting down the hours until I can fly back to him.

I felt guilty for weeks after that trip (I have Irish Catholic blood; we pour guilt on our cornflakes). I wondered if I should have helped Rhi out, been the older role model, at least held her hair back when she spewed into the water feature later that night.

I reassured myself I hadn't been in the position to offer any aid. I was swept in a riptide with no superfluous energy. I managed to mutter one line of guidance when we said our goodbyes at Luton airport:

**Make sure you've fallen in love
with the person, not their potential.**

As we've seen, it's damn near impossible to peel yourself away from the virility and charm of a Controll at the beginning. Even if it takes you a few months, when you start to see red flags, feel the ground shake, lose your footing, do all you can to bring yourself back to that question . . . do I love them, or do I love what I think they could be?

LEARNED HELPLESSNESS AND THE UNETHICAL DOG EXPERIMENT

When FrenchWeddingGate happened, I was well and truly pinioned into learned helplessness.

In the 1960s, American psychologist Martin Seligman developed the construct 'Learned Helplessness'. Seligman devised an experiment with dogs to look at the behavioural and psychological impacts of uncontrolled traumatic events. Right, this experiment is not that ethical, but stay with me – when you understand this concept it'll blow your mind and help break the cycle of toxic relationships.

Ready? Let's go.

Seligman worked with two different groups of dogs. I'm going to call them Group A and Group B. Group A were given electric shocks but they could escape from them. The other group – Group B – were also given electric shocks but were put into something called Pavlov's Hammock, which is a device that restricted their movement and ability to escape.

After a time, Group A all realized they could escape, and did so, but Group B – the dogs in the hammock – soon gave up trying to avoid the shocks. They understood there wasn't a way out and resigned themselves to taking them.

Both Group A and B were then moved into a new enclosure. Here, A and B were again administered shocks, but this time there was no hammock. That's to say, all dogs were free to leave. Seligman discovered that Group A – the dogs who had never been in the hammock and thus the ones that were taught to *avoid* the shocks – freed themselves from the enclosure quickly.

However, Group B, who had previously been in the hammock and conditioned to accept the shocks just lay still and whimpered until the pain ended – **even though there was a way to get out**. This is what Seligman termed 'Learned Helplessness'.

The only cure for the dogs in Group B who were suffering learned helplessness was 'directive therapy'. This is where they were put on leads and actively pulled away from the shocks. After a few attempts, the dogs understood that they could in fact avoid these shocks and, eventually, found their own way out.

Let's look at this in regard to the cycle of Controll partners. Over time the abuse suffered – physical, emotional, financial, sexual, etc. – is similar to the electric shocks. We teach ourselves that not responding, sitting with, taking and accepting the abuse is the only way to deal with it.

We subconsciously tell ourselves this is the way it's got to be.

Effectively, what we are doing is stepping into the Pavlovian Hammock: we become Group B. Conditioned to the abuse. And if another toxic relationship happens, we stay lying on that floor, taking the shocks.

When there is a way to escape – perhaps we see our worth, the signs of infidelity are too much to ignore, or someone shows us a way out – we do not act on it.

We have learned helplessness.

THE SOLUTION

What's the answer, then? Well, we need to find 'the dog lead', that directive therapy that guides us out of learned helplessness. It might take a few tugs at first but, eventually, we'll be shown that in fact toxic relationships with a Controll *are not* to be tolerated. We don't need to lie down and take them.

That 'dog lead' could come in the form of:

- Supportive, positive friends and family
- Taking time between relationships
- Understanding our behavioural habits (i.e. codependency)
- Setting boundaries
- Self-esteem building
- A great therapist
- Awareness (like this book)

It took several attempts for the dogs in Group B to see that there was a way for them to escape their shocks. You have to keep answering to the yank on the lead.

BAD BOYS, BAD BOYS, WHATCHA GONNA DO?

Shortly after the trip to France, I connected with Rhi on social media and saw she was newly single. I was glad for her, pleased that, in whatever way it happened, she'd opted to notice the pull of the lead. What happened to her Mystery Liar on the phone?

No doubt he went on to throw another girl's heart into turmoil. Or was this a case of impassioned young love? Was there a difference between Damien and Mystery Liar?

Rhi's line 'I love a bad boy' bothered me. I'd heard it escape my mouth on more than one occasion. What did she really mean? What is this infatuation we have with bad boys?

When you think of a bad boy, what comes to mind? Leather jacket, coiffed hair, tight white tee? Maybe they're covered in tattoos, open-collared, with rugged good looks? Perhaps it's a guy with a smouldering gaze who'll smack your ass in public but never be there when you actually need him? Whatever you dreamt up, bad boys have got a way better rep than they deserve.

**Ultimately bad boys are the Alpha,
hyper-masculine, emotionally unavailable,
overtly sexual fuckboys that we hate to love.**

In our teens we're attracted to them because we think they'll make good GCSE coursework and, oh boy, do we love a project. They display themselves as 'zero fucks given' guys that have bunches of bravado, their vulnerabilities are an exclusive for you. 'I can fix them!' we holler in synchronicity, dashing our actual homework out the window. As we grow up, these lads remain rooted in boyhood. You'll have a handful of 'U's' and not much else to show for your high school dateploma.

In the animal kingdom it's the most powerful Alpha males that find the mate. It's not the serially monogamous lion who is good at keeping a tidy den that gets all the lionesses. It's the lions that can fight and fuck that win. It's no different for human-kind. We think bad boys represent strong genes – warriors that need a little taming. An Alpha can come in all shapes and forms. They can present as intellectually on top, harness sporting prowess, perhaps even appear the ultimate do-gooder.

We've been flung the trope of 'devastatingly desirable bad boy' since storytelling began. 'So what if there will be infidelity, brutality and criminality – he's the lovable rogue we gotta have,' sing the painfully young Hollywood starlets cast against the love interest that could be their grandad.

No matter what you say, the thought of swooning into the arms of a man who has just defended your honour is sexy as hell. Perhaps we can blame it on our ancestral sisters who wanted the strongest, toughest genes for their offspring?

THE BELATED MESSAGE

Going back to Seligman's dog lead, it will take some training, some yanking of the lead for our tastes to change, for bad boys not to make us drool and slide off chairs. Some of us get bored of them, others aren't so lucky.

A long time after the wedding, on an afternoon scroll this time, Rhi popped up. I thought again what I would have said, had I not been so emotionally battered, and I messaged her this:

3.11 p.m.
Hey Rhi,

How are you? I know this is a little late, but I've had time to think . . . Here's my (maybe uncalled for) advice:

Being selective is sexy. You don't need to be 'won over', 'love struck' or 'swept off your feet'; it's the ones that move slowly to look on favourably.

Choose fact over feeling. Write the truths about them: are

they happy, stable, generous and kind? How do they make *you* feel about *yourself*, rather than noting only how you feel about them.

Bypass the heart-whomping, soul-shaking, coochie-chafing feelings, and forage fact first.

I hope this resonates.

Catch up soon.

Maddy xx

Well anyway she left me on read. So that's that.

Now, did you ever hear the one about the girl who saved her life using only gut instinct?

CHAPTER FIFTEEN
THE NOSE KNOWS
Gut Instinct

'Instinct is the nose of the mind.'
– Madame de Girardin

*It's Damien's work's night out and we're heading across London.
He's not allowed a guest, so I'll leave after we have some
drinks. Yes, I know he can invite a guest really. I'm not stupid.
Or can he? It doesn't matter. Won't you just let me enjoy this?
It's progress.*

*We don't hold hands on the bus but that's not unusual. He
doesn't like public displays of affection. I've wondered if it's in
case a woman sees us that he's . . . it doesn't matter. I'm
probably wrong. I get like this – all paranoid. It spoils things
and starts a fight. I never used to be this jealous and needy. I
don't know what's got into me.*

*As the 279 lurches to the next stop my thoughts are racing a
million miles a minute. Hypersensitive to his body next to*

227

mine. *What's he thinking? Is he angry? Have I done something wrong? I hope I look good. I really made an effort. My black dress hangs on my stomach, it used to be tight, which is a shame because he likes curves. I don't have them any more.*

A wild woman boards the bus. She has missing teeth, spiky blue hair that looks self-cut and she reeks of body odour and booze. She sucks what's left of her lower lip then leers towards us. I'm tense. Tenser than I was before. He didn't want to get the bus, I told him it would be OK. Now this crackhead is going to spoil it for me. For us. He's going to get cross. I can already hear him. Quietly, just to me: 'See why I don't get buses, Maddy?'

The wild woman sits in front of us. Her stench is overpowering. Real Me would have compassion, perhaps subtly move. I don't know Real Me. She's long gone. Me Now bristles as Damien exhales air sharply from his nose. I'm furious at her for doing this to me. To us. I wanted things to be peaceful.

A bit to wait. Two more stops and we get off. I hold my breath. It's not because of the smell.

Made it.

This is fun. We're out together on Oxford Street. It's a mild evening. A man with dreads to his knees sits at the entrance to Carnaby Street and expertly plays empty kegs and plastic buckets as drums. Tourists, couples, young families intermingle, fluidly moving as one, only stopping to stare through glossy shop windows. All celebrating the privilege of being.

I'm very happy.

I don't know where we're going but I'm thrilled to be in this moment. Excited for the drink that will soon hit my lips. Damien allowing me in his presence. I have to be cautious with alcohol and Damien. I used to be a lightweight but not any more. I often drink alone when he's not around. So, as I say – often. But tonight I don't want to drink too much in case I say something stupid. I have to remain on guard, or I'll spoil things. Again.

We dip into an expensive bar, just off Beak Street. It's lit with warm, amber lanterns that hang from gold chains. Colourful statues of tigers sit next to red velveteen wallpaper that laces all the way up to the high ceiling. Tinkles of cutlery and glasses cut over the chatter and laughter. The host greets us. She's a tall, curvaceous, pretty brunette. My breath stalls in my chest. Another to watch. Another to make me insecure. Another for Damien to chase.

Don't spoil it.

The mixologist – a thin young woman with a sag of skin from a removed ear plug which almost touches her shoulder – mixes our drinks. Damien loves cocktails so that's what we have. He sits on the deep red wine sofa and picks at the buttons that cinch tightly from one pattern to the next. I sit opposite. There wasn't room next to him, he said. He likes to look out into the room but I'm fine, all I want to see is him. I'm inhaling it all. It could always be like this. It should always be like this. It will always be like this.

Three cocktails down and it's starting to get late. We're laughing and catching each other's eye. It's like before. This is all we needed, one night together. He's barely been on his phone. I feel important. I think he's forgotten about his work event. Or maybe he doesn't care! Maybe he's decided I'm better than that and we go home together!

Suddenly, a squeal fills the air, then another. The large crowd

*of punters are momentarily silent. The couple next to us turn,
as do I, to see three women. Two petite blondes, one taller with
waist-length sandy hair. They wear clothes you see on fashion
shoots, but you can't actually wear in public, or you'll catch
hypothermia and break an ankle. They're heading straight over.
Damien rises, a huge grin on his face, arms open as if waiting
to receive a puppy. He stands in front, trying to hide me. I
attempt to crane my neck but all I see is a triple-woman pile
on. I'm choked with cheap perfume, stale roll-ups and top-up
Impulse bathroom spray.*

*Damien falls heavily to his seat, still grinning. There's no
hiding me now. I can't disappear. Unlucky for him. You can
probably see my heart beating. The leader of the pack – the
taller one – steps past me and squeezes cosily next to Damien.*

He told me there wasn't room.

*Now I see her. She has too-thick matte lipstick which is
smeared onto her crooked front tooth. I'm trying to find flaws.
She's beautiful.*

*She smiles at me. 'I'm Em!' She cocks her head and turns to
Damien, placing her hand on his thigh. Her two friends flank
me like I'm about to be escorted out by the aerosol squad.*

*'I'm Maddy. Damien's girlfriend.' I see a micro-wince on
Damien's face. I am absolutely not allowed to do that.*

'Girlfriend!' The two flankers giggle above.

*'As if you could hold one down!' Lipstick Smear pokes
Damien's chest.*

Serially unfaithful.

*'We should head, no?' she says. I hate it when people do
that. End their sentences with a question as if they're uncertain
of everything.*

'The guest list opened half an hour ago.' Smear stands, Damien moments behind her. He hasn't looked at me since they arrived. Who are they?

I know who they are.

On the bus home I put sunglasses on to hide my tears. I'd rather passengers think I've dropped a pill and have eyes like manhole covers.

I trawl Damien's social media. I unfollowed him years ago. Too many times his exchanges with women had been so brazenly flirtatious that they left me breathless. I didn't want to see it then. But now I'm actively searching. I want to get proof.

Why?

What am I going to do? Will this be the ounce of strength I need to leave? Unlikely.

Pathetic.

Found it.

In his replies. It's her, she's stood next to him. A huge, wonky smile, I can't make out if the lipstick stain is still there. They're virtually on top of each other. He has both arms tightly under her breasts as he kisses her cheek.

Screenshot.
Open message.
To: Damien
Send photo.

What did I do? My heart hammers in my throat. Mouth is dry. I shouldn't have.

Delete the message. Quickly.

Two blue ticks.

Delete for everyone.
Offline.

Fuck.

Everything will be turned. I can't keep up. Weak. Dry mouth. I can't deflect the words. Can't defend myself fast enough. There will always be something I have done wrong. I stepped out of line. I said this. I did that. He says I have an ego. An ego! I have so little self-esteem, I would be deliriously happy for a scrap!

Anything I say or do doesn't matter. He will be smarter, faster, stronger. More intimidating, bullying, ruthless. I will never win. Everything will be squeezed, spewed, squashed. I am one woman. I will never win. I don't know how to make it stop.

My body is riddled with tension, it solidifies me like rigor mortis. When I get home, I need alcohol. I drink half a bottle of white wine standing at the fridge. I have no one to call.

He doesn't come home that night. In a strange way, I'm glad. Now it's him who can be on the back foot – even momentarily.

It's a seesaw; I can tip it my way for a second. I don't sleep. He'll tell me I fucked it up. He'll tell me he's a grown man and he can do what he likes. He'll tell me to get out of his business. My gut instinct is feeble. Even if I strained, put my ear to the door and really listened, I'd still not hear her.

By 11 a.m. the next morning I get back into bed, I haven't slept a wink. I wake up from a fitful sleep to keys in the front door.

I brace like an air raid siren sounded.

This pattern persisted – clear indications of his cheating, woman-izing and so on became more blatant. Was it that I chose not to see, or did I decide it was less painful if I left it unspoken? A bit of both.

I began to realize he might be taming me by pushing me further and further with each occurrence of infidelity. Trying to get me to flinch. But by then I was in such a state of self-denial I could curtail Lady Gut Instinct by hissing back a line to her I'd been told so often myself: 'You're paranoid, it's nothing.'

I'm sure it's not much of a spoiler to tell you that this entire episode transpired to be my fault. I couldn't begin to explain why – I didn't understand then and I don't get it now. What was undeniable was that the more energy I put into defending myself, apologizing and backing away, the more energy was taken from having the chance to listen to my intuition.

Through gaslighting, negging, sleep deprivation and many other Controll tactics . . . you'll start wondering if everything you thought you knew was wrong. Every experience you've had was incorrect. Every memory conceived, opinion stated, action taken was not what was. Eventually, you'll question you ever had opinions, memories, actions of your own. They've all been skewed, squashed and stomped into a neat cube like a car crusher at a junk yard. Crunch.

But there is something that has the capacity to genuinely save your life. Something that will help you get back to reality and feel that beautiful sense of groundedness again . . .

Gut instinct. Sixth sense. Hunch.
Intuition. Inner voice. Self.

Whatever you want to call it, we all have it. Some of us are attuned to it, others ignore it. What's for sure is that if you lose contact with it, you're in danger.

FIGHT OR FLIGHT AND
STRESS RESPONSES

Gut instinct, or Lady Gut Instinct as I like to call her, has been intrinsic to the survival of humans since the beginning of time. Our primitive brain is doing its best to protect us from dangerous situations. Our ancestors relied on 'fight or flight' as a sixth sense, alerting them to the need to escape predators.

Fight or flight – also called acute stress response – refers to the body and brain's natural response to peril. The nervous system is triggered, which releases hormones such as adrenaline.

Our brain is basically telling our body: 'Based on previous experiences, plus my general wisdom, kindly get the fuck outta here before we get eaten alive.'

PHYSICAL SIGNS OF STRESS

Physical signs of acute stress response can be:

- Pale or flushed skin
- Trembling or shaking
- Sweaty palms
- Dry mouth
- Dilated pupils

- Fast heartbeat
- Increased urge to urinate

If the reaction is severe it can lead to a panic attack. When up against near-consistent states of terror in the hands of a Controll, our natural stress responses are activated. In most circumstances these are useful. They are priming us to be ready to protect ourselves. However, fleeing a situation where the Controll is displaying intimidation can sometimes make them angrier and ramp the situation up. We want to leave but, from past events we understand this could escalate things. (Welcome back, learned helplessness.)

Our central nervous system is thrown into a confusing overdrive.

Our gut instinct is telling us this is not a safe situation, escape quickly, but we are under such immense pressure that often it's easier to suppress it altogether. Sit tight and brace.

THE SECOND BRAIN

Scientists worked on the correlation of the brain and the gut and were astounded to see a direct link. So much so that the gut is often named the 'second brain'.

This 'second brain' is called the Enteric Nervous System (ENS). Although you can't set the ENS working on becoming fluent in Spanish whilst you tackle the day job, it still steadily communicates with the brain in our head.

The study of the communication between the 'two brains' has produced astonishing results.[1] Scientists found a direct link between gastrointestinal issues like IBS, constipation and general gut health and emotional problems like anxiety and depression.

For years scientists thought that gut issues were heightened by anxiety and depression, but the study suggests it could be the other way round. Researchers have uncovered findings to show that issues in the gastrointestinal system could directly send messages that alter mood. This works for positive emotions too; at times of excitement, for example, when we feel that 'flutter' and 'butterflies' that something brilliant is about to happen.

More often than not, victims of Controlls will suffer weight loss or gain, abdominal issues, cramps and so on as a direct cause of the build-up of inner turmoil, anxiety and depression. I consistently suffered gut issues when in relationships with Controlls, and I lost a hell of a lot of weight. If this is you too, listen to it. Lady GI along with your second brain is trying to tell you something.

OUR VERY CLEVER EMOTIONAL WAREHOUSE

Gut instinct is based on unconscious assessments that our brain makes in every situation, with every person. We look at how they talk, walk, act, and then match this with our inner database to create meaning and 'short-cut' what our reaction to events and people should be like in the future.

Our inner database is a warehouse of memories, recollections and emotions that we have been storing up since we were born.

The warehouse helps us keep a tab on what we like or don't like, what we respond and don't respond to, and what we should allow or avoid.

One critique of gut instinct is that it can be blindsided by cognitive biases. Cognitive biases are a preconceived notion of events or people that give us a 'subjective reality'. That is to say, how we see the world is a direct cause of a lifetime's worth of experiences, basically what we have in our warehouse.

There are many types of cognitive biases, one being Confirmation Bias. Confirmation Bias is where we deliberately select information we see and hear to back our existing inner beliefs. If we have the presupposition that, say, a person will be rude, and we thoroughly believe that – perhaps based on information we know already – then when we meet this supposedly obnoxious person, we'll notice actions, words and so on that support our thesis.

I can already hear the Controlls yelling: 'That's what you're doing to me! Making me out to be the bad guy, told you it's all in your head!' Conversely to what the Controll is banging on about, what actually happens in a relationship with a Controll is that we hold onto the good stuff. We want our original decision of selecting them as our mate to have been a smart one. This is why when the Controll does one mediocre decent deed, or uses occasional indulgences, we use this to shush Lady Gut Instinct: 'See – I told you he's a nice person! This can work out! Just a weensy bit more investment from me and then I'm sure we're onto a winner!' It's the fallacy of sunk cost – you continue a behaviour because of previously invested time. It's like staying on a premium rate phone line. We know that our minutes and money are ticking away but we think – 'look, we've got this far, keep going! If I give up now I really *will* have wasted all my resources.'

The burying your head in the sand 'ostrich effect' is not necessarily because you point-blank don't want to look at it, but because it's too painful to, and you're up to your neck. Think about it – wouldn't it be far easier if the Controll was a wonderful person that you hadn't squandered all your energy on? Of course it would!

Look, it's all well and good to say to someone in a relationship with a Controll to 'trust your gut', but what that is not taking into consideration is the fear, exhaustion, anxiety and lack of self-esteem the victim is plagued with, which are all blocks to getting anywhere close to Lady GI.

Here's the thing:

If you're having doubts, if you feel the need to investigate and suss that person out, if you're reading this book because you're worried . . . then it's highly probable you have legit cause to be concerned.

Your very actions, searching for answers, rooting for some golden solution, are a manifestation of Lady Gut Instinct saying: PLEASE BLOODY HEAR ME!

LADY GUT INSTINCT SAVING A LIFE

Having trust in your gut could save your life. In 1978 Rodney Alcala was a contestant on the TV matchmaking show *The Dating Game*. Rodney, in his mid-thirties and from Texas, was pitted against two other men in a bid to win the heart of one

female contestant, Cheryl Bradshaw. Cheryl asked the three men questions from behind a screen to try and suss out who would be the best match for her. Alcala's boldness, confidence and charm won Cheryl over and the two stood side by side at the end of the show ready to sail off into the sunset.

Backstage after the show, Cheryl recalled how Alcala's behaviour was odd. She noticed his on-camera uber-machismo was still turned on; she commented how his demeanour 'felt practised'. In an interview she stated: 'I started to feel ill. He was acting really creepy. I turned down his offer. I didn't want to see him again.' Although she wanted to meet someone, she remarked she had to 'go with her instincts'. Alcala was furious when the producers informed him Cheryl would not be attending the date.

What neither Cheryl nor the show's producers knew yet was that Alcala had been convicted of raping an 8-year-old girl and had already murdered four other women before his appearance on the show. The fact Cheryl held on so tightly to her gut instinct not to go on a date with Alcala very likely saved her life.

Cheryl was totally in tune with her intuition, she trusted it and let it guide her.

THE THINGS STANDING IN THE WAY OF YOUR GUT INSTINCT

Aside from the stress you are under in a relationship with a Controll, there are some other factors that may block you from your intuition:

'**Need**': If you feel the *need* to make your relationship work because of age/financial pressure/every other relationship has failed, then you will be less inclined to listen to your gut. These motives to stay have probably been fed to you over time from unfit and outdated sources, like your Great Aunty Petunia telling you she was married at 11. Next.

'**Previous trauma**': Here's a tricky one. Sometimes past trauma works against you and can force your gut instinct into a state of panic that previous abuses are back in another form. Now you can see why this is an issue – when dating post-Controll it is possible to chuck previous trauma into an actually non-threatening situation. It's also conceivable you may ignore your gut instinct and call it 'previous trauma' when it's trying to tell you something. The solution? Set clear boundaries, make sure you are 100 per cent 'whole' and ready to date.

'**Everyone else likes them**': Ah, the old 'perhaps they can see what I can't'. May I remind you that these Controlls could storm any glitzy awards ceremony with their acting prowess. Of course other people think they 'aren't too bad', 'seem friendly' and 'are a good guy/girl/person' – that's what they're trained to do; it's exactly how they've manufactured their public-facing persona.

The best place to be at with your gut instinct is becoming . . .

THE CURIOUS OBSERVER

When we are the curious observer, we lean on our gut instinct for guidance, stepping back and assessing the situation that is presented to us. Curious, receptive and interested, but cautious, all the same.

There's a great exercise to help you retune your gut instinct at the end of the book.

Now, quick quiz question: What word do you think Brits say on average 4,380 times[2] a year, yet I'm sure for you and me it's more like 10,911 times?

Answer coming right up.

CHAPTER SIXTEEN

SORRY SEEMS TO BE THE EASIEST WORD

Toxic Shame and Self-blame

My feet make no sound as I climb the beige carpeted flight of stairs to our flat. I don't know what time it is. Time isn't really a concept. I reach the entrance; the silver-coloured number 13 is bigger than I remember. The door is slightly ajar, which is strange because it's heavy and normally shuts on its own.

There are faint sounds from inside.

Someone's in there.

A man groans with pleasure.

I push the door wider. It's microseconds before I deduce what's happening. In what feels like one step I'm stood over our double bed.

Shit. He's with her. His hands on her back. She tries to jump off him.

I knew I wasn't crazy.

I'm panting when I wake up. Judging by the soft, white light seeping through the linen curtains it's about 5 a.m. Damien is next to me. His face is soft when he's sleeping, almost as if, as soon as he rouses, he takes a hardened expression from the bedside drawer like you would a morning vitamin.

These dreams are regular. They alternate between catching him with one of his many mistresses to him punching me full in the face. I know what they mean. If I could only see him with another woman, if he could really leave a mark, that would be enough. But it wouldn't, would it? It's more than that. If there was a bruise there would be physical evidence, I would have confirmation this is not in my head. There would be proof.

That evening Damien is guest speaker at an upscale charity event for children with leukaemia. I almost don't go; I'm not sure I can bear a roomful of adoring gazes in the direction of a man they think they know. But I go. I haven't been out in months, and I've been looking forward to making myself look nice.

The charity fundraising gala is in a cathedral out of town. The vast, ornately beautiful stone walls are lit with deep purple theatre lamps. Multicoloured, towering stained-glass windows radiate with amber lighting from outside. Banners bearing WE CAN FIGHT IT TOGETHER are strung from one side of the stage to the other.

There's a projector looping images of gorgeous but poorly, hairless children, sitting up in their hospital beds, smiling for the camera. I swallow and look away.

I notice a few familiar faces chatting and laughing as silver-service waiters and waitresses glide between them, champagne on trays. Apparently, there's to be a talk from the charity's CEO followed by numerous guest speakers and then a raffle. Damien says we need to leave after his speech, he has to be up early. So that's that.

I like how dim it is in here; I feel hidden. Like I could get away with anything amidst the established guests, then pop off in an Uber home.

Damien heads outside for a cigarette. I want to go with him, but he tells me I'm too needy, so I take a seat at a table covered with purple velvet, accidentally knocking an empty champagne flute as I do. A woman in her forties, with long, dark hair, glimmering with gold jewellery, at the far side of the table grins at me. I smile back. Maybe I'm glad I came. She leans over, 'Samaira, hi!' she says.

Before I can reply, barely cutting over the sound of the chatter I hear:

'Maaaaaaddy!'

I turn to see a face I'd long forgotten, but one that fills me with joy: Andreas. He's a colleague from over eight years ago. He was the most fabulous soul I'd ever met and, even from ten feet away, I can see he still is. He rushes over, arms outstretched. I forgot how lovely it is to feel wanted.

'I knew it was you! Dreamboat!' He kisses me on the mouth. I laugh, quickly looking for Damien's eyes. He wouldn't like that.

'God, you look great! You've lost so much weight; I barely recognize you!' I guess I have. Three dress sizes in a year.

Andreas plonks himself onto the seat next to me, waves to Samaira and skirts his chair inches from mine. I feed off his effervescence.

Even though Andreas came with other people he shrugs them

off. 'Way rather be with you, babe,' he says, with a Dame Edna wink. We stay together, adopting Samaira to join our exclusive crew. It's magical; I haven't felt this alive in a long time. Damien sits three seats away, not getting involved, shooting dark looks over. For once, I choose not to be fazed by it. I feel a little more powerful with Samaira and Andreas beside me.

Damien steps up to the stage to do his speech. He's articulate, captivating, and at one point falters on his words, choked by emotion. His self-assured hubris makes me want to vomit. Everyone, even Andreas, is enraptured by him. Why aren't I proud? Why do I struggle to buy it? Is it because I see a side reserved only for me? Is it that I hate how easily everyone is gulled?

When it's over, he's showered with cheek-kisses, hugs and applause, which he pretends to be far too humble to accept. I'm surprised at my anger. I want to tell Andreas what he's like. I want to shout it so everyone will listen. But I know I'll come off as the mad woman. No one will believe me. What do I show them? Wait for him to look a bit mean and manically shout: 'See! There, he's doing it! Look at his face!'

Andreas has managed to get a bottle of champagne at the table; Samaira, he and I are merrily gossiping away, hatching plans, and cackling like the Moët Musketeers. I have no idea where Damien is, he must have left without me. Deep in the pit of my stomach, dread lifts its ominous, ugly head but I push it away with more fizz.

After the raffle, a jazz band starts. It's made up of three suited men, each with an instrument – a sax, trumpet and drums, and a glitzy blonde woman with a tall navy feather in her hair; they take over the stage doing jazz and blues *renditions of hits. When they cover 'Hey Ya!' Andreas leaps from his seat, hauling Samaira and me to the dance floor.*

As we tumble towards the stage, we bump into people, we're the Moët Musketeers, we don't care. I'm giggling away, but when we get to the front, I feel shy and stupid. I look to the other two, jiving at each other. I used to be like that, the life and soul. I don't think I'll ever find her again.

This venue is amazing. I hadn't really looked at it until now. Something about this space, steeped in history, reverberating with modern sound. A nod to the future, hot stepping from the past. It makes me feel electric. Before I know it, I'm cutting loose. Andreas throws himself on the floor and attempts a snake. He looks more like a smashed slug. We're howling with laughter, pulling our new-found pack tighter.

3 a.m. comes and goes, we're the last punters. I'm soaked with sweat, feeling like I've been purged of evil in this godly place. I grab my handbag, hidden under the table, and root around for my phone. The hours that passed have been bliss. No Damien. No fear. No anxiety. Before I look at the screen, I already know what I'll see. I breathe in liberation for one last lungful.

It's worse than I imagined. Far, far worse. I'll need to break this down so I can try and work it through myself.

Whilst I was engrossed in dancing, 'a female friend' of Damien's took it upon herself to film us and send it to him. She was apparently aware I was 'acting inappropriately with another man'. It didn't matter that the man was the furthest from straight you can get, or that I had been surrounded by hundreds of other revellers, or indeed that I'd barely left the house in months.

I've been hit by a cyclone. Lifted off my feet and thwacked onto the cold concrete outside. I'm furious someone would steal those treasured moments of freedom, invade my privacy, actively put me in danger. Meddling bitch. Distraught that it could be over with Damien, yet terrified to ever go home. He stops replying, so furious, he says, he cannot type nor sleep.

There's no point rehearsing what I'll say, I'll forget it all. The unpredictability of him at the best of times has me quaking, but this is a whole new dimension. Trying my best to keep it together, I tightly hug Andreas and Samaira goodbye and wait for the N157 night bus. I say a silent prayer for it to break down, but it pulls up, the doors opening with a hiss. For once, the journey takes meagre minutes when I need days. I decide all I can do is take it. Whatever is about to happen. Whatever the lasting consequences. It's all too late now. It's been too many years, too much struggle. Too trapped. Acceptance is all there is.

CHARITY CASE

It's not uncommon for Controlls to take on charitable roles. In fact, it's the perfect place for them to hide. Why would anyone doubt the man who's just donated a vast sum of money to a heart-tugging cause? There's no way the person who actively and publicly supports women on social media would be a perp, is there? Pull the other one – you're telling me that guy in the public eye who is a national charity's spokesperson for violence against women is an abuser himself? No way! Way. Very much way. Curds and whey.

By no means am I saying that everyone who supports charitable causes has controlling tendencies. But think about it – if someone was to camouflage themselves as the last person you'd suspect to be abusive, then adopting the suit of a warm, articulate, altruistic person who supports charity would be genius. Wouldn't it?

Controlls hide behind large corporations, charities, and their publicly moral standpoints, because when they are seen as the do-gooder, they have even more power. The very same man that tweets: #Reclaimthestreets, #MeToo or #ViolenceAgainstWomen could be the man that has, will or is abusing behind closed doors.

THE GOD COMPLEX

I was angry that night that Damien not only controlled me, he controlled the room. I was pissed off people worshipped his charitable facade like he was some kind of a demigod. Because that's exactly what he wanted.

Controlls, especially those heading up the further end of the Psychometer, have what's called a **God Complex**. They see themselves as an all-divine, benevolent deity. They expect people to fall at their feet and are irate if they don't. Ironically, Controlls may call you privileged, spoilt or entitled but no one could ever match them. They have a colossal chip on their shoulder, convinced they deserve the utmost praise, validation and respect. Then as soon as they step out of the public eye, their mask drops, and they become the abuser you know only too well.

When you add up all of the above, it's not surprising that victims of Controlls are crippled by self-blame and toxic shame. The vast majority of perps *ensure* they are loved by communities, sometimes for their charitable deeds, other times because they are so good at being effusive and charming. Meanwhile, the victim sits feeble, traumatized and alone, cast in the shadow of their Controll.

Victims deduce they would be defenceless if they ever did seek help or report their abuser. It seems the whole world has this person on a pedestal, how could one, drained, victim knock them down? Often, that's not even what the victim wants anyway. We don't want to destroy them, even though they've destroyed us. We don't want to see them suffer, even though we've suffered at their hands. We don't want them to lose their jobs, even though we may have come close to losing, or have lost, ours.

No, all we want is someone to trust us. Someone to say, 'I believe you. I believe you have been victimized, abused, raped, manipulated and coerced.' Well, you know what? You do have someone because:

I BELIEVE YOU

I believe what you went through, or what you are still going through. It's real. It's not in your head, you aren't mad, paranoid or delusional.

WHAT THE LAW SAYS
ABOUT COERCIVE CONTROL

On 29th December 2015, thanks to Women's Aid, Section 76 of the UK's Serious Crime Act created a new offence of controlling or coercive control in an intimate or family setting.

The government's definition of coercive and controlling behaviour reads:

- Coercive behaviour is an act or a pattern of acts of assault, threats, humiliation and intimidation or other abuse that is used to harm, punish, or frighten their victim.
- Controlling behaviour is a range of acts designed to make a person subordinate and/or dependent by isolating them from sources of support, exploiting their resources and capacities for personal gain, depriving them of the means needed for independence, resistance and escape and regulating their everyday behaviour.

OK, great. We're making steps. But how could you actually prove coercive control in a court of law? I for one know that I meticulously deleted messages, voicemails, pretty much all trace of my Controlls because it was too excruciating to revisit, and I wanted a total detox. What then? The short answer – it's difficult.

Not impossible, difficult.

As you can imagine, there's a lot of 'their word against his' going on; and if we're looking at, let's say, a man of supposedly great moral stature, cherished by communities, against a woman so broken she can barely string a sentence together . . . who are we going to back?

The pattern of abuse suffered in coercive control is insidious, cyclical and, most importantly, *subtle*. There are very rarely any other witnesses, except the victim. Even then, they're gaslit that it's all in their head. It takes a lot for a victim to come forward and seek any sort of justice. The main thing any prosecution will look for is evidence.

In court, whether that be civil, which pertains to family, individuals or organizations; or criminal – usually when the government brings a case – there needs to be what's called 'a burden of proof'.

In a civil court a burden of proof basically means that the court needs to know that the abuse happened 'on the balance of probabilities' i.e. they must be reassured that it's more likely that the abuse did happen rather than didn't. However, if the case is taken to a criminal court this burden of proof is elevated; this is where you will hear the phrase, familiar from TV shows, that it must be proved 'beyond all reasonable doubt'.

It depends what the case is as to which court it will go to. If the victim is seeking an injunction against her perp this will go to the civil court. If, however, the perp is charged with a criminal act then this will go to the criminal court. Coercive control under Section 76 can go to either the civil or criminal court.

I've chosen not to get too law-chat-heavy, because I don't want those who are considering the next steps to be put off. The National Domestic Abuse Helpline (0808 2000 247) can help you decide the safest move.

WHAT IS EVIDENCE
OF COERCIVE CONTROL?

The fact we cannot ignore is that evidence in cases of coercive control is extremely problematic to come by.

Examples of evidence that could be used to prove coercive control are:

- Proof of financial control through bank statements, changing wills, or evidence of being cut out of accounts
- Witnesses testifying to instances they saw or heard of abusive and controlling behaviour. This could also come from their children
- Threatening and manipulative text messages, emails, other forms of communication
- Bodycam footage from police
- Journals kept by the victim
- Proof of tracking devices installed by the perp
- Emergency call transcripts

I remember times I recorded my Controll's violent outbursts, not for evidence but merely hoping if I could play them back to him 'when he was in a calm state', he would change his ways. Needless to say – that didn't happen. As we know:

They won't and they can't love you.
They won't and they can't reform.
They won't and they can't change.

The toxic shame that surrounds all cases of coercive control is poisonous to the victim. Over time, you've been made to believe that if only you were prettier/thinner/smarter/less emotional/kinder/funnier/richer/sexier, none of this would have happened. You may think you should have stopped the abuse, left earlier, spoken up. Because it's easier that way, isn't it? When things are our fault, at least there's only one person who can fix the wrong: Us.

THE 'S' WORD

I need to flag a word here, a word so embedded in our vocabulary we barely pay attention to it, but it's a term that stems from trauma, abuse, conditioning. That word is . . .

SORRY

'I'm sorry I made you angry'

'I'm sorry I let you down'

'I'm sorry I was paranoid'

'I'm sorry I didn't believe you'

'I'm sorry I called you out on your shit'

'I'm sorry I exist'

'Sorry' is our riot shield. We're so used to saying sorry to pacify, defuse and placate that it slips out like a fart after a vindaloo. Ooops. Sorry. And yes, you got it – 'sorry' is the word we say 4,380+ times a year.

Listen, sis, we must make the choice not to be sorry for our whole lives. We hold up 'sorry' in the hope it'll keep us safe when in a relationship with a Controll. That it'll cushion some of the blows. Sometimes it works, doesn't it? When you're being verbally assaulted all you can do is apologize for something you haven't done. I did it too. Because shouldering blame for something you're not guilty of is a whole lot more attractive than standing up to a Controll.

POST-TRAUMA APOLOGIZING

Once we're out of the relationship 'sorry' stays with us; and we need to watch that. It's post-trauma talk. It's natural that we feel flighty, on guard and ready to go on the defence. If we've given ourselves adequate time, sought therapy, practised self-compassion and we're ready to slowly go into another relationship, then that word 'sorry' might not just disappear. It could take years. If the person you're with really cares about you, they're attentive, kind and gentle, then they won't cuss you for your constant apologizing. They'll softly explain:

You have nothing to be sorry for.

Oh, and on another note – it's not useful to say to the over-apologizer, 'STOP SAYING SORRY!' It's an inbuilt defence mechanism.

Phrases that are useful are:

'No need to apologize. Is everything OK?'

'You've done nothing wrong!'

'I'm sorry too. Wait, why are we apologizing, we have nothing to be sorry for!'

We've shaken off the shame and diluted the self-blame with compassion. What's the opposite of sorry? The antonym for sorry is: 'glad'. What does 'glad' really mean? The definition, according to Merriam-Webster is: '**Experiencing pleasure, joy, or delight**'.

That's where our focus needs to be – where you find pleasure, joy or delight.

Nice uplifting way to end the chapter, right? I thought so too.

Hey, I've just thought of something. I don't know why it didn't come to me sooner. If it's so bad . . .

WHy DoN'T yOu jUSt lEaVe hIm? ☺

CHAPTER SEVENTEEN

WHY DON'T YOU JUST LEAVE HIM?

The Cycle of Abuse

We're both leaning on the graffitied wall outside Friese's Presse und Tabakshop, adorned with three eight-foot images of an eyeless astronaut. The newsagent was meant to open at 9 a.m. but it's gone half past. You'd think it was dawn in Alexanderplatz as the Sunday morning streets lie near-deserted, bar a few bleary-eyed construction workers chatting and smoking. Next to us, a five-storey building rigged with scaffolding looms skyward, blue sheeting quivers in the light breeze.

Five glorious days ahead filled with nothingness. Although it's September, it's 24 degrees and we're cheating seasons: mustard leaves heap street corners, lying below naked trees, with the temperature of early summer.

Damien is wearing a black bomber jacket and dark jeans. Effortlessly suave. I'm in battered white pumps and a red checked shirt dress I picked up from a charity shop in an expensive part of London. One woman's junk is another woman's treasure.

Damien turns to me: 'Let's get pastries and sit in the park.' Then, after a beat, he adds, 'Fuck it. We'll get a bottle of bubbles too.'

I don't know what we're celebrating but I'm like a woman that's cheated cancer, won the lottery, then eaten a Nutella pancake. Euphoric.

When Damien clutches my hand as we cross the street, I think my heart will explode out of my ears. I love this man. I adore the bones of him. I'm totally and utterly addicted. When he wants to, he can love me like nobody else knows how. Times like this, all the rage, the bitterness, the cheating is forgotten. This is all I need and he's the only vendor.

Electricity runs from my hand to his. Just like that first night. Fingers sparking like they're being welded together. It's all I can do to stop myself from bursting into ecstatic tears. I never factored we'd get back here. I was sure it was over. Who would have thought after the terror that unfolded only days earlier . . .

I'm in my Marigolds on the street outside the studio flat in North London, picking up sodden tampon boxes and empty tuna cans after a late-night fox feast. It's dusk and Damien has just arrived back after a week's work trip with a spring in his step. I'm certainly not going to dull it and ask why.

His suitcase lies open on the bed. I see an M&S carrier bag stuffed with what I presume is dirty washing. Whilst he freshens up, I set to work sorting laundry, chucking it in the machine. There's chana masala in the slow cooker and *homemade mango chutney proudly sat on the kitchen table. I light some candles. I'm pretty sure I've aced this.*

In under five minutes everything is chaotically upended. The 0–60 must win some kind of world record. I'm in the bedroom, my bashed purple suitcase now next to his. Blinded by tears, I can't see what I'm flinging in. He's standing at the door, watching me, convulsing with rage. My hands are shaking as I grope in my underwear drawer for at least a week's worth of pants.

I'm not doing this any more. Enough.

Fear dilutes anger.

I need to end this. The week he'd been away gave me space to become resolute: things are going to be different.

He moves forward, backing me into the wall. I try to side-step like a cornered animal.

Why did you go in my bag? / I was . . . / You breached my privacy, I'm a grown fucking man. / What are you talking about? / Are you fucking deaf? Get your hands off my stuff / I was doing the washing, what's wrong with you? / There's something wrong with me, now? / No, I . . . / This is why I can't be with you. / You can't be with me? / Yeah, go on, here's the waterworks. / I was doing the washing. / No fucking respect. / I do respect you! / Perhaps I'll break your fucking jaw, then you'll learn some respect for me. / I can't . . . / Yeah, bye bye. Good luck finding anyone like me. / I don't want anyone else . . . / You'll always be alone, go on, fuck off.

Step round. Suitcase zipped. Where's the keys? Wallet. Pull my green backpack from the hook on the door. Stuff a coat in. I need my phone. Hands trembling. Where do I think I'm going?

I don't remember being at the front door. I blink and I'm halfway along the main road. Lit by golden street lamps. Free-fall tears, my suitcase trundles behind me. My backpack on, like a poor man's Dora with nowhere to explore.

I try and connect what happened. There's no first draft. The rages smack you in the face at exhilarating speed. I don't know where I'm walking. Up ahead, behind some huge square wheelie bins, I suddenly see the shadow figures of men, exposed by the glow of their cigarettes. I cross the street. One of them starts to follow. Another calls out: 'You need help, baby?' Actually, I do. I really do. I put my head down and move on. I don't look back.

As I reach the junction that takes you from one borough to another, I pull out my phone:

11.46 p.m.

Nearly three hours have evaporated. I scroll through my contacts in an attempt to jog a memory of a place I could shelter. I fall on:

Annelisa Franks ☺ (NEW – From Work)

I haven't spoken to her in over two years, but she used to live around here, could be worth a try before I give up and return home. I don't want to go back. What are the chances she's close by? What are the chances she's still awake? What are the chances she remembers who the hell I am?

Hi, Annelisa. This is Maddy. How are you?
  Weird one . . . are you up?

What am I doing? Wandering around the streets of London in the middle of the night, frozen fingers, carrying God knows what on my back.

My phone pings.

Maddy! Hi! How are you? Long time! Yup I'm awake. You OK? XX

How do I explain this? I'll say I was locked out. No, that's stupid. Why would I have a suitcase stuffed with a random selection of summer dresses, thermal socks and a Wonder Woman costume?

Sorry to ask you this . . . Are you still in Seven Sisters? I need somewhere to stay tonight. Don't worry if it's not possible. It's a lot to ask. MX

I wait, standing next to a desolate 24-hour Budgens. I realize the cashier, a young Asian man, is looking at me. I move on.

Typing.

Typing.

Jesus, I'm so tired I could weep.

Oh no! Yes, I'm still here. You can come. My lodger is back tomorrow early though. 45A Brooklyn Road. Take a right by the Chicken Cottage.

Before I reply the address is in Google Maps. Ten minutes' walk. I can do this.

Thank you SO much. Be there in 10. Thank you xcx

A night bus pulls up next to me and three lairy thirty-somethings get off. They blaze past like I'm invisible. Oh, to be them. So high on life and substances they can't fathom the comedown around the corner.

When I arrive it's after midnight. Annelisa opens the door with a spent roll-up between her fingers, black hair in two plaits draped around her head, dressed in a delicate, green silk kimono, looking like an out-of-work Hollywood starlet.

In the living room, she places a thin mattress on the floor with an emaciated orange quilt and a couple of grey cushions from the sofa. It looks fit for Tracey Emin but to me it's Ritz luxury. I roll my sad suitcase flat on the floor and pull out an odd pair of pyjamas. Annelisa asks no questions. She flicks on a Himalayan salt lamp then heads for bed.

As I lie on the ground trying to soothe myself in the womblike incandescence of the lamp, my heart finally has time to break. It's already broken. It splinters. I check my phone: nothing from Damien. No worry, no apology, no love.

Midnight bleeds to morning. A constant lump in my throat. I'm not sure if I've slept. The spotlights in the kitchen turn on and I watch the feet of Annelisa's lodger patter in, pause, then continue. I decide to play unconscious. My head throbs. I hear the kettle switch on as the lodger lightly hums 'What a Wonderful World'. Of all the songs.

I realize my phone is clamped against my chest. I bury my head under the thin quilt to open it. Four messages from Damien. My tired heart sings.

I no longer have a say over my body and mind. The sensible, steered head would say: 'fuck you'. But I don't run this ship any more, he's at the controls. Why I'm elated to see his name as I

lie crooked on a stranger's floor, as he reposes in our cosy bed, I
don't know. That's the dials he's chosen to twist this grey
morning.

> 06.34 a.m.: Morning, out about 12.
> Call when you're up. X
>
> 07.10 a.m.: Hey, you alright? XX
>
> 07.30 a.m.: OK then . . . Still asleep?
>
> 08.16 a.m.: Hey?? I'm leaving for work around midday but would
> be good to see you before I go. X

A trillion questions swirl around my foggy brain: 'Before
I go' as in, you're leaving me? Why are you not asking where
I am? Don't you care where I slept? Do you remember what
you said to me? What will happen when I come back to the
flat?

The riptide is frenzied and furious. I don't pause to thank
Annelisa for taking me in. Like I say, I'm not at the control
panel any more. I pack my things, waiting for the lodger to
leave for work. I'm desperate for the loo but it's right by
Annelisa's bedroom. I'd rather give myself a UTI than wake her.
I need to get out, to get to Damien.

On the way back to the flat I make-believe I'm returning
from a gap year or teaching English abroad. Off to reunite with
my friends and family. My hair is knotted into a messy bun
and, as I approach the flat, I lick my fingers, drawing them
under my eyes, as if that'll remove the black circles that have
been building for years. I push my key into the lock and inhale.

I hear BBC Breakfast News and smell toast. My heart is throbbing in my ears. Him not being in eyeline feels like walking into an open space with a sniper on the rooftops. I close the door and catch sight of myself in the gilded hallway mirror. I'm drawn, pale and thin. Damien steps out of the bathroom, smelling of expensive cologne, mid-shave.

He looks at me, smiles and kisses my cheek, throwing me completely off guard.

'Brekkie there if you want or crumpets in the bread bin.' I . . . I can't scrabble for words. Last night's furore has dissipated like boiling water in sub-zero. Hiss.

'I'm heading out but if you're here later shall we get pizza?'

I must look like a dog who's realized her owner is pretending to throw a fake ball. Head cocked.

No comment on my suitcase. My backpack. Nothing. I haven't gone this far before. Never been this close to leaving.

'OK, well, I'll let you readjust . . .' he says. Readjust! Readjust! He makes me sound like a woman adapting back to the community after being sectioned. To be fair, I strongly affiliate with her.

'And Mad, next week, you and me – Berlin. What do you say?'

And just like that, it's forgotten. His threats, intimidation and castigation, hoovered up and popped in the bin outside with the half-eaten takeout, ready for the foxes to devour.

If I had a pound for every person who asked me: 'Why don't you just leave him?' I'd have enough for a lifetime's worth of therapy and a Freddo.

It's frustrating, isn't it? Of course you know you shoul leave. You get it – they're bad for you. You're definite you should end it. But you can't seem to find the strength. Something keeps dragging you back. Don't worry, it's not just you. I felt it too. I was haunted by it. LEAVE, I thought. But I never did. I never could.

I once wrote an article about this very subject – escaping your toxic partner – and I was horrified to receive a blunt, victim-blaming response from someone I had considered a friend in television who called me a 'coward' for not 'just leaving'. Instead of running into the sea I worked on some points for you to understand what is really happening.

Welcome to the unseen chemical world of Trauma Bonding.

THE CYCLE OF ABUSE:
CHEMICALLY BONDED

You've heard the phrase 'trapped in an abusive relationship'. Well there's more at play than physical, financial or emotional bonds tying you to your Controll. There are chemical ties too.

Let's take a look at the **Cycle of Abuse**[2] that happens in a relationship with a Controll.

Hormonally speaking, when we are stressed, i.e. in the **TENSION** phase, **cortisol** floods our body. Cortisol is a steroid hormone responsible for 'fight or flight'. It tells our body when we are in danger. We get anxious, our blood pressure rises and heart rate increases. It gives us the sensation of being totally on edge. Pepped up for a fight.

TENSION
Tensions increase,
walking on red-hot coals,
victim is hyper-tense and
tries to placate the perp.

CALM
All is forgotten –
put out for the
foxes. Back to the
honeymoon phase
that initially hooked
the victim.

INCIDENT
'The Blowout'. Huge
argument, physical,
emotional, verbal,
sexual abuse. Threats,
intimidation, volatility,
violence.

RECONCILIATION
The Controll loosely
apologizes, perhaps gives
and expensive gift or
gaslights the victim into
believing it was their fault.

When the **INCIDENT** phase hits, the victim is already plagued with nervousness and burnt out from the cortisol produced in the **TENSION** phase. **Adrenaline** will then be rushed into the victim's system. Adrenaline and cortisol are produced by the adrenal glands; both of these hormones help limit bodily functions that are not essential in a dangerous situation. When these hormones are 'kept running', i.e. in near-constant use, they can cause devastation to the body, including heart attacks, strokes, anxiety and depression.

The victim is in a perpetual state of fight or flight for the first two stages of the Cycle of Abuse, and they are desperate for a release. That comes in the final two stages – **RECONCILIATION** and **CALM**. This is where the reward hormone **dopamine** is released. You may know dopamine as the 'happy hormone': it's also discharged when people have a hit of drugs. There's an old-school belief that dopamine is addictive – it's not. However, the body understands that dopamine is connected to rewarding experiences, therefore signifying to the brain 'you're gonna enjoy this'.

You can understand then why this Cycle of Abuse very quickly traps victims.

**It's a hormonal helter-skelter
which is near-on impossible
to disembark.**

I hope that has gone some way to comforting victims on why you stay or return. I got you. I've been there, I know why you're dwelling, I experienced it too. These chemicals are strong. Even if they're not good for you.

THE OTHER REASONS YOU ARE STAYING WITH YOUR CONTROLL

Chemicals aside, there's an overabundance of reasons you remain.

You stay because:

- You love them.
- You are dependent on them.
- You think they'll change.
- You think you can change them.

- You have no money/they control your money.
- They've convinced you you'll be alone without them.
- You have children together.
- You're married and don't want a divorce, perhaps for religious reasons.
- They've isolated you from any support network.
- You're exhausted and disorientated.
- You've lost all self-esteem and personal power.
- They've manufactured it so they're your entire world.
- You think you deserve it.
- You think there's no better.
- You're scared of being alone.
- You're worried what they'll do to you/your children if you leave.
- You're anxious about what they'll do to themselves if you leave.

This barely scratches the surface on reasons you stay. It is not your fault if you remain in a relationship with a Controll but there are steps to take to process whether leaving is the best option (it is).

Firstly, you need to understand this brutal truth:

Your situation will only get worse.

I'm sorry to say there will be no improvement on what you're tolerating. No 'working it out', no 'better days ahead', no 'sticking it through'. This is it. I know you're barely holding on; I know you're shattered, scared and unsettled.

You have been conditioned by the Controll to normalize these abusive patterns. You fluctuate from thinking their behaviour is acceptable and manageable to unrelenting and painful.

It's no wonder you're broken and depressed. These are valid states. You don't need to hide it from anyone and pretend everything is fine and dandy.

There's that unwavering nagging feeling that this is not right, but you're hooked, swept under, treading water in the hope they'll change their ways and pull you out. They won't.

THE MERCILESS BREAK-UP/ GET BACK TOGETHER PATTERN

In the **INCIDENT** phase a Controll will often threaten breaking up with you if they feel you pulling away. I was broken up with more times than I dare to count. This is to warn you how traumatized you'll be without them – ironically, the complete opposite is true. Eventually you start numbing to their threats, and then, guess what happens? They'll sense this and the threats will only get more conniving and intimidating. By constantly blackmailing you with leaving:

They are consciously making you feel unsafe.

Tell me – have you ever asked yourself if your partner actually likes you? Do you honestly wonder, due to their words and actions, if they sincerely despise you? It's all part of the **INCIDENT** phase. They lash out, torment, abuse, chastise, weaken and bring you to your knees.

Is this the measure of someone who loves you?

Those words of reassurance you tell yourself – 'it's because he/she cares', 'they had a bad day', 'tomorrow will be better' – are phrases the Controll has drummed into you in the **RECONCILIATION** phase. Without even knowing it, you're longing for any kind of resolution followed by **CALM**.

It. Is. Gruelling.

The Controll conditions, normalizes and terrorizes. There are so many subtle ways they keep you from lifting the veil of realization. They may constantly tell you stories about how they have been abandoned by their mothers, fathers, teachers, exes, siblings; it doesn't really matter. As long as you are fully ingrained with the notion that they are the poor souls who have been discarded, then it's enough for you to question how you could ever add to that list and desert them too.

It's likely, especially early on in the relationship, they will tell you stories about their 'paranoid' and 'crazy' exes who all acted completely out of character and made their lives hell. 'Huh,' you'll think, 'they really do sound like they were batshit mad. Poor thing.' You're reinvigorated with the thought you'll do all you can to never become one of his Controll exes. Oh, but you will. I'm afraid to say you're next.

If you're lucky enough to get out, it'll be you looking back, comprehending that it wasn't that all their exes were crazy – they were *driven* to *insanity* by the Controll!

They – and you – were merely chemically addicted to the cycle; and let me tell you, rehab is a far nicer place to be.

OK, time for a quick chat with those who have loved ones in toxic relationships, desperate to get them out.

TO FRIENDS OF LOVED ONES TRAPPED WITH A CONTROLL

I understand why people ask the question: Why don't you just leave? They see their friends, loved ones, family fade away. Become shells of themselves. The bright, bubbly, lovable souls now secretive, distant and quiet. You know exactly what's happened to them, or rather, *who* has happened to them. It's obvious to everyone bar them what they need to do: escape, block, heal, move on. It's frustrating, isn't it? You've said it repeatedly, listened, advised, sent links, even paid for counselling, but nothing will make them leave their toxic partner. It breaks your heart. They're in a cult for one. Unreachable.

Perhaps it was something you did wrong? It's human nature to blame yourself. Maybe your friend or loved one really does want to stay, so you should step away? You question if you should stop making it your problem at all.

To those concerned their friend or family member is trapped in a relationship with a Controll:

Your loved one is not staying in this relationship because they're stupid, unlovable, cowardly, addicted to the drama or codependent.

They persist because they have been subjugated to a form of brainwashing and this is no *Matrix* make-believe; these are methodical, manipulative mind games that strangle self-esteem, diminish dignity and extinguish energy. It is *never, ever* as simple as 'just leaving'. Deep down, in a long-buried part of themselves, they know what you say is true, but they're so far in, so coerced, so controlled that it's not easily accessible information.

Rewrite the rules

Normal rules do not apply when you suspect someone is in a relationship with a Controll. The victim is not disobeying you by staying; they are not ignoring your advice or cutting the ties between you; they don't dislike or disregard you. This wasn't your fault, and it isn't theirs. *They are only trying to survive.*

The emotional abuse and control they are living with does not necessarily present as bruises, black eyes, or scars. Perhaps it barely even manifests as shouting or yelling in public. It is subtler. So, don't get irritated, frustrated or pissed off that the person you are trying to help isn't paying attention. It doesn't work like that.

The number of calls you make, interventions you stage, videos you send is inconsequential – they won't 'just leave'. I get it – it's agonizing to sit back and watch them disintegrate, I am not asking you to do that. You need to aid them by loosening the stranglehold the Controll has them in. There's hope.

HOW TO GET THEM OUT OF
A TOXIC RELATIONSHIP

Reach out

We understand a powerful tactic used by the Controll is isola-tion. When the victim is isolated, they are cut off from support networks, in this case – you. Get ready to start being pushy. You don't want to hound the victim but make a point of drop-ping them a text every few days, perhaps a call once a week. Even if they don't pick up, you are laying down lines of commu-nication that say: 'I'm not going anywhere, I'm paying attention and I care.' Make sure the victim knows you are interested in their life, not only their situation. Ask them about work, the weather, a TV show – anything but 'how's the dickhead?' Respect that they are bonded to their perpetrator and you casting judge-ments will only drive a wedge between you and the victim.

Listen

When you meet up or talk with the victim be prepared to listen. This is not Therapy 101, you may come off preachy and the victim will be sick of hearing it. By all means, once the conver-sation is flowing, steer it round to the subject of their partner, but if it doesn't happen on that occasion, don't force it. If they do start speaking about their partner be ready to listen. The more they trust you, the more they will open up. Even shaking your head or raising your eyebrows can be seen as condemna-tory. You could say things like, 'I'm sorry this is happening', 'How did that make you feel?' and 'What did you think when that happened?' Which leads me on to . . .

Highlight abusive behaviour

I don't mean stand on a table, scream, and set off a firework when they let you know some of the shit their partner has put them through, but if they mention behaviours by the Controll which clearly highlight coercive and abusive tactics then shine a spotlight on them. Don't let them pass it off as 'maybe I am paranoid'. In a safe and reassuring way comfort them and let them know that what's happened isn't normal, loving behaviour. If they want to move on to something else or appear tired from talking about it, let them.

Focus on positive past times

Find subtle ways to remind the victim of a time before the Controll. You could send photos of you together, recount funny memories or even get them to visit an old haunt. Anything that nods at a more content stage when they were at ease and happy is useful in guiding them towards a belief life can be healthier.

Deliver solutions and serve a Safety Plan

Note down ways they could leave – you are effectively writing down their escape plan. Remember, it's unlikely they will have the time, energy or capacity to do this. When it feels right you could gently suggest safe ways to back out. Keep their options open; if they pull back, don't push. The victim will need time to calibrate and may initially feel unsafe.

Your Safety Plan could be something like:

1. I will put £500 on this bank card for you.

2. You pack a bag and I'll collect you after work.

3. Once you're out, we will let the Controll know you will not be returning and call the police if he/she gets volatile.

4. We will call the Domestic Abuse Helpline for support.

Make sure the victim's safety is your first priority, which doesn't necessarily mean getting them out quickly.

Expect them to go back

For the love of God, if you are lucky enough to bear witness to them leaving, do not even dare think, let alone utter the words 'I told you so'. Anything that makes them feel small or stupid will play straight into the hands of the Controll. They have been made to feel worthless for their entire relationship; do not re-inforce this rhetoric.

Expect they may go back. Soon we will look at Hoovering – manipulative tactics used by an abusive partner to lure victims back. This is extremely common. Do not be surprised, and certainly do not blame the victim if they return to the Controll. Be there for them if they do. Let them know you don't judge them. Be the itch the Controll cannot scratch: persistent and irritating as fuck.

Understand this:

**A mammoth reason
victims stay is fear.**

Fear of the unknown, fear of being alone and fear for their lives. According to the Femicide Census, 2020: 41 per cent (37 of 91) of women killed by a male partner/former partner in England, Wales and Northern Ireland in 2018 had separated or taken steps to separate from them. 11 of these 37 women were killed within the first month of separation and 24 were killed within the first year.

That is staggering. The numbers speak for themselves, so to an outsider, when someone may seem mindless or reckless for staying in an abusive relationship, understand this could be the level of danger they are dealing with.

LEAVING WHEN MARRIED TO A CONTROLL

If you're married to a Controll, you may have the words of your vows ringing in your ears, likely amplified by them: 'for richer, for poorer, in sickness and in health, to love and to cherish, till death do us part'. You've got to stick with it, right? Wrong. Are they sticking by their pledge to love and cherish you? Nope. I'm not going to start dissecting religious vows, but I can tell you one thing for sure, your safety, mental health and life count more than all oaths combined.

You have been made to believe you have no choices. You've been told in so many ways that life without your Controll is not worth living. They are your world. You fear even *thinking* about where you could go, let alone having a penny for any court system, especially if they control all the money. But it is possible to live a fulfilled, happy and healthy life again, without them. Leaving is an option. You have choices.

There won't be a 'right' time but it's never too late to leave.

There are laws in place to protect you from danger from your abuser. It is true that the stats of serious harm and murder from the perpetrator rise significantly after you leave, but the flipside to this is that thousands and thousands of victims of coercive control become survivors; they escape and build better, safer and happier lives as a result.

For victims of Controlls with children and little or no access to money, here are some steps to take to move towards the life you and your children deserve:

Get organized, carefully

It is important your Controll does not know you are even *thinking* of leaving. If they do, they could become volatile and dangerous. As best you can, act as close to your normal as possible. Start by putting aside an emergency bag of essentials for you and/or your children. This could have some wash things, a few changes of clothes, a phone charger, official documents like birth certificates and passports or ID. If possible, leave this with a trusted neighbour or friend. If not, keep it totally out of sight, yet accessible.

Arrange a place to stay

You may still be in contact with a family member or friend, so let them know you need a place to crash and stress the importance of keeping your plans confidential. If you do not have a place to stay, there are refuges available. Contact the National Domestic Abuse freephone line, operating 24/7: 0808 2000 247.

Women's Aid also has a comprensive directory of local support organizations on its website, www.womensaid.org.uk/domestic-abuse-directory, or you can contact them via their Live Chat. There's also help for male victims of domestic abuse here.

Travelling by train
For those who need to travel by train, Women's Aid founded the Rail to Refuge scheme in March 2020. Once you have a space in a refuge, they will help to organize this for you, free of charge.

Codeword scheme
Many pharmacies participate in the 'Ask for ANI' (Action Needed Immediately) scheme. Go to the counter and ask for 'Annie'; they will be ready to help and will give you a private place, a phone and help with contacting the police or domestic abuse organizations.

Orchestrate an exit strategy
The main thing to consider when taking the action to leave is your partner's routine. When are they at work? Is there a time they aren't in the house for several hours? Spend a few days working out what is the best time to escape and make any calls to domestic abuse charities.

Set the day, but don't stick to it
When you can set a date and time to leave, with a place to stay secured, start mentally preparing yourself. This will feel over-whelming, but you are capable.

Expect doubts. If something happens that means it's unsafe to leave when you had planned, don't be disheartened. Contact those you need to and rearrange.

If you are in immediate danger, call 999 in the UK. If you are in another country, research online and source emergency help.

If you are trapped in a relationship of any kind with your abuser, with or without children, it is never too late to leave. Being a good parent is loving, nurturing, and keeping your child safe; this is not viable in an abusive household. Choosing to get help, whether that be through a domestic abuse charity, the police, or another service, is giving yourself and your children the lifeline they need for fear-free lives, away from the abuser.

Research has consistently shown that 30 to 66 per cent of children living with domestic abuse are themselves being abused – either physically or sexually – by the same perpetrator.[1] You need to get yourself and your child safely and securely out of this harmful environment.

The family courts in the UK are a shambles. I am not going to rose tint and tell you it's going to be an easy ride. It isn't. But there is support out there for you.

A FINAL WORD

Big deal, you've broken up and returned more times than you can remember. Who cares if this Controll is the last in a line of fifteen toxic partners? You're only predicting your remaining friends and family will roll their eyes. You're doing this for you, and if you have children, you're doing it for them too. **This is you ending the cycle.**

You deserve genuine love. You deserve happiness. You deserve someone who is worthy of you. The longer you stay in a relationship with a Controll, the further you are from this merited abundance. And you know that, don't you? I knew it. It doesn't mean I left, though. And that's OK, for now, because you're beginning to awaken. Awareness will be your armour.

Very quietly and taking as much time as you need, start making your way towards the EXIT sign, honey.

CHAPTER EIGHTEEN
MIND BLANK

PTSD and Disassociation

ONE YEAR AFTER THE RED WINE ANGEL.

This is a colossal waste of time. I could be job hunting, putting the starting touches to a novel I won't finish, or watching Dr Pimple Popper. Instead, I'm hot, sweaty and late. Lost in the arse-end of nowhere. I reckon I've missed the turning. I probably did that subconsciously so the counsellor will tell me I've forfeited my slot. Fingers crossed.

As I pivot the other way, I'm startled by a man inches behind me. I think he appeared in a puff of smog. He's middle-aged, wearing a beaten NYC baseball cap and a blue Donnay fleece that's clearly been circulating since the eighties. He has an unkempt, greying beard, interwoven with what looks like porridge. I take 'Days Like This' out of my ears. 'Sorry!' I say, for absolutely nothing.

'S'nice walking behind you,' he says.

The residential street is dead, bar a skinny-looking tabby cat in a window. I don't think that's the pussy he's after. My heart accelerates. I step off the pavement into the road in an attempt to dodge him, but he blocks me. 'Don't go. What's your name?' he says.

We're so used to this shit, aren't we? Our ability to make lightning-speed judgements on the safest reply is honed to a tee. This time my brain is telling me: 'Keep walking, say nothing.'

As I quicken my pace, he thankfully falls back. Maybe the porridge slowed him down. But not without hollering: 'Fucking slut. Ugly bitch. Only asking your name, stuck-up cow.'

I take a well-practised steadying breath. I'm back on the high street. Off a side road I see arrows to 'NHS Psychotherapy'. I reluctantly follow them, wanting to put off any stirring up of the past six weeks. I've been dealing with it all just fine. Totally fine.

Today is good. I've left the house, which is huge. Sometimes I can't believe all this shit is still going on. Almost twelve months to the day since he left me, yet he's only really just gone. An entire year he's dragged this out for. Well, I let him drag it out for. I never guessed it would come to a head the way it did.

The Red Wine Angel. Then Jesús. For someone struggling with their mental health I'm surprised it didn't tip me over the edge.

I push away the gnawing feeling I should run and hide back in bed and force myself to head through the automatic doors. Within seconds of sitting down, a young woman, curly hair, dressed more Brighton than Brixton, pops her head out of a door. 'Maddy?' she says, with a light Irish lilt.

Her room is effectively a glorified broom cupboard. I plonk myself onto a bobbly, green armchair. On a tiny, grubby windowsill sit dead yellow tulips in a frosty pint glass. A peeling poster on the wall says:

TALKING IS THERAPY. LET IT OUT.

The egg sandwich I wolfed down on the tube for breakfast is already repeating so I'm not sure that was the best thing to read.

The therapist, perhaps only a couple of years older than me, introduces herself as Nicky. I'm boiling but decide to keep my coat on to stress that I don't want, and don't need, to be here. If I must suffocate to prove it, so be it.

'Really lovely to meet you. Shall I take your jacket?' I shake my head. It seems you lose the ability to speak after reaching a certain temperature.

'It's great you sought help, Maddy,' she says.

I find my voice: 'I didn't.' Then cross my arms.

'You didn't?' She cocks her head.

'Well, I did but . . . I called when I wasn't in the best state, and yeah, maybe then I wasn't fine, but I couldn't be more fine now. Finer. I couldn't be finer,' I say.

I don't know why I'm acting like a petulant child. My whole being is repulsing every second of this. Give me a crayon already.

'It wasn't long ago. That you called, though?' she says kindly. I raise my eyebrows. She's right but I don't want to go there.

'Well, shall we do this session, then assess if you need more or not?' she continues, realizing she's going to be carrying the full weight of the conversation.

'Good. Well, as I'm sure you've gathered, I'm your NHS

Counsellor. We'll be seeing each other for six weeks. Unless of course, you're "absolutely fine", then we'll stop. If you do the whole six weeks, I need you to keep your appointments; if you're sick, that's OK but please let me know in advance.'

'Yup', I say, now pulling imaginary feathers out of a small hole in my sleeve.

She draws a clipboard with sheets of paper from a cabinet and hands it to me. There's a gnarly biro attached to it by an old piece of twine. As if anyone's going to nick it.

The questions ask me things like:

Over the last 2 weeks, how often have you been bothered by any of the following problems?

1. Having little interest or pleasure doing things:
   - Not at all
   - Several days
   - Most of the time

2. Suicidal thoughts, perhaps that you would be better off dead, or hurting yourself in some way:
   - Not at all
   - Several days
   - Most of the time

I get to the second question then put the board flat on my lap. 'Right, this is stupid. Sorry, I'm not being rude, but I'm not depressed or suicidal. We're not even together any more. Everything is completely fine. Someone else can use this better than me. I'm fine. Totally fine.'

*Half of Nicky's mouth upturns; she's trying to suss me out.
I don't like it.*

*'What?' I snap. I think the demon of my old secondary
school bully was in that egg sandwich.*

*'You can fill it out at the end, no problem.' She's like an Irish
Miss Honey. Her gentleness is making me weak.*

She takes a beat, then tries a different tack.

*'When you called us, because you needed help . . . shall we
talk about that?'*

*'We can. I mean, back then I was . . .' I drift off. Back then.
'Back then' was only a short time ago, why am I talking like it
was years?*

*I guess I've figured it's best to keep everything inside. Because
that's how he wanted it. How he manufactured it. Even a year
ago when he left, what followed was twelve months of using me
in whatever way he wanted. I was still silent. I've kept this all
in: the Red Wine Angel, Jesús, the money, the desperate desire
to end things.*

*'Maddy, I read your notes. You've been through a lot of
trauma. Domestic abuse can have—'*

*'It wasn't domestic abuse!' That came out a little louder than
planned.*

*She pauses then begins twiddling an NHS Trust pen between
her fingers like a tiny baton.*

'What makes you say it wasn't?'

*'He didn't hit me or anything. I don't even want to—' Big,
sloppy tears spill over my cheeks. Where the hell did they come
from? My inbuilt sprinkler system is faulty. This is so humiliating.*

Nicky leans towards me. 'Where would you like to start?'

I don't respond. I can't respond. Where do I begin?

Then something very weird happens. I try and think back on the night of the Red Wine Angel, to Jesús, the money, my twin saving my life, anything at all, but I can't remember it. My mind is a big vat of nothingness. Men in Black have stepped in with their neuralyzer. Zzzzhoink. I can barely utter a sentence to Nicky.

An hour or so later I come out of the session feeling like I've done a double HIIT class after an all-nighter. I don't even want to eat, which is my usual go-to trauma-blocker.

I sit on the train with my head in my hands, vaguely staring at my warped reflection in the toughened glass opposite. For someone whose mind is normally whirring, the numbness that fills it is disconcerting. I'm shattered.

A man sits on the seat opposite. My heart double somersaults then belly-flops.

Fuck.

It's him.

My head is still down, now fixed on his Fred Perrys. Maybe he hasn't noticed. My hands are shaking uncontrollably, I can barely hold my head up. My heartbeat is in my throat. I can't breathe.

Why is everything black? I tilt my chin up. We're stuck in a tunnel.

An announcement crackles.

'Ladies and gents, apologies for the slight delay whilst we wait for the station up ahead to clear. Should be on the move again shortly.'

Flashbacks flick through my mind like a terrible old movie. He's snarling, backing me into a corner. His hands on my throat as he has sex with me. His rage. The cheating.

Made to feel like I'm insane. The tension. Walking on red-hot coals.

I can't. Breathe.

The train jolts. He stands and walks to the tube doors. I have to look up, be ready to protect myself. White spots float before my eyes, my mouth is bone dry.

It's not him.

A manic chuckle shoots out of my mouth. He turns around. He's over 50. It's not him. This is hilarious.

It's. Not. Him.

Fuck. Maybe I am losing it. In that moment a strong urge pulls me to go back home, to my family, the countryside, nature. I've got to remind myself how to breathe.

It's time to start healing.

You'd be surprised how many times this happened. The whole seeing him on public transport thing. It wasn't only there, it was bloody everywhere. One time I swear he was disguised as Minnie Mouse trying to chug money off me for the British Heart Foundation on a street corner.

After the breakdown or loss of any relationship it's totally normal to be reminded of that person through smells, sounds, sensations. That 'missing them' pang is because they're hardly off your mind, so it's not surprising you manifest doppelgängers. But what I was experiencing was something very visceral. And deeply carved with fear.

Damien and I didn't break up and cleanly split our intertwined lives like you'd gut a fish backbone from its flesh. Nope, I was choking on bones for months. So to speak. You see, there was a definite break-up but what followed was a prolonged period of Hoovering (we'll cover this in a sec) and once that finished the shit really hit the fan.

All in all, when it peaked, a full twelve months after the Red Wine Angel and Jesús, it really and truly was time for me to seek therapy.

During the messy, drawn-out break-up period I began to suffer something reminiscent of agoraphobia. A distinct desire not to leave the house. If there was little option other than to go out, I'd be thoroughly distracted. 'What do I do if I see him?' 'Where's the nearest exit?' I became as paranoid as he'd convinced me I was.

I'M FINE-ING MEETS THERAPY
(AND JOEY FROM *FRIENDS*)

I didn't want to go to therapy. Not only did I think I didn't need it, I believed I didn't deserve it. There are people way worse off than me, I thought. But as the weeks, months and years went on, I saw how emotional abuse by its very nature has you keeping schtum, wrapped in your tiny bubble, make-believing that every-thing is completely fine. You've been using a spot plaster to cover a disease.

Therapy slowly starts pulling off the layers. I like to think of it as that episode of *Friends* where Joey puts on all of Chandler's wardrobe, you know? Even though you're scorching, uncomfort-able, chafing to fuck and weighed down, you just keep walking around pretending you're A-OK.

Therapy starts peeling off the overcoats, and as each is removed, you get to the core of the situation. You begin to feel freer, lighter, less burdened. That's not to say it's pain-free, oh no, it can be agony at times. There will be sessions you don't want to turn up to, sometimes you'll be angry, sad, hysterical, knackered. Many instances, I felt a million times worse coming out than when I'd gone in; but slowly, layer by layer, your independence and self-esteem return.

I had no idea I was at crisis point until I found myself in Irish Miss Honey's broom cupboard. Needless to say, I deserved to be there. I *was* the one who required her time, and *you* are worth your own Irish Miss Honey too.

Therapy is the single most compassionate thing you can do for yourself.

It's also nothing to be ashamed of. If a relative, friend or colleague grimaces and pats you on the head when you say you're in therapy, you can reply, 'Deirdre, I have no shame that I take care of my mental health, I also care for my house plants. More to the point, perhaps we should discuss why you kill three a week?'

The healing process wasn't all chips and gravy. In multiple sessions I struggled with my memories. It's like my brain put down shutters and then, in any place that was not that broom cupboard, they opened up and came flooding back in gruesome glory. After the first few times that happened, I learnt to journal so that I could pull the layers off, dissecting them with Irish Miss Honey.

Funnily enough after my fifth session, as I began to not feel so much like a tiny, unimportant mouse, her room got an upgrade. We moved down the corridor to a bigger office with a prayer plant and windows to the paved area outside. We grew and found space together.

DEALING WITH DISASSOCIATION

Those mind blanks weren't down to shit memory. Although I had been accused of having amnesia many times over the years. No, it was something quite different. It's called **Disassociation**.

Disassociation and Post-traumatic Stress Disorder are linked, and common in survivors of trauma. Disassociation is effectively a disruption in the piecing together of recollections. It has its own spectrum, not too dissimilar to the Psychometer. We have all experienced disassociation to a greater or lesser degree, because at number 1 on the spectrum of disassociation is daydreaming. Those times you find yourself absent-mindedly drifting off to a beach or the chores that need to be done. It's pretty simple to snap yourself back to reality then, isn't it?

The closer to 10 we get, the greater the experience of disconnection with self. It can be distressing to feel so far removed and, the further up the scale, the harder it is to bounce back to the present.

Disassociation is an inbuilt protection system in the brain. It's part of that fight-or-flight response.

Disassociation is most common in children but can certainly happen for adults too. If someone has been exposed to prolonged or repetitive traumatic events – like emotional abuse – then the brain concocts disassociation as a coping mechanism. It's essentially saying 'don't worry, I got you – I'll blank this to protect you'.

Just like how a smell, sound or sensation can hark back to a person you miss, a non-threatening, seemingly incongruent situation can act as a trigger for dissociation, and you may not even realize why. This is the reason counselling after a relationship with a Controll is crucial to your healing. Even though you technically could be out of harm's way, your brain will still be in defence mode, and it may not allow you to live a full, happy and healthy life until you have worked through your trauma with a trained professional.

It's worth noting here it's fine to 'shop around' with therapists. It's easy to be put off if you jar with a counsellor or you find them unhelpful, but be persistent. There is an Irish Miss Honey for everyone.

THERAPY AIN'T JUST FOR THE RICH

At that time in my life, I had no money, which I thought meant no help. To me, a therapist sat in some mahogany-clad office, shelves of degree certificates, charging £200+ an hour. It was only because I fell to rock bottom that I attempted to reach out.

I went online and searched 'free therapy near me' and was surprised to see it wasn't just a shady geezer operating out of his van in return for a blowjob. No, quite the opposite. The NHS runs 'Talking Therapies', which is a free counselling service for everyone, in most places within the UK. See what's available near you if you don't live in the UK. A GP can refer you or, like I did, you can make contact via their 24-hour, free helpline for those in crisis. Although there may be a waiting list, I strongly urge you to look them up if you are in need. Search 'NHS Talking Therapy' and you'll find your way there.

The mental health charity Mind can also assist you with support. Visit www.mind.org.uk. You certainly won't need to go bankrupt or pay in oral to get the help you deserve.

PTSD, YEAH YOU KNOW ME

Another side of post-Controll is **PTSD**. Not everyone who escapes a coercive relationship will suffer from PTSD or disassociation. In fact, after a few weeks they may finally feel back to their old selves. That doesn't mean they're discounted from therapy. It's likely there's much to uncover under the surface. Yes, that's right, I'm talking to you.

PTSD, Post-traumatic Stress Disorder, is exactly as it sounds, an after-effect of a highly nerve-racking situation. Soldiers can suffer it and so can survivors of Controlls.

Think of it like this – you suddenly find yourself locked in solitary confinement with a very violent and aggressive guard, who tells you what to wear, intimidates you and convinces you that you're delusional. Then one day your 'stint' is over, and you're released. Do you think you could instantly, merrily function again in the outside world as if nothing had happened? I doubt it. Because coercive control, or in this analogy, being kept in solitary confinement, terrorizes you from the inside out. You would have found unique ways to cope, and your mind would have normalized this to try and protect you. Simply because that set of physical circumstances are eliminated doesn't mean you won't mentally return to these dark times.

Indirect effects of the stress suffered whilst in the hands of a Controll can present as depression, anxiety and PTSD.

What does PTSD do to a person? Well, PTSD can carry a wave of symptoms, and some may be very subtle and hard to spot. They could be things like:

- Nightmares
- Flashbacks
- Insomnia
- Intrusive thoughts
- Feeling jumpy and on edge
- Emotional outbursts such as upset or anger
- Sweating, tingling or tremors

Normally the symptoms develop a month or so after the traumatic event; however, there could be a delay of several months, or even years.[1] PTSD can affect day-to-day activities and you should always seek help from a trained professional if you notice indicators.

Many, many years after my first meeting with Irish Miss Honey I was living alone in a basement flat. At 5 a.m. on one dull morning I was woken by a thud. My curtains were thin and white, backlit from a housing estate on the other side. What I saw stopped my heart mid-beat. It was a satanic Punch and Judy. A Hitchcock where you can't hit 'stop'. The shadowy figure of a man trying to lift my bedroom window. Thankfully, after several attempts, he did not get in. But that didn't stop the subsequent weeks of flashbacks and stomach-flipping fear I felt in that flat. As the lease was coming to an end, I gladly moved out.

The terror of the attempted break-in would have been traumatic for anyone, but for me it was also linked to a deep-seated learned helplessness, which we covered earlier. That feeling of 'if I just lie here, soon it will stop'.

I am convinced that my many years of therapy prior to this allowed me to refind my grounding and cope far better than I would have done otherwise.

HOW TO BACK AWAY FROM THE EDGE

In life, shit happens that you can't prevent. You may get angrily shouted at by an uptight colleague, get into a disagreement with a drunk or even be harassed on the street. The only thing you can control is your reaction. If you survived a relationship with a Controll, it's probable you'll be on edge, perhaps fearing men and wary of any intense or aggressive situations. Now put yourself back in one of those 'shit-happening situations' above, as a survivor who hasn't taken the time to seek therapy. Can you see how something like that may just be the trigger that tips you over the cliff edge?

Therapy means you can:

Safely back away from the precipice.

Yes, you'd still be pushed closer to the drop by something unpleasant happening but, if you've had therapy, you're less likely to topple because you would have already been retreating to safer ground. Do you see? Here's a demonstration:

I'll be the first to tell you that if you escape a relationship with a Controll and don't take time to heal, another Controll in a new skin will soon be around the corner.

It's OK to be jumpy and fearful of aggression, especially after a run-in with a Controll. If you jam yourself back into a new relationship with no time and no therapy, you'll find unwanted remnants of your toxic ex cropping up. It's like washing a pair of jeans with a tissue in the pocket – that crap will get everywhere.

Trauma and post-trauma are nothing to be ashamed of. You don't need to hide and pretend nothing happened. In fact, I'm going to ask you to do the opposite:

OWN YOUR TRAUMA

It's part of you now so you may as well choose to accept and nurture it. Nurse it like you would a baby, really care for it. That means when it's squealing out for attention, take it to therapy, hear what it's asking you for. In time you'll actually be proud of it. See how strong you are because you gave it the love it deserves.

We're making great progress, right? Things are starting to look up.

Wait. Watch your back, babe.

This isn't over yet.

CHAPTER NINETEEN
BREAKING THE CYCLE

Hoovering and Cutting Ties

ONE MONTH AFTER THE RED WINE ANGEL.

I might start smoking again. Maybe try a little crack. Any other addiction to replace this emptiness. There's no point trying to substitute the longing with exercise, I haven't got the energy. I googled 'buy sedatives' the other day. I was thinking it could be the ideal way to erase the next three or so months. However long this miserable cold turkey takes.

Eight whole days without contact. Things ended a month ago. Four weeks since the Red Wine Angel and I've been coping fine. I guess that was down to the fact he'd been in touch on and off. Now it's all changed. This communication vacuum is a new level of pain. I've tried, I can't suck it up. This is the longest we haven't spoken in God knows how long. Most days have been spent in bed. I want to talk about him all the time, which is a shame because I have no one left to speak to.

I hate him but I love him. Emotional ambivalence. Except the two states don't cancel each other out, they coexist. He's my cancer and my cocaine. I wish I'd never taken that first hit.

Yesterday I forced my sorry ass to Sainsbury's and burst into tears in the aisle holding a meal for two, because it's now a meal for one. The state of me. I haven't seen a hairbrush in over a week. I've been wearing the same joggers for three days.

I've spent hours watching him pop up on WhatsApp. He's constantly online. He always was. When we were together, in a moment of weakness, I asked him about it and he looked at me, poker-faced, and said: 'What is wrong with you? It says "online" when the app is open. You sound insane.' Well, I got my friend Harveen to practise with me and that's actually not true. Who is he speaking to for all those hours? I play silly games with myself like: if I turn my phone on silent then he's guaranteed to message. No, wait, I'm going to switch it off for an hour and I bet he'll have texted. I never make it more than five minutes.

At the end, just after the Red Wine Angel, Damien held my face between his hands and told me everything would be all right, but I don't think even he believed it. In that moment I was back to the first night we met. There on the escalator staring deep into his eyes, trying to guess the future. So much promise. I can't imagine a world without him. Although it was tumultuous, terrifying at times, I was handling it. I could have kept handling it.

I'm in a shared flat now. I moved out of my studio. Too many memories. Damien is meant to be here. But now I live with Rachel, who insists I call her Ray-Ray. I hadn't met her

*before, I found her on Gumtree. She said she was an
'easy-going professional seeking female housemate for
occasional wine nights and a peaceful life'. Well, we've been
sharing for some time and there's been no wine night, just lots
of pass-ag notes like the one I found in the kitchen this
morning:*

PLEASE WIPE
CRUMBS UP
AFTER USING
TOASTER!!!!!!!!!
Ray-Ray
☺

*Nine exclamation marks. I know because I stood there and
counted them. Nine exclamation marks doesn't seem very easy-
going to me, Ray-Ray. To be fair, I don't think she expected to
move in with a cracked-out Casper. The way she's seen me –
pale-faced, floating out of my room to get water then scurrying
back. Must give her nightmares.*

*I haven't bothered telling 'Ray-Ray' . . . Hold on, I can't call
her that. It's making me queasy. I haven't bothered telling
Rachel about the Damien saga, she doesn't seem the sort to
understand. She stipulated she must have a flatmate who was
single because the last woman she lived with had her girlfriend*

over every night and, quote, 'soiled every surface with bum prints'. Last thing she needs to hear about is an erratic, demonic ex.

3.34 a.m.
Still awake. There's a weird underworld that comes alive at this time. You can find them on Twitter posting things like:

Anybody else up, or just me? #tired #yawn #cantsleep

And then many creatures of the night will scuttle into their replies:

Yes! Me! Talk to me I can't sleep #insomnia #helpme

I wonder if I should join in— oh God. It's him.

Hey. You still awake? Just seen you online . . .

I could cry! Damien! I ache for you. There's no point playing it cool, I might lose him all over. I reply:

Hi! Yes! Can't sleep. You OK? Xxx

4.10 a.m.
I'm sitting upright in bed wearing a full face of make-up and a cheap, synthetic nightie that's aggravating the rash I gave myself by dry shaving my bikini line.
I've told him not to ring the bell, I don't want to wake Rachel. Or her exclamation marks. I didn't think I'd be this nervous. The rule of thumb is: 98 per cent of the time, if you've

got to hide what you're up to from your friends, you probably shouldn't be doing it at all. Unless it's a surprise birthday party. Well, I wouldn't want a soul to know what I'm doing tonight so it's pretty clear what that means.

Drop call. He's here. I get a last-second wave of shame that I'm dressed so scantily and pull on a holey black sweater. I bet my hair's gone static.

He looks glum. He always looked glum. There's no small talk. We know what he's here for. I dressed up for it. Is that all I think I'm worth nowadays? I can't even pin the 'girlfriend' label to this sloppy shit show to retain a little dignity. This is perfect for him.

Gagging. Hands on chest. Around my neck. Spits. No love in his eyes. Was there ever? Am I only noticing this now?

He's yanking up his jeans. I got him those socks. Fred Perrys on. He knows I don't like shoes in the house. Why would he care? I can feel his semen drying on the inside of my thigh. I wipe what's still liquid on my Habitat bed sheet. I washed these yesterday. This is fucking grim. He's not even looking at me. Deathly quiet.

Is he summoning a . . .?

'Four minutes. Mercedes E-Class. Nice,' he mumbles to himself.

Should I get up?

'Why can't you stay?' I say. It comes out far more desperate than I'd hoped.

'I don't think that's a good idea.'

I don't think any of this is a good idea.

He moves his mouth in what I guess is supposed to be a smile but looks more like a grimace, opens my bedroom door then shuts it without a glance back. The yellow gown I picked up on our trip to Brighton falls off the hook.

I hear the front door slam. Rachel coughs from upstairs, meaning: 'I've been woken up and yes, I'll mention this in the morning.'

I come to at 9 a.m. Make-up smudged, contact lenses still in. I painfully peel them out, ghostly face, dehydrated skin. Dredged of everything.

Not even a 'thank you' text. The silver lining is, I'm far too gone to feel used. There's nothing more to take.

Will it always be like this? Cast aside, picked up and used when he needs to fill a hole and then flung aside. All I want is to give my love and feel someone else's. To be protected, supported, and know – I mean really know – that I'm not in this alone. That someone loves me enough to fold their world into mine.

Controlls are like boomerangs: they'll persistently rebound until your communication is permanently snapped.

I didn't block my Controll. Oh, sure, I told anyone who would listen that I had, but I did not think I was tough enough to actually do it. If only I could go back, lift the chin of my broken little soul, and say, 'Hey, honey – if you *don't* block them now then you best expect an avalanche of agony to bury you up to your neck very soon.'

It's 99.9 per cent impossible for there to be an amicable break-up with a Controll. There will not be a conversation that goes something like:

SFX. Birds chirping.

INT. Morning. The hallway of the house you share.
YOU stands, luggage by their feet.

YOU

I love you, but I can't do this any more.

CONTROLL

I love you too. I know this is toxic and I
respect your choices.

YOU

You're . . . you're OK with calling it a day?

CONTROLL

Of course. Thank you for all the good times.
I'll miss you but you can be sure I'll
disappear. I won't harass you for six months,
I certainly shan't spread false rumours and
there's not a chance I'll intimidate you to the
point of breakdown.

YOU

That's so thoughtful, thank you. (Beat.)
Goodbye.

CONTROLL

Goodbye.

CONTROLL vaporizes. YOU smiles, picks up suitcases and wanders out into the sunshine.

FADE.

Even in a non-Controll relationship these conversations are few and far between. There will always be heartache; it will be ugly. But with a Controll it's a different playground entirely. Over the months, years, decades you have been together, they have ensured that you leaving is an impossibility. They've gnarled your self-belief and obliterated your safety network.

HELL HATH NO FURY

Because you say it's over does not mean it's done. Even though you've been through the most gruelling time, you're battered and bruised. Take a deep breath. Because there's more.

Controlls need to feel superior. You ending things is one of the greatest embarrassments and they will do everything in their power to stop it. Everything. Hell hath no fury like a humiliated Controll.

It could be that they discarded you, as happened in my case. Well, guess what? Even if they dumped you, it *still* doesn't mean they'll let you be, they'll *still* find a reason to be indignant with rage.

BLOCK COCK

Let's say you're out (congratulations!). It doesn't matter how you escaped, if they left you, or vice versa. Freedom is close. But you aren't safe yet. Setting aside all the healing that you need to do in the future, in those first few days, weeks and months of separation you are extremely vulnerable.

There's one small step you can make to help ensure your future is non-toxic and you are as protected as possible.

Block them.

I mean it. On everything:

- WhatsApp
- Text and phone
- Email
- LinkedIn
- All social media

Be ruthless, leave no stone unturned. If you're a fresh escapee I know what you're thinking. There's a voice deep down saying, 'But . . . But I want them to get in touch. If I block them, how will they contact me to apologize?'

Scary how I know that, huh? I know it because that's exactly what I thought. When he discarded me, it was so frightening, so awful, that I couldn't possibly fathom it. I figured it was all a giant ruse, yet another instance where he'd threaten to leave, but really, he'd return. I was certain I'd rather cope with the pain of being with him than the agony of being without. Trauma bonding is real, and fuck me, it's painful when you go cold turkey.

Well, I'll let you in on a little secret. It's really nice on this side, post-Controll. It's light, tension-free and you won't sear your feet on red-hot coals. Come on, there's room for you, pull up a pew.

Ask yourself this:

- Do I want to stop repeating this tortuous cycle?
- Am I worth more than being intimidated, spat and sworn at?
- Wouldn't it be nice to be fear-free in my own home?

I hope the answer to all of those is a resounding YES. There's one promise you have to make in order to stop the cycle:

NOT EVEN ONCE

I never thought I'd be quoting Nancy Reagan, but here we are. Not even once: that means when you're out and safe you cut ALL TIES and do not communicate *even once*.

Let's go back to the idea that when in a relationship with a Controll, you become addicted to them like a drug. If you've managed a short time cold turkey, then one small hit – a text, a WhatsApp, sending a damn pigeon, will have you hooked all over. You'll think 'it's only a quick hello', but trust me:

When you take a tiny hit, it's game over.

Don't say I didn't warn you. These Master Manipulators know *exactly* which buttons to press, and let me tell you, this relapse will give you the most brutal comedown yet.

You're probably desperate for them to repent, see the error of their ways, learn to love you 'again' – but they won't, so you may as well make peace with that. You don't need their apology and hopefully you've understood by now, they cannot and will not change their ways.

SQUAD GOALS

I know what you're thinking. If you have a house or child with the Controll, how can you simply stop communicating? It's time to start building a network. Extricating yourself from a Controll is no mean feat and it's even more challenging to do alone. I know you've been isolated so you may think that rebuilding a support system will be next to impossible, but it isn't. To begin, you only need three main people to lean on. There's no need to be ashamed about asking for help.

It's time to assemble (please hum action theme tune) . . .

YOUR SAFETY SQUAD.
Your Safety Squad has three main positions open:

1. Safety Spokesperson: a trusted friend, police officer, lawyer, domestic abuse worker who is your go-to if* you need to communicate with your ex-Controll. (*Stop making excuses as to why you need to talk to them.)

2. Accountability Ally: a reliable person, this could be a friend, neighbour, relative, colleague, who you make a pact to be 100 per cent honest with and who you know will not judge you.

3. Compassionate Counsellor: it may take you a little while to find the right therapist, but stay with it. They will be a big part of your healing process.

These three main team members are going to be your ticket to a Controll-free life.

I write this with bitter experience. I was certain I could handle things alone. Yes, my family did all they could to help, but I was resistant for a long time. Hindsight is a beautiful thing and had I allocated a Safety Squad from the off then the many months of Hoovering . . . and what you're about to find out post Red Wine Angel, most likely would not have happened. Use me as your mistake, make the right choice.

SUCKER PUNCH

All righty, so we're in agreement that blocking them and building your Safety Squad are the best moves towards healing. That's not enough, we need to be smarter. Even if you block them, barricade yourself in a steel fortress or choose to live the rest of your life down a dark well, that Controll won't be done with you yet. You are too good to fully dispose of. There's always more fun to have with people in the eyes of a Controll.

Remember, they need others to function; without them, they are nothing.

Once upon a time, you served as their elite ego masseuse, boy you were really good at that job. I'm talking world class. When the dust has settled after the break-up, they could perform what's known as:

THE HOOVER MANOEUVRE

Hoovering and the Hoover Manoeuvre are terms coined to illustrate how Controlls start sucking you back in once you've managed to escape. They want you for another round, another cycle of abuse. Even if they were the ones who disposed of you, it won't be long until they remember that ego massage and start finding ways to manipulate you again.

Don't think for a second they'll be shiny, reformed versions of themselves (even if they convince you they are). Oh no.

Here are some of the ways they may attempt the Hoover Manoeuvre:

Emotional blackmail
This could be anything to pull at your heartstrings. 'I am lost without you', 'You were the best thing I ever had.' Whatever makes you care about your poor baby Controll.

Threats of harm
Threats of hurting themselves, threats against you or your children. You must *always* take these seriously, don't pass it off as 'they don't have it in them'. Trust me, they do. Call the police if you think you or your children are in danger.

Threats of taking their life

Telling you they can't live without you, saying it's your fault and they are going to end their life. As above, always take these threats seriously. Call the police and give them as much information as possible. BUT they are still not your responsibility. Do not go to them.

Minimizing master

They'll make sure to downplay what happened. Gaslighting, what are you doing here? We didn't miss you. They may say things like, 'Sorry if I was a bit mean', or 'We only had a few small arguments'. You'll begin to wonder again if it really was all in your head, if you made it worse than it was. It isn't and you didn't.

Sudden illnesses

They may tell you they are suffering with a disease, have broken their leg, sprained their ankle, or hurt themselves. Nothing is out of the question. Their sole aim with this is to make you empathize and end your silence. Don't. If they are unwell, it is not up to you to care for them.

Pedestal push

It will miraculously dawn on them that you are incredible. They will tell you, or get a friend to let you know, how highly they think of you. Suddenly 'repentance' is their middle name, how could they have been so foolish? They will flatter you, tell the world how wonderful you are and make you believe it will be a fairy tale if you get back with them. Sorry to burst your bubble: it won't.

Financial abuse

They'll magic up money that you owe them, or it could be possessions of theirs you have that they desperately need. You may even hear them throw around the word 'thief'. They will try and frighten you with pressures of court, police, bailiffs – do not crumble. If you do have anything that belongs to them, your Safety Spokesperson can offer to return it in a public place, or have it sent to them.

Overblown gifts

Oh, hi there, old friend, we remember you from the very start. What does that signpost say? 'Love-bombing part II'. Huge bouquets, showy presents, designer goods, gold-wrapped Swiss chocolates, overstated displays of affection. Anything to try and destabilize you and lull you into thinking a new relationship with them will be roses and caviar.

Advice needed

They require guidance in order to proceed with their life. People love to be asked for advice, it makes them feel special, but when your Controll asks you 'how the heating works', if you could 'help them understand a bill', or 'use the washing machine', don't fall for it. There are advantageous tools we call 'search engines' that can answer almost any question.

'The new partner'

'Hmm,' they think, 'none of my Hoover Manoeuvres seem to be sucking up anything decent, let's try this one.' It's human nature to display a little healthy jealousy. No doubt, over the course of your relationship you were made to feel delusional that they were cheating. Now they may showcase their 'new-found love' on social media or happen to parade them in front of your workplace. Take a deep breath. What they enjoy most is the false superiority of people fighting over them.

Choose peace, let them go.

The friend

If you've blocked them (as we made a pact you would), the Controll will struggle to contact you. This doesn't mean they'll give up. You may have mutual friends, even relatives of yours who are misinformed and still talking to them. These manipulating moguls will use their power to get your mutual acquaintance to sweet talk you into communicating. Gently explain that unless they want to chat to you about something else, you are not in a position to have a conversation. If they can't understand what you went through, or you don't want to speak to them (which is totally fine), then leave and surround yourself with a squad who truly have your best interests at heart.

If I was to say the single main thing that helped me move from trauma to tranquil it would be: **HONESTY**.

You must be truthful with at least one member of your Safety Squad. That means if you communicate with and/or lose your nerve and agree to meet your ex-Controll, *you tell someone in your squad.*

This may seem like you're gifting control of your life just as you're starting to reclaim it, but it's not. This squad are only necessary for the first six-ish months after leaving. This is a period of time when you are the most targetable, prime for a second Controll swipe. Being transparent with someone you trust will help keep you safe and ensures you take an extra moment to question if the action you're about to take is conducive to the life you deserve.

IT'S DECISION TIME

It's natural to feel unsteady after a break-up of any kind, but especially with a Controll. Be careful, any one of the tactics above could floor you. You may be suffering with panic attacks, your emotions in disarray, intrusive thoughts that will only remind you of the good times; their words that you'll 'always be alone' and you 'aren't good enough' echo in your ears. Journal to remind yourself of the terror, tension and torment. It's natural for us to want to recollect happy memories but when you really think about it, they all came at a cost.

Keep as sharp as you can to the Hoover Manoeuvre. Hopefully, now you know the telltale signs, you can flag them and file them as spam. Ultimately, though, the decision is yours . . .

Short-term gain for long-term pain
OR
Short-term pain for long-term gain.

Make your choice. You may think reinstating communication with them is the quick pain-release you so frantically crave, but it will only end in lasting pain.

Shoulder the hurt, keep strong and maintain your fight temporarily for the enduring gain of a healthy, happy and free life.

The option is yours.

OCTOPUSSY

What's our eight-legged pal got to do with Controlls? Well, as momentarily marvellous as the Hoover Manoeuvre may have made you feel, it should come as no surprise that you aren't the only one they are hoovering. Oh no, the more sources they can siphon, the better. They can't get enough. When you feel hopeful that they are finally giving you their undivided attention, this is actually what they are doing:

Many fingers in many pies, many hoovers between many thighs. It's important you know of the Controll's tentacular ways, not because I'm trying to make you feel worse, but because I want you to be crystal clear about the fact that:

Their words are meaningless.

The sooner you know that, the less likely you are to fall for them. I was sequentially suckered. Time and time again. Every instance I responded to my Controll's Hoover Manoeuvres, I thought it would be the moment he'd fall right back in love with me. Instead, I was treated to microcosms of what we once had, the love-lacking sex, the rage, the happy times, and repeat.

BOOZE BLUES AND THE CONTROLL HOLE

Soon after the Red Wine Angel, the reality of what had happened became so raw I had to find a way to numb myself. I was drinking and partying more and more.

This is not unusual for victims. When one addiction leaves, we want to fill that Controll Hole. It could be shopping, alcohol, gambling, drugs. The original addiction – the Controll – although terrible for us, gave us an aptitude for desensitizing. Remember the chemicals in the Cycle of Abuse?

Whilst it is true that men who abuse alcohol or drugs are six or seven times more likely to be perpetrators of domestic abuse,[1] what we often forget about are the victims who self-medicate to anaesthetize from what is happening to them.

Alcohol is the easiest to attain drug in the world. You can get it, day or night, without so much as a second look from the cashier. But boozing to escape is a slippery slope. I like the analogy that Allen Carr uses in *The Easy Way to Stop Drinking* where he likens alcohol to a pitcher plant. A pitcher plant is carnivorous, it lures insects in with its sweet-smelling nectar. Once a bug is halfway down, enjoying all the sickly goodness, they realize they've fallen further than they intended and it's become virtually impossible to get out.

When you're in a relationship with a Controll, your nerves are frayed, and you are counting down until the next time they become emotionally or physically violent and lose their temper. You are understandably left shaken and stressed from the build-up and release of their aggression. Alcohol has long been a way to try and relieve stress. There are several studies which look at chronic stress and drug use and addiction, all drawing the conclusion that the two are inextricably linked.[2]

Alcohol is a depressant of the central nervous system, which means for a short time it does ease anxiety by slowing your heart rate. However, when you're already strapped into the hormonal helter-skelter of a Controll relationship, you're dealing with a hell of a lot of chemical signals telling you that you're under fire. When you add alcohol into the mix, that chemical imbalance is yet more vigorously swirled. If you are turning to alcohol every time the Controll has you feeling unbalanced (which will be shit loads), then you are stepping very close to the risk of dependence.

It took me a long time to figure this out. It wasn't until many years later that a random cracker in the street started yelling and swearing in my face and I went home and had a strong desire for alcohol to calm down. I recognized how linked high-pressure, violent situations and alcohol were for me. It's possible to work through this dependence, but it takes time. I'm not an

AA counsellor, but if you are worried you have a problem with alcohol or drugs, you can visit www.nhs.uk/live-well/alcohol-support or www.alcoholics-anonymous.org.uk for non-judgemental and free advice. You can also raise any concerns with your GP, a trusted friend, or find local support via www.alcoholchange.org.uk.

There's no shame in saying alcohol, drugs or something else has become an issue. Don't hide it – air it and get the support you deserve. I've been there – I'm right here with you.

It may not seem so yet, but post-Controll is a very exciting place to be. We've gone through it and we're about to be stronger for it. This is the start of your journey to a new, safer and infinitely happier you.

OK. I've avoided this long enough.

I was in such a state I thought I could be hallucinating, but the purple plastic beaker still at the back of my junk cupboard tells me different.

It's time you encountered them too.

Red Wine Angel, Jesús. There's someone here to say hi.

CHAPTER TWENTY
THE RED WINE ANGEL
How to Leave Your Psychopath

THE NIGHT OF THE RED WINE ANGEL.

I want to kill you. I want to be dead.

I'm on life support. You're playing with the mains lead like it's no more than a phone cable.

A tempest is brewing. It's rolling in. The air is dense. I wish you'd sit with me and we'd watch it pass together, Damien. You look through me, not at me. I'm nothing but an inconvenience. An obstacle you skirt around. A misplaced cone on the M25 about to get splintered by an HGV.

How did we end up like this? When I look in the mirror, hollow eyes stare back, turned dark like yours. Whatever you have is infectious. I used to be able to love. I was kind and compassionate, but I'm empty now. No room for empathy.

I exist.

I know something is coming because you've stopped caring about your traces. The Viagra, the messages, the condoms. All

317

signs of a sordid life outside of us. Hidden in plain sight. They were always there, but I grew to accept them. Made them my fault. Gulped down with a large glass of cheap rosé from the corner shop.

You're sitting on our sofa as I pack our lives into cardboard boxes. But you aren't really here though, are you, Damien? Not emotionally. Checked out, caught the last train, and ripped up the return.

When I think of our good times my breath catches in my throat. I reimagine you, on that same sofa, head in my lap, permitting me to hold you, letting me tell you everything was going to work out. Twisting your red hair around my fingers. Tracing my fingers over your nose and lips. You let me in.

But not now.

I try and make noise whilst I pack, hoping you'll shake off whatever you're thinking. How very British. Obviously, I could just ask: 'Damien, love, so sorry to bother. I've been packing our things for four straight hours, it'd be wonderful if you got off your arse and helped.' I can't, though.

I can't because we're treacherously treading the threshold. Threshold of what? I'm not sure yet. You're not angry. If you were seething, I'd know what to do. But we're past that. This is disturbingly alien. There's just nothingness.

In a few days we move into the flat you wanted. It's meant to be our bright, new beginning, but you can't even be bothered with the ending. Let it happen, Damien. Release whatever you're holding onto. Whoever she is. We could have it all. Why can't you see that?

He gets up and places his phone on charge next to where I stand. No, no, no. This isn't what's supposed to happen. Is he trying to show me the other women? I know, Damien. I don't want to see.

Charlotte Sudbury calling

Please, Damien. I can live with it, I'll keep pretending I don't know. I won't survive. He glances at me, then the phone. Did he plan this? Did he message and get her to call? Deliberately wanting me to see?

He grabs the mobile. He's barely out the room:

'Babe, I can't talk right now.'

The front door opens and closes. I hear his conversation peter out as he heads down the stairs.

Damien. Don't.

I grip the fake black marble countertop to steady myself. I suppose this feeling is meant to be anger, or jealousy, but there's nothing.

When you're in a relationship that swallows you from the inside I swear you get ultra-senses. Your hearing becomes a superpower as you strain to judge what's happening behind your back. Struggle to deduce the mood they're in. Always ready. No relaxing. Need to know what's next. Hypervigilance.

He's coming back up. Padding the beige carpet. He left his key. It's here. I see it. Sitting on top of the microwave. This could be it! Ridiculous thoughts of me deciding never to open the door flood my brain. I could live here alone again in my studio flat, amongst the boxes. He would leave and I would heal.

Before I know it, I'm turning the fingerprint-smeared gold latch. Even though he's a mere foot in front of me, he avoids my gaze. Look. At. Me. Damien. He heads to the kitchen and pulls his trench coat from behind the door.

Where is he going? Damien. Look. At. Me.

'I . . . I can't do this any more. I don't want . . . this.' He waves his hand in the air like I'm a bad smell.

No, he doesn't get to do this. He doesn't get to suck me dry then be the one to leave. Surely there's some unwritten rule that the last shred of dignity – saying goodbye – comes from the one most wronged?

'OK,' I say.

OK? Is that it. Panic surges. Moments after that cool-sounding 'OK' I'm shuddering, weeping. Brought to my knees by emotion. I always thought it was fake when they did it on the soaps. Real hammy acting. But it turns out that's exactly what happens.

He doesn't come to me. Hands outstretched on the lino at his feet. A poor, pathetic pool of past.

'I need a cigarette.'

He must've left.

I have to keep packing. We're moving in the morning. So much to do. I couldn't find the kitchen spray to scrub the fridge. I can't use that cream stuff because it'll leave marks. I stand and grab a J-cloth and some cleaner. It's an under-counter fridge so I have to kneel, that's fine for me. I'm unsteady so it works being closer to the floor. Fuck. This is polish. I've sprayed furniture polish in the fridge. Fuck sakes.

I smell the cigarette smoke clinging to his clothes before I see him. He says I look crazy down here. I stick my head further into the fridge. The bloody plastic egg carton things are impossible to remove.

'Fucking listen. I'm talking to you.'

So much to do. Should I have defrosted before I did the freezer?

He kicks the fridge door which bounces off my head.

In that nanosecond I've had enough. Rage swoops up my body like vertigo. I'm dizzy with it.

I'm so fucking angry. I duck out of the fridge and stand. Feel his breath on my forehead. His stupid fucking blank face. 'Fuck you, Damien. You fucking, womanizing piece of shit. I hope you get what you deserve.'

'What's that?' he sneers. Effortlessly cold.

I've never been this livid. Never sworn at him like this. I don't do that. But he's pushed me to every limit. Enough. Enough sneaking around, making me feel worthless, intimidating me. I've carefully edged around his moods for years, now he can try it. God, I'm so mad, I'm scaring myself. This is the aggression he continually warned I had. Hah. Well, seems you finally manifested it, Damien. I could punch him straight in his condescending mouth.

'Go on then, hit me,' he mocks, as if reading my raging thoughts.

His words jolt me back to the present.

I see me. This is what I've said. So many times. Woeful, non-violent me. 'Go on then, hit me.' Terrified but defiant, I uttered that exact phrase. Because if he did hit me, I would leave. Wouldn't I? But he never did. And I never left. He was smarter than that. Stealthy supremacy snaked around my soul.

He has destroyed me. Mercilessly destroyed me.

All that justified anger vaporized by five little words. Go. On. Then. Hit. Me.

Halfway down the stairs now. Hands in the pocket of my old uni hoodie. Leavers 2010. Pyjama bottoms. Trodden-down Reeboks. I'm having some weird out-of-body experience as if all the pain and tension from the past few years has made me mad. He did warn me I was insane. Perhaps this is it. The grip of lunacy.

Outside. It's dark. It's the kind of fine rain you can only see when you look up at a street light, illuminated in a soft haze.

I stand in the middle of the road and I'm wailing. Actually wailing like a professional mourner. Or some bonkers banshee from the eighth century. It's like it isn't happening. A parallel dimension. I drift up and observe this broken woman from above in her hysteria. I'm sure I'll rejoin her and return upstairs shortly. Look at Damien vacantly like nothing even transpired.

I pull out my phone, desperate for . . . I don't know what. Scrolling through the numbers, there's someone I know I need to hear. Someone I've shut out. A man who has been there for me since the day I was born. My greatest protector, if only I'd been able to let him in.

Calling: Dad

I have no idea what time it is. What I'm planning to say.

'Hi, Mad?' His voice breaks me again, but for a totally opposite reason. I can't even begin to tell you what I say, I utter singular words. He thinks I've been raped. In a way, he's not wrong.

An hour goes by, maybe two. Damien is still up in our flat.

What once was my flat. All I can focus on is the rain dripping off my nose mixed with tears. My dad represents a fishing line of strength. We make a plan, I'll pack a bag then come home. Even though I agree, I can't face it. Damien and I are moving to our new house in days. The removal van tomorrow. The promise of returning to calm. It's all capsized.

I sit on the wet pavement and feel the dirtied water seep into my thin, checked pyjama bottoms. A sadistic Love Actually. Where's the fucking man with the placards?

A car zips past, splashing me with a filthy puddle.

I want it to be over.

I try and picture what's ahead. Where I'll live, how to put myself back together. Then it comes to me: maybe there is no ahead. I try and fathom what my parents would do without me. They don't know a quarter of what's gone on. I can't even wrap my head around it.

I'm so deep in dark thought I barely notice two cream, fluffy slippers float next to me. When I do, I jerk and crane my neck up.

The figure is wrapped in a maroon fleecy dressing gown with bare legs. So close I can see the stubble. The street lamp is directly above them so their hood casts a shadow over their face. In their hand, a purple plastic beaker. Like something you'd take camping. A voice drifts out. A warm, northern drawl.

'Not be rude or nothing but I heard you. Crying an' that. I wa'nt listening, mind. I thought you might need . . .'

The figure leans forward, their face still obscured, and hands me the beaker.

'S'red wine. All I had.'

I stare down at the opaque liquid in this child's cup, unsure what to say.

'I . . . I don't like red wine.'

What? That's it!

'Sorry, I don't know why I said— I'm not thinking straight.'

'You're all right,' the Red Wine Angel says, with a little laugh. ''Ere, have a fag too.' The Red Wine Angel pulls a bent roll-up and lighter from their fuzzy pocket and stoops to offer again.

I look at these two objects in my hand, all social skills out the window. The lighter reads: BUY YOUR OWN FUCKING LIGHTER. At that very moment it's the funniest thing I've ever seen. Tears turn to chuckles. I can't stop myself.

'You're all right,' Red Wine Angel reassures me for a second time. Drying my laughter to titters and then silence.

''Ave a drink. 'Ave a smoke then go back and live ya life, hen. No one's worth this. You're OK.'

I put the roll-up in my mouth and struggle for a few moments with the lighter. When the cigarette is finally lit, I take a long draw. It's heaven. I watch a spindle of silver smoke kink in front of me. I follow it skyward with my eyes and realize the Red Wine Angel is gone. All I see is that misty rain catching in the glow of the light. I haul myself to my feet, sodden trousers sticking to the pavement.

The Red Wine Angel is nowhere.

I walk out into the middle of the road and look up and down the street, but it's dead. Not even a fox. So silent, I am deafened by it.

I twist to look behind me at the flat, our flat.

The lights are on but nobody's home.

The damp roll-up falls from my fingers. It's so quiet I can hear it sizzle as it hits the wet tarmac.

Now it's just me.

Suddenly, something happens that to this day I struggle to put into words. I'm hit with a sensation I have never experienced in my life. The only way to describe it is like being lifted from above but my feet stay firmly planted on the ground.

This isn't some hippy religious cult shit. Yeah, I know I'm drained, drunk on emotion, but there's something going on. It's other-worldly.

For the last four years I've been tied by my ankles to a truck driven by Damien. Anytime he chose to slip it into third and career over rocky terrain he could. I was at his mercy. Sometimes, I could actually describe it as fun, yet all the while I knew it was his foot on the accelerator. But now the ignition is off.

In this space, this new stillness, I'm washed with an awareness that makes my shoulders drop from my ears. So clearly, I comprehend:

'He doesn't love you because he can't love you.'

I physically spin on the spot. I don't know what I'm expecting to see. But I have to do a full 180.

All at once I get it: Damien isn't capable of love. It feels transactional because that's all people serve as to him: things. Not beings with overflowing hearts.

Things.

I guess you could call it some kind of enlightenment.

Standing there, in soggy pyjamas and holey trainers with the backs broken down, the words of the Red Wine Angel reverberate inside my head: You're all right. You're OK.

The morning after.

He sits on the other side of the room, eating the Meal Deal I carefully selected because I knew moving day would be hectic. I didn't envision it would be cataclysmic.

I watch him drag a piece of rocket from his mouth and drape the slug of its half-chewed remnants on the cardboard sandwich packet. Still chewing, he opens a bottle of Coke. I wish I'd shaken it.

My prawn sandwich sits next to me, overheating in the morning sun. Dewy beads form on the inside of the plastic. He lets out a small burp and screws his rubbish into the open backpack at his feet.

Now what? Are we waiting for him to finish his food and then it's officially over? Is that how this works?

The removal man is nearly an hour late. I pick up my phone to call him again. Straight to voicemail.

I slept about thirty minutes last night. I can't imagine taking all these boxes down the stairs. It's like doing a full day shift after a bender. The thought alone makes me shudder.

Last night, as I lay in our bed for what I thought was one final time, I heard Damien ripping open sealed boxes and callously extracting his belongings. I should have seen the signs. Was it me? Would it have been different if I hadn't asked him to move into my studio to 'see how it went'? If I'd kept some distance? When I look at him there, with three bin bags of his belongings from a whole flat, next to thirty neatly labelled boxes of my things, I want to smack my head against the wall. His paltry possessions compared to a mountain of mine. If ever there was a symbol of how much I gave him, and what he offered in return, it's this.

My phone rings. I haven't saved the number, but I guess it's the removal man. He has a deep Mexican accent and sounds like he's just woken up.

"Ello, you called?' His voice is faraway and grainy.

'Yes, a removal today in Seven Sisters, it's Maddy.' I'm so exhausted, my voice is no more than a whisper.

In that second, I'm taken back to the day Damien moved in with me. Me merrily puffing up the stairs, Damien grumbling about the ascent behind. It's not even that warming a memory but still tears prickle my eyes. The removal man is still on the line muttering some excuse about mixing up days and the clocks changing. He'll be there in thirty, he says.

I hang up and wipe my eyes with the sleeve of my grey hoodie, leaving dark gunmetal stripes. Damien is tapping away on his phone. Totally detached. Totally impassive.

'The removal man will be here in half an hour,' I say meekly. Damien doesn't look up but nods.

'Do you need a hand?' he says. Is he for real? Do I need a hand cleaving my life from yours?

What's obliterating me is his total lack of empathy. Transactional.

'No. I'm fine,' I say. Classic 'I'm-fine-ing' when, in reality, I'm buckled, gripping my knees as I crouch on the rubble of my life.

'OK. Well, we'll meet soon. Once this is . . .' He hasn't even got it in him to finish his sentence.

I need him to say this isn't forever.

'Maybe in a few weeks, or . . . ?' I don't care how desperate I sound.

'Yeah. Yeah, definitely,' he says, standing and grabbing all

three bin bags in one hand then launching his backpack onto his shoulder.

It's all so futile. Four years. Flattened. He may as well put me in one of those bags and sling me out for tomorrow's rubbish collection. Tears free-fall down my face. I can tell it's making him uncomfortable. He hates it when I cry. For once, I don't hide it.

He walks over, dumps the bin bags on the floor and holds my blotchy face between his hands. A role reversal of what I wanted to do all those years ago on the escalator.

'It's going to be all right,' he says half-heartedly. He's moved on to his next acquisition and I'm stalling him for time.

He can't love me. That's what's hurting the most.

His phone pings, he pulls it from his pocket, glances down, then picks up the bags again.

Then, just like that, I'm alone with his ghost.

Heaving, guttural sobs emerge from my stomach. I don't even compute at this point how much he's facilitated that everything starts and ends with him; and now it's ended, there is no beginning. Like a master craftsman, all memories conceived, opinions stated, actions made, were not mine. He's warped the eyes I see out of, and now that he's discarded me, I'm blind.

I'm startled by the buzzer in the hallway. I stumble to my feet and head to the door, lifting the receiver. It could be Damien, he's changed his mind, wants to forget any of this happened.

'Maddy? It's Jesús.'

What the fuck? Is someone trying to make me lose my mind? It's too late for that. First the Red Wine Angel, now Jesús? I'm not even religious. Moses'll be delivering a Hawaiian next.

A high-pitched reverb emits from the speaker. It makes me grimace.

'Removal?' the voice says over the crackle.

I realize who it is and press the entry button. 'Sixth floor, sorry there's no lift.'

A few hours later and I'm sitting in the front of Jesús's messy Luton van. He's having a very loud, in-depth conversation on his Bluetooth. I don't mind. I can't face him talking to me.

He has shoulder-length dark, long curls and tanned skin. Really smashing that Jesus look. I'm in a daze, mindlessly watching a bobbing Our Lady with an oversized head stuck to the dash, her arms outspread.

He has an A4 piece of paper stuck to the inside window. I translate the reverse wording. It says:

Removal, Man in Van.
Discount service.
Jesús Saves

I'm sure the irony is not lost on him. Jesús finishes his call, removes one of his earphones and turns to me.

'Everything going in storage?'

I bite my lip, desperately trying not to crumble in front of this stranger. He glances from the road to me again. 'You OK, miss?'

All I can manage is a nod. I look at the satnav and see fifteen minutes until we arrive at the storage unit. Fifteen minutes is a long time to hold this in.

I decide it's best to give up. 'No. I'm not,' I say. Then it all comes tumbling out. Whilst I'm bawling and waving my hands in the air, Jesús shakes his head, wrinkles his brow, nodding faster than Mary, taking it all in, deeply immersed. When I run out of steam, I see the Big Yellow Storage sign up ahead.

'Shall I go round again?' he asks. 'S'OK,' I reply, no capacity to be ashamed.

Jesús drives the Luton up the ramp and turns the ignition off.

'Lady,' he says, turning to me. 'Some of these guys they filled with hate, you know? Angry, fighting all the time, evil spirits, if you wanna believe that. No good for anyone. A woman gotta be your queen. If you stay around these ones too long, they kill you.' He draws an ominous cut-throat gesture across his neck, like Bill on the train. 'Maybe not for real, but make you wish you were dead, you know?'

Jesús had nailed it. Excuse the pun.

The open wound in my chest seals ever so slightly. This man, Jesús, has shown me more understanding, hospitality and compassion than I've had in years from Damien.

Without a fuss, Jesús helps me Tetris my boxes into the storage unit. When I need to stop, he takes a pre-rolled cigarette from a rusty tin in his top pocket and leans against the brick wall outside. He hands one to me. Looks like I smoke again. The whole job takes far longer than it should have done, but he doesn't mind. Here is the most empathetic man gifting me room to speak and silence to compute.

When I'd invented the last job I could think of to keep Jesús with me, I take £100 out of an ATM, fold and give it to him. He shakes his head, but I push it into his hand.

I know what's next and I have no idea how I'll face it. As I watch the broken tail lights of his Luton pootle down the road, *then disappear from sight, I'm more alone than ever.*

*Earlier that day, Jesús had waited outside Crum & Co.
Estate Agents whilst I dropped two sets of keys off and checked
out. What they didn't know was that I had an extra 'safety' set
clasped deep in my pocket. I had no idea what I would do with
them but appreciated the option.*

*I'm glad I kept them. Even for one last look at our old flat. I
pull out the shiny key, grab the handle of my purple suitcase,
look up and down the street then head inside.*

*The flat is cavernous. I see marks on the floor where my
table and desk once sat. The only furniture that remains is the
sofa and white goods. Greasy marks the size of a penny spot
the walls: they once held motivational posters like 'YES YOU
CAN' and 'H IS FOR HAPPY'. Blueprints to a former life.*

*I'm spaced out. Feeling like I may faint, I quickly slump on
the couch. My worn black handbag containing a lip balm,
purse, my charger, and uneaten, now soggy sandwich is next to
me. My battered purple suitcase stands at the door, containing
a few changes of clothes, some wash things, and an old pair of
Converse. Ample, I thought, to last me the few days before
heading to what was meant to be our new life.*

*I'm staring at the space where the TV was as if there's some
mind-numbing reality show to distract me. Evening is drawing
in. I'm afraid to turn on the lights; I'm not supposed to be here,
the landlord could come anytime. It's nearly 9 p.m. There's no
way anyone will visit now, is there?*

*I'm like a dog who's been dumped in a cardboard box at the
side of the road. Rejected because they are no longer cute or
fun to play with.*

There's no bedding here, it's all in storage. The longer I'm in

our empty flat, the more frightening the outside seems. I keep
hearing footsteps. What will I say if the agent or landlord
comes in? 'Apologies I'm still here, my partner decimated my
life, is it OK if I have a kip?'

My phone vibrates and startles me. It's Dad calling again.
I've been so absorbed, prioritizing getting my things in
storage, that I hadn't checked in with him. 'We're all worried,'
he says. I'm suddenly comforted ever so slightly with an
awareness of the love that was always there, but I was too
smothered to see: the love of my family. I reassure him I'm
fine, I'm safe. I'll come home soon. I don't know whether
that's true, but it soothes me, and I think my dad too. I make
a promise to call in the morning, but now I am too spent to
speak.

I edge across the now dark, vacuous living room and take
the black cardigan out of my suitcase. I lie on the sofa,
attempting to drape it over myself, and somehow, at some hour,
manage to fall asleep.

Did you know that the first few microseconds after you wake
up you can be clinically insane? I don't know where I read that.
As I come round, pain shoots into my temples, I'm dehydrated
and stiff. Did I drink last nigh— Oh fuck. The weight of where
I am and the events that unfolded hit me like a mallet. Thunk.
Straight between the eyes.

I slowly sit up. I'm weak and wobbly. Haven't eaten for days.
No messages or calls from him. Zero concern.

That moist prawn sandwich keeps me going for a further
three days. With no cups I drink straight from the tap. I ration
the last roll of loo paper and, with no towel, I use an old
T-shirt to dry myself after tragic sink washes. It's like a poor

man's SAS Survival. Could probably teach Bear Grylls some things. I'll start using the bed legs for firewood soon.

I'm living in a paranoid, hallucinogenic state, certain Damien, the estate agent or the landlord will come knocking. I learn a new way of doing things. Squatting in the shadows. I can't bear to face anyone. I don't want anyone to see me. To see what I've let him do to me.

I call my dad and twin, doing my best to assure them I'm OK. I hear myself say 'it's a passing moment', 'just a blip'. I don't feel like that, though. This is not only a break-up. This is the dogged degradation and manipulation of an individual and the decision to toss that person once they're too crippled. But that is not a thought that articulates in my mind for a very long time. In this moment, I live on second-by-second empty promises to my family that all is well. The Queen of Minimizing.

Still no messages or calls.

On the morning of day four, I spend over an hour dredging up the courage to vacate the flat. I can't remain in this quasi-existence. With close to 500 deep breaths, another sit-down because I've made myself all spacey with the deep breathing, and then a heave up again, I eventually leave.

I close the door and post the keys through the letterbox, blinking into the early autumnal sun.

I walk down our street.

This street.

For the very last time.

Days become weeks, and weeks become months. Although the Red Wine Angel and Jesús marked the end, it doesn't mean

Damien and I are done. Perhaps, had I known this in my sorry squatting state, I would have picked myself up. It could have been nice back then to kid myself Damien & Maddy II HD was potentially incoming.

Damien starts getting back in touch. At first, it's the odd 'hello', which I grab, still nowhere near healed. His 'hellos' graduate to late-night, soulless sex visits. He comes, cums then cut and runs. I allow it. Feeling wretched, used and dirty, swearing it'll be the last time, but he tempts me with flashes of the high highs from our relationship, enough for the door to be opened again.

Autumn turns to winter, winter to spring, and then summer arrives. It's been almost twelve whole months since the Red Wine Angel.

Though Damien and I are not officially together any more, I am certainly not rehabilitated. I still bounce unhappily from the pittance Damien offers in the form of sex, piteously impersonating some form of what we had. I bury myself in hedonistic, wild nights out, unable to face any stark truth of the situation. I sprinkle every conversation with 'I'm fine's. My days are hangovers, comedowns dangling on the fake existence I lost with Damien. There is no joy.

Damien and I had a separation practice run. Eight agonizing days of nothingness, broken by one more soulless sex visit. Now he's been away on a business trip for almost six weeks. Six whole weeks.

Without grasping what's happening, each day I wake a little freer, marginally less broken. When his name pings into my WhatsApp messages weeks later, my heart does not flutter. I don't somersault over the bed to grab my phone. I do not have to steady my breath. I also don't reply. The more distance that's formed between us, the more I'm ready to live without him. I am very, very slowly starting to see my worth. I conclude that if morsels are all he's offering, I'd rather do without.

Damien does not like this. In a matter of days, his messages come in thick and fast. I can track his feverish rage, growing more violent by the second. Grateful not to be in his presence this time, I try to shut it out, but it's like a loud siren zooming past when you're on the phone. It gets in. Stops everything. Takes centre stage and deafens you.

I'm afraid. He's unpredictable and, though he left me, in his eyes my not responding is turning the tables for vengeance. It is making him ferocious. The truth of it is that I just want it to stop. I don't want revenge. I never wanted retribution. I want it to be over. His messages are blazing and constant. I do my best to extinguish them.

One day, when he rings, I'm weak, I pick up. He calls me every name under the sun, and spits vitriolic, wild allegations, nonsensical venom. I take the phone away from my ear, too terrified to hang up. But I listen; it's self-harm. There's a part of me that is still latched on, thinking I deserve this. He's a madman, now loose.

Then it appeared. I pre-empted it. Although I didn't know exactly what 'it' would be, what the final curtain would hold. But I understood him well enough to know he would not go quietly.

It was a demand for money. Over £2,000 in total. He had placed amounts in my bank account to help me pay the rent for the flat he didn't stay in, due to leaving me the night before moving. It was a flat where he was named on the contract. On *top of that, over the past few months, in order to keep that 'plaything' door open, he'd often deposited small sums into my account. I'd always been anxious about taking them but pinioned by debt. Promising repayment with half-baked IOUs – written more for my own sanity that one day I'd be strong enough to get out. Each time I was effectively being paid for sex, but degradation was long overshadowed by his other actions. This was the money he threatened I now owed him.*

In the cold, hard light of day, his inflammatory accusations of me being a 'coked-up thief' were ludicrous and would have no place in a court of law. But days of unstoppable terrorizations continue. He does not get tired, whereas I am a broken, paranoid outline of my former self, now in huge arrears. He threatens he will ruin me. Doesn't he get that he did that long ago?

In a desperate state I make a call that I'm not sure I'll be here to even follow up. Doggedly crawling into bed.

One morning, at 5 a.m., I awake, officially annihilated. I decide this is my end.

I can't do it any more. I can't pay him; I will never escape. This state is a carbon copy of the night of the Red Wine Angel; twelve months have passed and, in reality, very little has changed. I know there is only one way out. How I'll do it, I don't know.

I fold.

I acquiesce.

I surrender.

You win, Damien.

I'm standing on the green woven rug in the living room of the flat I now share with Rachel, as she sleeps soundly upstairs.

I think about how she'll find me later, how I'll destroy her life too. I don't want that, but I can't do this. There's no point running, he'll never let me go.

He'll think I'm weak. Damien could never understand emotions. Forever thinking people were masking something malicious or that they were pitiful if they expressed vulnerability. No trust in anyone. Forever angry about something. So much hate. It doesn't matter what he thinks any more though, does it? Maybe this will set me free.

My phone vibrates.

He can't be up at this time, can he? Didn't you hear me, Damien? I said, you win.

It's my twin brother. Our twinstinct has been powerful since we were wombmates.

In under ten minutes, my twin has saved my life. That's twice now. Once when we were ten and went to a swimming pool party at the local leisure centre, I slipped and my head got caught underwater between two eerie, giant clown inflatables. He somehow knew I was in trouble and heaved me from the darkness. Drowning again, here he is. The money he says he'll pay, with a written contract for Damien to never contact me again. My obligation – to block Damien. Categorically, this time.

Three hours later there's a knock on the door. They answered the call I wasn't sure I'd be able to follow up. I'm calmer now due to tea, Shreddies and my twin's voice. I see blotchy high vis through our front door's frosted glass.

I let them in.

Detective Inspector Rawlands from the Metropolitan Police Domestic Abuse Unit. She says I can call her Zoe. She's stern, hair wound in a tight bun, fake eyelashes glued with what must be Gorilla glue. She's ready to listen.

I don't concern myself that Rachel may soon be up. Maybe it's finally time to be open about everything. Zoe sits on a wooden dining chair. I look at her dirty boots, wishing I'd asked her to take them off before she walked on the rug but reminding myself that's not what's important right now.

In only half a day, it's all over.

I am frail and fragmented, but ready to be reconstructed. I need to talk to someone. Professionally. I make a vow that this is the end. I have £11.34 in my account. With hands so pale and thin I can see the tracing of blue veins, I type 'free therapy near me'. I pull up the number of a therapist through NHS Crisis Counselling. In ten minutes, a gentle-sounding Irish woman has booked me in to see her.

SIX MONTHS LATER . . .

I love this place. Puffs of nebulous clouds are piped across the infinite sky, carefully positioned over a continuum of blue. A buzzard circles above; sighting his next prey, he swoops in a sudden downward arrow. On one side you can see out to sea, on the other, expansive, rolling hills.

There's so much S P A C E.

Anyone could breathe here, and I am.

Breathing.

I am present and I am safe.

I have left my Psychopath.

EPILOGUE

We Made It

I hope I have been as large a part of your healing as you have of mine. We're all in an ever-constant cycle of healing/repairing; neither stage is a disadvantage. When you're in a toxically cyclical relationship with a Controll where patterns are systemically stabilizing then destroying you, it's difficult to see a world outside. A life that isn't reliant on another person's mood, where you aren't at dial 10 alertness, trying to estimate not only what they're up to but what you could possibly do wrong next. But it exists. We're waiting for you. It's gorgeous here.

PTG – POST TRAUMATIC GROWTH

You've taken the stress, tension, red-hot coals, and survived. There is nowhere else for you to go than to grow.

Welcome to Post Traumatic Growth.

Developed by psychologists Richard Tedeschi and Lawrence Calhoun, this term signifies that after a turbulent, traumatic struggle we can experience soul-affirming growth. You can

341

expect a new appreciation for the life and love that is to come. You will find pride in your own strength and begin to see new possibilities opening up for you.

I never thought I could write a book about my experiences with the world's best literary team, become a Women's Aid ambassador and help so many other strong, brilliant people, but it happened. I went through my own PTG, and suddenly, anything was possible.

THREE KILLER QUESTIONS

Let's revisit those three questions from the top:

1. How did I get into these controlling relationships?

2. Why didn't I leave them earlier?

3. How can I stop the cycle?

THREE KILLER ANSWERS

1. Not by choice. Not because I was addicted to the drama, dating only bad lads or desperate for love. My tendency to jump quickly from one relationship to another certainly didn't help. Neither did my infatuation for being the Fixer. Nor my codependent tendencies. But ultimately, it wasn't my fault – and it's not yours either. Yet I took accountability, and I am certain it won't happen again.

2. Short answer: It's not that easy. Long answer: We're dealing with chemicals, dependency, addiction, and self-esteem battering. This isn't like choosing whether to leave your umbrella at home or not.

3. You're already a huge way there by reading this book and building awareness of how and why you attract and are attracted to Controlls. We keep learning. About ourselves, our habits and why we are the way we are. We're doing great.

DATING POST-CONTROLL

Wait a minute. What are *you* doing here? We aren't quite ready yet. This one is to come and it's a bloody Tinderbox. See what I did there? *Once* you're ready to date again, it may be tricky. Dating me now is like the toughest obstacle course there is. Men will convince themselves they can hack it, there'll be blood, sweat and tears. Those with weak heart conditions and a large savings pot get a head start. May the best man win.

But how about we wait on all this? For now, I'm happy you, your friend, your loved one have escaped, or are very close to freedom.

A FINAL WORD

Perhaps in the future we may be able to spot the early risk factors associated with psychopathy and treat them. More emphasis needs to be put on early interventions – environmental interventions. I think empathy could be taught in schools, for example. We're fighting toxic masculinity, narcissism and psychopathy – this isn't a conflict, it's an almighty war.

There's no harm in feeling empathy for a Psychopath. I love this description of a Psychopath:

They know the words, but not the music.[1]

We get to enjoy all the pleasures of the emotional world, literature, art, music. But to a true Psychopath, these mean nothing. They will never understand the sensation of being whisked away by a book, dreamily gazing at a Gauguin, or having your heart filled by watching a sunset. They'll never know the pain of watching Eurovision. Let's celebrate us: we're the lucky ones.

SOME PRACTICAL EXERCISES TO HELP US

My mantras

Please repeat the below mantras to yourself a minimum of five times a day. You can do this while you're making toast, in the shower, walking to the bus. Out loud, in your mind, recorded and played back, whatever method works for you.

I am worthy of compassionate, kind and gentle love.

I am sane, stable and sound.

I trust my gut instinct and I act on intuition.

Create your own:

....

....

....

....

....

....

My boundaries

Right, I'll start you off, but this one's on you. You have to be super clear on what you will and will not accept. Boundaries can be tested every now and again but not on repeat, several times a week.

We set boundaries so we understand what is and isn't acceptable; they strengthen our Awareness Armoury.

My new unmoving boundaries as of . . . / . . . / . . .

1. I will not accept being physically attacked by my partner.

2. I will not be threatened, sworn at, or intimidated by my partner.

3. If my instinct tells me to be wary, I will give myself the space to think about what to do next.

4. ....

5. ....

6. ....

7. ....

8. ....

9. ....

10. ....

AN EXERCISE TO CHALLENGE
YOUR SELF-LIMITING BELIEFS

Without perhaps realizing it, our brains may be stuck on negative, unhelpful thought tracks about:

- Ourselves
- Others
- The world

These are self-limiting beliefs and they impact us and our choices daily. Let's dismantle them.

An example for each could be:

Ourselves: *I'm unlovable and often irritating.*

Others: *Most people I date think I'm loud and brash.*

The world: *You only get what you want in this world if you're under 25, beautiful and thin.*

I'd like you to spend ten minutes, without censoring yourself, writing all yours down. Really dive in and pull them out.

Done that? Good. Next, put them into a table that looks like this:

SELF-LIMITING BELIEF	ROOT	CLAPBACK
I'm unlovable and often irritating.	My primary school teacher.	I'll never forget the first time we met but I'm going to keep trying.
Most people I date think I'm loud and brash.	My asshat ex.	This is called a personality, sunshine; you should try one.
You only get what you want in this world if you're under 25, beautiful and thin.	Almost all media.	Earth is too full of brilliant people. Go home.

Root = where it's derived from. Sometimes this will be hard to pinpoint but really try and get an answer in there, even if you need to sleep on it.

Clapback = you standing up and defending yourself now. What would you say as the strong, powerful person you are today?

SELF-LIMITING BELIEF	ROOT	CLAPBACK

You'd be surprised how ingrained some of the name-calling and negging you went through is. This exercise is like a giant brain colander, keeping all the helpful bits and getting rid of the unhelpful gunk.

Exercise to reconnect with Lady Gut Instinct

Read through all of the instructions before you begin and get ready to have Galentines with your Gut.

1. Find a space where you will be undisturbed for at least fifteen minutes. Sit cross-legged, preferably on a cushion on the floor with your back against the wall. Get a blanket and put it over your knees; if you have another, drape it over your shoulders. Even better if it's weighted. You want to feel as warm and protected as you can.

2. Allow your palms to rest open on your knees, align your spine and rest against the wall.

3. Take a nice, deep breath into your stomach. If you like, you can place your hand just below your belly button and breathe into that space. Take three deep breaths, in through your nose for the count of three, out through your mouth for the count of four. Allow your eyes to close.

4. Work down from the crown of your head to your toes, holding tension and then releasing. You want to be in a place of complete relaxation, ready and open to start listening.

5. Bring to your mind the person, event or circumstance that you are deliberating and want to listen to your intuition on. See their face or the situation as clearly as you can in front of you. Allow yourself to be in that moment; you can remind yourself you are safe.

6. Start listening in to the physical sensations of your body and ask yourself this question:
   Do I feel open or closed?

Closed will feel like a contracting energy, a tightness, a resistance like you want to shutter down and protect yourself.

Open will feel like an expanding energy, a release, a readiness like you want to receive.

If you haven't listened to your gut instinct in a while, be patient with yourself. It may take a few attempts to be in touch with anything at all. This is a development of a Third Eye meditation I was taught. Over time, you can train yourself to be fully acquainted with your gut instinct. This all takes time, it's like reintroducing yourself to an old friend, trying to be as close as you used to be. It takes concerted effort!

You could also journal and make notes on every time you felt Lady GI was trying to tell you something. Perhaps she pops her head up to point out that he's hiding his phone again – note it down. All of this will begin to make you more intuitive.

The potential partner checklist (the PPC)
When you're ready, start drafting your PPC. This shouldn't include too many things about their appearance, although of course it can factor. No, what I really care about are things like:

Kind
Empathetic
Funny
Compassionate to animals
Early bird, or at least not nocturnal

Now you fill in some more:

....

....

....

....

....

....

Good luck. You got this. You're stronger than you think you are, and if you're not yet, don't worry – we're all in this together.
    Peace and love,
    Maddy
    Xxx

NOTES

Chapter 3. Spill the Genes: Why Are Psychopaths, Psychopaths?

1 Study from the University of Haifa by Dr Simone Shamay-Tsoory, 2011, https://www.eurekalert.org/news-releases/627192

Chapter 4. Don't Be Afraid of the Narc: Narcissistic Personality Disorder

1 'Regret and its avoidance in psychopathy', Arielle Baskin-Sommers, Allison M. Stuppy-Sullivan, Joshua W. Buckholtz, Proceedings of the National Academy of Sciences, Dec 2016, 113 (50), 14438–14443; DOI:10.1073/pnas.1609985113
2 'Psychopaths fail to automatically take the perspective of others', Lindsey A. Drayton, Laurie R. Santos, Arielle Baskin-Sommers, Proceedings of the National Academy of Sciences, Mar 2018, 115 (13), 3302–3307; DOI:10.1073/pnas.1721903115
3 'The Dirty Dozen: a concise measure of the Dark Triad', Peter K. Jonason, Gregory D. Webster, University of West Florida, University of Florida, Psychological Assessment © 2010, American Psychological Association 2010, Vol. 22, No. 2, 420–432, 1040–3590/10/$12.00; DOI: 10.1037/a0019265

Chapter 5. Prey for Me: How Controlls Find Their Prey

1   First published May 2009, research article by Sarah Wheeler, Angela Book and Kimberly Costello, Brock University

Chapter 6. Miss Codependent: The Ins and Outs of Codependency

1   Ross Rosenberg, M. Ed., LCPC, CADC. Essay, 'The codependent/narcissist dance: the perfect partnership', www.humanmagnetsyndrome.com

Chapter 8. The Shame Game: Controlls and Shaming

1   'Relationships between shame, restrictiveness, authoritativeness, and coercive control in men mandated to a domestic violence offenders program', City University of New York, April 2018

Chapter 9. Sleepless in Seven Sisters: Biderman's Chart of Coercion

1   Ergun Cakal, LLM. PY, 2018/08/01 T1, 'Debility, dependency and dread: on the conceptual and evidentiary dimensions of psychological torture'

Chapter 10. Money, Power, Respect: Financial Control

1   'Controlling money, controlling lives: financial abuse in Britain', Citizens Advice Bureau, Nov 2014
2   2015 Study: Refuge, in partnership with the Co-operative Bank

Chapter 11. Sex with a Psychopath: Sexual Coercion

1   A.J. Bridges, R. Wosnitzer, E. Scharrer, C. Sun, R. Liberman, 'Aggression and sexual behavior in best-selling pornography videos: a content analysis update', *Violence Against Women*, 2010;16(10):1065–1085; DOI:10.1177/1077801210382866

2   Philip Larkin, 'This Be The Verse', *High Windows*, London, Faber & Faber, 1974

Chapter 12. Like Father, Like Son: Interparental Coercive Control

1   Jane Callaghan, Joanne Alexander, Judith Sixsmith, Lisa Fellin, 'Beyond "witnessing": children's experiences of coercive control in domestic violence and abuse', *Journal of Interpersonal Violence*, 2015

2   Dargis M, Newman J, Koenigs M. 'Clarifying the link between childhood abuse history and psychopathic traits in adult criminal offenders.' *Personal Disord.* 2016;7(3):221-228. DOI:10.1037/per0000147

Chapter 15. The Nose Knows: Gut Instinct

1   Jay Pasricha, MBBS MD, Director of the Johns Hopkins Center for Neurogastroenterology, Professor of Medicine 'The Brain-Gut Connection'. www.hopkinsmedicine.org/health/wellness-and-prevention/the-brain-gut-connection

2   Study commissioned by chocolate biscuit bar PiCKUP!, 2019

Chapter 17. Why Don't You Just Leave Him: The Cycle of Abuse

1   Department of Health, 'Women's mental health: into the main-stream: strategic development of mental health care for women' (London: 2002)

2   American psychologist Lenore E. Walker first documented the theory of the Cycle of Abuse in 1979.

Chapter 18. Mind Blank: PTSD and Disassociation

1   NHS Guidelines, September 2021, https://www.nhs.uk/mental-health/conditions/post-traumatic-stress-disorder-ptsd/overview/

Chapter 19. Breaking the Cycle: Hoovering and Cutting Ties

1   R. Yu, A.J. Nevado-Holgado, Y. Molero, B.M. D'Onofrio, H. Larsson et al., 'Mental disorders and intimate partner violence perpetrated by men towards women: a Swedish population-based longitudinal study', *PLOS Medicine* 16(12) 2019; e1002995

2   Rajita Sinha, 'Chronic stress, drug use, and vulnerability to addiction', *Annals of the New York Academy of Sciences*, vol. 1141, 2008

Epilogue: We Made It

1   Karina Blair, R.A. Richell, Derek Mitchell, A. Leonard, John Morton, Robert Blair, 'They know the words, but not the music: affective and semantic priming in individuals with psychopathy', *Biological psychology*. 73. 114–23. 10.1016/j. biopsycho.2005.12.006

RESOURCES

**If you are in immediate danger,
please call the police on 999**

Domestic Abuse Helplines

- **The National Domestic Abuse Helpline** is a freephone
  24-hour helpline which provides advice and support to
  women and can refer them to emergency accommodation.

  0808 2000 247.

  The National Domestic Abuse Helpline is run by Refuge.

  There are translation facilities if your first language is not
  English. The Helpline also offers BT Type talk for callers
  with hearing difficulties. The Helpline worker contacts the
  Type talk operator so that the caller can communicate
  through them.

  Website: www.nationaldahelpline.org.uk

- **Women's Aid**

  For practical and emotional support, contact https://chat. womensaid.org.uk 10am–6pm seven days a week.

  There is a plethora of information, including *The Survivor's Handbook* on their website: www.womensaid.org.uk.

  They also run a website to support children and teenagers who may be living in a home affected by domestic violence, or who may be in a violent relationship themselves. Check out www.thehideout.org.uk.

  For information on keeping safe as a teenager in relationships, visit: www.loverespect.co.uk.

- **Refuge**

  Their helpline offers advice and support to women experiencing domestic violence.

  Refuge also provides safe emergency accommodation through a network of refuges throughout the UK, including culturally specific services for women from minority ethnic communities and cultures.

  Their website also includes some information for men who are either being abused or who are abusers.

  Website: www.refuge.org.uk

- **Solace**

  For free and confidential advice and support for women in London affected by abuse, you can call Solace on **0808 802 5565** or email advice@solacewomensaid.org.

- **ManKind Initiative**

  Male victims of domestic abuse can call **01823 334244** to speak to ManKind, an initiative available for male victims of domestic abuse and domestic violence across the UK as well as their friends, family, neighbours, work colleagues and employers. www.mankind.org.uk.

  Alternatively, the Men's Advice Line can be reached at **0808 8010327** or emailed at info@mensadviceline.org.uk.

- **Ashiana Sheffield**

  This is an organization which focuses on helping black, Asian, minority ethnic and refugee women and children in England, Scotland and Wales who are in danger because of domestic violence, 'honour'-based violence and/or forced marriage – phone **0114 255 5740**, email them at info@ashianasheffield.org or contact them online: www.ashianasheffield.org/contact-us.

- **Forced Marriage Unit**

  The government has a **Forced Marriage Unit** which seeks to help those at risk of and those who have been a victim of forced marriage – phone **+44 (0) 20 7008 0151** or email fmu@fco.gov.uk.

- **Galop's National LGBT+ Domestic Abuse Helpline**

  This is a service offering support for lesbian, gay, bisexual and transgendered people who are being abused – phone **0800 999 5428**, email help@galop.org.uk or visit www.galop.org.uk/make-a-referral.

- **RISE**

  RISE operates an independent domestic abuse helpline in Brighton & Hove.

  The helpline **01273 622 822** is open Monday evenings (5–7pm), and Tuesday and Wednesday mornings 9.30–12.30pm.

  Alternatively, email helpline@riseuk.org.uk letting them know a safe contact number on which to call you.

  If you are seeking **LGBTQ+ support**, you can speak to their specialist caseworker on a Monday evening on **01273 622 828** or email lgbt@riseuk.org.uk

- **Finding Legal Options for Women Survivors (FLOWS)**

  FLOWS gives legal advice to women who are affected by domestic abuse; they also give advice to front-line workers.

  Website: www.rcjadvice.org.uk/family/flows-finding-legal-options-for-women-survivors/

- **Southall Black Sisters**

  Southall Black Sisters provide advice for Black (Asian and African-Caribbean) women with issues including domestic abuse, forced marriage, immigration and homelessness.

  Website: www.southallblacksisters.org.uk

- **Respect – Men's Advice Line**

  The Men's Advice Line is a confidential helpline for all men experiencing domestic violence by a current or ex-partner. They provide emotional support and practical advice and can give you details of specialist services that can give you advice on legal, housing, child contact, mental health, and other issues.

  Freephone **0808 8010327**

  Website: www.mensadviceline.org.uk

- **SurvivorsUK**

  This is a helpline for men who have been victims of rape or sexual abuse.

  They may be able to arrange counselling or a support group if you live in the London area, or provide details of an appropriate service if you don't.

  Chat via SMS text: **+442033221860**

  Website: www.survivorsuk.org

- **Everyman Project**

  The Everyman Project offers counselling to men in the London area who want to change their violent or abusive behaviour. It also has a national helpline which offers advice to anyone worried about their own, or someone else's, violent or abusive behaviour.

  Call: **0203 642 8850**

  Website: www.everymanproject.co.uk

- **Rape Crisis**

  Rape Crisis (England and Wales) is an umbrella organization for Rape Crisis Centres across England and Wales. The website has contact details for centres and gives basic information about rape and sexual violence for survivors, friends, family, students and professionals. Rape Crisis (England and Wales) also runs a freephone helpline: 0808 802 9999 Website: www.rapecrisis.org.uk

- **Honour Network Helpline**

  The Honour Network Helpline is a national helpline run by Karma Nirvana, a national charity which advises victims and survivors of forced marriage and honour-based abuse.

  Website: www.karmanirvana.org.uk

- **Action on Elder Abuse**

  Action on Elder Abuse gives confidential advice and information to older people who are victims of violence or abuse. A relative or friend of the person being abused can also contact the helpline on behalf of the older person. The helpline can be used in the case of older people who live at home, in a care home or who are in hospital.

  Call: **0808 808 8141**

  Website: www.elderabuse.org.uk

- **National Stalking Helpline**

  The National Stalking Helpline can provide advice on how to deal with any type of stalking behaviour. This includes advice on how to report the behaviour to the police, and what you can expect if you report something.

  Website: www.stalkinghelpline.org

- **Respect Phoneline**

Respect Phoneline offers information and advice to partners, friends and family who want to stop someone's violent behaviour.

Website: www.respectphoneline.org.uk

- **SignHealth – Domestic Abuse Service**

SignHealth provides a specialist domestic abuse service to help Deaf people find safety and security. You can find out how to contact them on their website.

Website: www.signhealth.org.uk/with-deaf-people/ domestic-abuse/domestic-abuse-service/

- **Respond**

Respond work with children and adults with learning disabilities who've either experienced abuse or abused other people.

Website: www.respond.org.uk

- **Revenge Porn Helpline**

Get in touch for confidential support and assistance with reporting content that has been shared online. The helpline cannot guarantee removal of all images online but hold exceptional partnerships with industry partners. Open Monday to Friday from 10am until 4pm. You can email at any time and they will respond during normal working hours.

Email: help@revengepornhelpline.org.uk

Telephone: **0345 6000 459** open Monday to Friday from 10 am till 4pm.

https://revengepornhelpline.org.uk

- **Financial Abuse**

  https://survivingeconomicabuse.org/

  Freephone 24-Hour National Domestic Abuse Helpline: 0808 2000 247 or visit www.nationaldahelpline.org.uk

Drugs & Alcohol Helplines

- **NHS Alcohol Support**

  Find services near you:

  Website: www.nhs.uk/live-well/alcohol-support

- **Alcoholics Anonymous**

  For impartial help, advice and support.

  Visit their website: www.alcoholics-anonymous.org.uk

  or call their free helpline: **0800 9177650**

They will also guide you through to Narcotics Anonymous, or similar if required.

- **Alcohol Change**

  You can also find local support: www.alcoholchange.org.uk

ACKNOWLEDGEMENTS

Anna Pallai

This book would still be knocking about in a cobwebby corner of my mind were it not for the boost that my superb literary agent Anna Pallai gave me. She endlessly encouraged me and relentlessly worked through edits on a first draft that, really, I had no idea what I was doing with. Thank you for your wisdom and helping me share this important story.

Also, for being my agent, confidante, and friend. (I suppose I should also thank Sam for the intro. Sam – you know how brilliant I think you are.)

Carole Tonkinson

I'm still not 100 per cent certain that this woman isn't some celestial being sent to me for good behaviour and doing lots of recycling. It's wrong to say Carole was enthusiastic about this book from the off – no, she was positively *passionate*. Fervent about bringing this to the hands of those who needed it most. Thank you for your dedication to the cause and being not only a superb editor, publisher and friend but also a strong sister-in-arms.

HOW TO LEAVE YOUR PSYCHOPATH

Jess Duffy, Sian Gardiner, Jodie Mullish, Katy Denny and the whole team at Bluebird

I realize how lucky I am to have a roomful of brilliant minds behind this book. Your determination, belief and backing are what has kept this book buoyant. You are creative powerhouses, with endless superb ideas and, together, we are changing the world for the better! Thank you, from the bottom of my heart.

Teresa Parker, and all at Women's Aid

Where can I begin with your excellence? Not only have you supported and nurtured me on my journey, both personally and with the book, you have lifted more women than you can know from despair. Thank you for giving us all not only hope, but excitement for the future. Please, everyone, donate here: www. womensaid.org.uk/make-a-donation

My family

Mum, Dad, Tom, Claire and all your wonderful babies and partners. God, I'm lucky to have you. Thank you for lifting me up, inspiring me and guiding me through this crazy world. I can't put into words how much I love you all.

Partner

Thank you for showing me what kind, compassionate, gentle love is. You have never tried to change me, always accepted me as I come and for that I am truly grateful. Thank you also for ceaselessly listening to me reading half-written paragraphs of the book at ridiculous hours. You're my penguin. I love you.

To you, the reader

I hope you know how brilliant you are? Thank you for stepping into this journey with me. Effectively I'm the over-zealous girl in the club toilets and I've just grabbed your hand and told you how great you look. I love how the book has united us.

I'm so glad we're mates now.

To past me

Thanks for knowing you were more than your circumstances and thanks for never giving up.

INDEX